C++ for VB Programmers

JONATHAN MORRISON

Apress™

C++ for VB Programmers
Copyright © 2000 by Jonathan D. Morrison

ISBN (pbk): 1-893115-76-3

Printed and bound in the United States of America 12345678910

Trademarked names may appear in this book. Rather than use a trademark symbol with every occurrence of a trademarked name, we use the names only in an editorial fashion and to the benefit of the trademark owner, with no intention of infringement of the trademark.

Editorial Directors: Dan Appleman, Gary Cornell, Karen Watterson
Technical Reviewer: Dan Appleman
Editor: Katharine Dvorak
Projects Manager: Grace Wong
Supervising Production Editor: MaryAnn Brickner
Production Services and Page Composition: Impressions Book and Journal Services, Inc.
Artist: Frank Giangreco
Cover: Karl Miyajima

Distributed to the book trade in the United States by Springer-Verlag New York, Inc.,175 Fifth Avenue, New York, NY, 10010
and outside the United States by Springer-Verlag GmbH & Co. KG, Tiergartenstr. 17, 69112 Heidelberg, Germany

In the United States, phone 1-800-SPRINGER; orders@springer-ny.com; http://www.springer-ny.com
Outside the United States, contact orders@springer.de; http://www.springer.de; fax +49 6221 345229

For information on translations, please contact Apress directly at 901 Grayson Street, Suite 204, Berkeley, CA, 94710
Phone: 510-549-5930; Fax: 510-549-5939; info@apress.com; http://www.apress.com

Acknowledgments

THIS IS THE SECTION OF THE BOOK THAT IS probably only read by those who are named in it, so I will try to stay informal. Here it goes:

First and foremost, I want to thank my Lord and Savior, Jesus Christ, for giving me the opportunity, talent, and stamina necessary to write this book (don't get nervous I'm not going to start preaching!), and for placing me with Apress, home of the best technical book people around. To my wife Kelly, thank you for being my source of encouragement and inspiration throughout this difficult book-writing experience, and more importantly, throughout my whole life. You have made it possible for me to write this book by being able to simultaneously run our household, keep track of our two-year-old son and carry the newest addition to our household in your womb all by yourself, while I was busy writing. Thank you honey, I love and appreciate you more than you know (or I show)! I am absolutely the luckiest man alive. You are my soul mate and my existence. I would also like to thank my two-year-old son Joda, for being a constant reminder that even though writing a programming book is important, it pales in comparison to the importance of being a dad. I would like to thank my, as yet unborn, second child—PumpkinDoodle—as named by Joda for the last nine months of joyous planning and anticipation.

Thanks to everyone at Apress. It was truly an honor to write for such a first-class publishing company. Special thanks to Dan Appleman for doing an incredibly thorough (and sometimes humbling) technical review and for always being available to answer my questions. Also thanks to Dan for writing the best technical books I have ever read. It was truly wonderful to work with such an awesomely talented person. Thanks to Gary Cornell for answering all of my "novice author" questions and for helping me and encouraging me through the whole writing process in general. Also to Grace Wong for being a patient, kind, and dedicated project manager, who was always available to listen to my questions and concerns regardless of how ridiculous most of them were. To Sarah Jaquish who did a great job of handling all the various marketing aspects of the book as well as tolerating all of my unschooled marketing suggestions. Thanks to Katharine Dvorak whose very gentle editing style helped make this book great without hurting my feelings about my grammatical and stylistic deficiencies. And with much gratitude I thank my best buddy, Frank Giangreco, for doing all of the illustrations for the book. Great job, Frankie!!

Next I would like to thank those that have mentored me either technically, professionally, or both, along the path of my career. To Keith Yarnell, thanks for believing in me and teaching me how to think like a programmer, not just to write programs. You gave me the foundation on which I have built my career. Thanks to

Dr. Phyllis Chasser for teaching me about computer science in general, but more for being a good friend and always supporting me. Special thanks to Priscilla Murphy (Aunt 'Cilla) for making me finish school instead of going on tour with my rock band, although I still have my spandex and hairspray in the closet just in case this programming thing doesn't work out. Thanks to Roger Collins for constantly challenging me with some of the wildest C++ problems I have ever seen, and for never accepting "just good enough" from me. I would also like to thank Ed Martin for helping me prepare mentally for the challenges of writing a technical book and explaining the various subtleties of the publishing business. To two of the most talented programmers I know, and two of my closest friends, Lazaro Ballesteros and Gilbert Rosal, thanks for everything guys! You have been a source of encouragement and inspiration to me always. I would also like to thank Mike Bracuti for getting me "really" interested in C++ in the first place, and for answering many of my C++ questions over the years. Also a big thanks to Mark at Zarr's VB Website (`http://www.zarr.com/vb`) for providing a Visual Basic community that has enhanced the careers and lives of Visual Basic programmers around the world. Thanks, Mark.

I would like to thank Berry (like strawberry) Crook from the Maxim Group for all of the "free" sushi lunches and other various encouragements along the way.

Last but not least, I want to thank my family for standing behind me and always believing in me. My mom, Deborah Morrison, I love you as if you were my own mother (Ha Ha!)! I love you mom. My sisters, Sarah, Rachel, Mary, and Hannah, I love each and every one of you with all my heart. I hope that I have been as much of an inspiration in your lives as you have been in mine. My grandmother, Evelyn Bozeman, you are the most "practical" person I know, and I wouldn't change a thing about you. Thank you for loving me and believing in me even though you didn't always understand me. My "other" parents (a.k.a. in-laws), Chip and Barbara Plank, thanks for making me a part of your family, and loving me as such. You are both very near and dear to my heart. To my "other" sisters, Kara Plank (who I can still beat at any water sport in existence today!) and Kristen Brown (who's hard editing work made this book even better than it should have been), I love you both. To my "other" brother (and international finance genius) Don Brown for the golf lessons and his general great-guy-ness. I love you Man! To "Doc" (a.k.a. Dr. James K. Isom, veterinarian extraordinaire!), you have been like a father to me and always encouraged Kelly and me in all of our endeavors. You will always hold a special place in our hearts. You truly have made a huge difference in my life and for that I love and thank you. To my closest friend and the best drummer in the world, Doug Miller, thanks for all of the free therapy sessions and the lifetime of great memories. You are a part of who I am today. To David Verost, thanks for always being there. I consider you both closer to me than brothers. And to the two men who took a part of me when they passed away: my granddaddy, **Robert Guy Bozeman**, and my father, **Lewis Alvyn Morrison**. I wish that both of you could have been here to share this happiness with me, but I know that you are in a better place today. I love, miss, and think about you every day of my life.

Foreword

by Dan Appleman

"SHAME! SHAME!"—I CAN HEAR MY FRIENDS CRY. "How could you, of all people, write a foreword for a book that teaches Visual Basic programmers to work in C++?"

I can see their point. After all, I have built much of my career on the idea that Visual Basic is the best language for Windows development. My own company, Desaware, is dedicated to providing tools that extend the power of VB to the point where programmers can do virtually anything they want without having to use C++.

Why then, would I not only write a foreword to a book that teaches C++, but act as the technical reviewer for the book as well? What could lead to such a radical change in approach?

Sorry to disappoint you, but in fact my approach to Windows software development has not changed at all. I continue to be a strong advocate of VB as the best software development platform for most Windows applications. But I have never suggested that it is the best language for all Windows development. There are many tasks that are better done in C++, and some that can only be done in C++. For example, most of Desaware's components that extend the reach of VB are written in C++ using Microsoft's Active Template Library (ATL) and the exact techniques that you will soon read about in this very book.

What I have opposed, and continue to oppose, is the idea that the choice of language is an all or nothing proposition. The idea that C++ is the best tool for creating Windows user interfaces is, in my mind, as silly as the idea that VB is the best tool for creating ultra high-speed pixel manipulation routines. The ideal Windows software development environment is, and always has been, one that allows you to use the right tool for each job that comes along. Visual Basic alone may be a nice language, but what makes it truly great is its ability to seamlessly integrate code written in C++ or other languages using components or external DLL calls with the Declare statement.

I believe many VB programmers would agree that mixed language programming is the best strategy for software development in Windows. Unfortunately, learning C++ represents quite an investment in time and effort—an insurmountable obstacle to many.

But why should this be? After all, as a language, C++ is in many ways simpler than VB. It has far fewer keywords to memorize. Why is it so hard to learn?

Well, one reason is that every book on beginning Visual C++ that I have seen focuses on using MFC to build C++ applications. That huge library is enough to intimidate anyone. And every line of every book that discusses MFC is a complete waste of time for VB programmers! Why should they learn to create user interfaces and dialog boxes using C++ when, in fact, smart VB programmers can create any user interface they need using VB and a handful of components, and do so in a fraction of the time with a fraction of the effort?

No, what VB programmers want and need is an introduction to C++ that allows them to write small, high performance code routines that can be called from their VB applications. In other words, what most VB programmers really want is the ability to create their own DLLs, and expose either function libraries or COM objects that can be used by their main VB application.

As I reviewed this book, I was impressed by how closely Jonathan focused on the real needs of VB programmers. The introduction to the C++ language assumes no prior knowledge of C++, but it doesn't waste time teaching concepts that every VB programmer already knows. He covers the fundamentals of classes and exporting functions from DLLs, and how to call them from VB. Then he shows how to use ATL to build COM components for use with VB.

This book won't turn you into a C++ expert. It won't turn you into an ATL expert. But that's the whole point—you don't need to be an expert to solve most of the problems that VB programmers want to address with C++. You just need to know enough to solve a problem. This book will teach you what you need to know and not make you waste your time learning techniques and class libraries that you're better off doing in VB anyway.

I think this book will make a real contribution to the VB community. I'm glad I had the privilege of reviewing it. I hope you enjoy it as much as I did.

Contents at a Glance

Contents

Introduction

ONE OF MY GREATEST FRUSTRATIONS AS a newbie Visual Basic programmer was the fact that while 90 percent of the functionality I wanted was available directly from Visual Basic, the remaining 10 percent was trapped in the Win32 API, which I had no idea how to use. Luckily, I discovered *Dan Appleman's Visual Basic Programmers Guide to the Win32 API* (Sams, 1999), which I read from cover to cover twice! I could not believe that all of the great functionality from the WIN32 API was at my disposal right from good old Visual Basic.

Instead of curbing my appetite, however, Dan's book made me want to learn even more. I was no longer satisfied with simply calling the Win32 API; I wanted to be able to write my own API. I realized that in order to achieve the level of knowledge I wanted to have, I would need to learn C++. So I started reading every C/C++ book I could get my hands on, but I was usually disappointed with the content. The books were either so basic they were useless for teaching me what I wanted to know or they were so advanced I couldn't grasp the concepts presented (which meant that they didn't help me at all in my ultimate quest—to become a more effective Windows programmer).

Finally, I gave in and learned C++ from scratch, and thereby ignored everything I already knew about programming for Windows with Visual Basic. This drastically increased the time I had to spend learning C++. I hope that no other Visual Basic programmer has to learn C++ the way I did. In fact, it is for this very reason I wrote this book. I don't believe that your existing knowledge of Visual Basic should be negated just because you're trying to learn C++. In fact, it should be exploited in order to reduce the time required to attain this new skill.

Most Visual Basic programmers want to learn C++ in order to enhance the applications they are writing in Visual Basic—not to replace them with applications written in C++. Being able to write DLLs that take advantage of C++'s low-level capabilities, having access to API's that use types not supported in Visual Basic, and writing ActiveX components that don't require a huge runtime library are a few examples of how knowing C++ can enhance your effectiveness as a Windows programmer. And that is the goal of this book: to make you a more effective Windows programmer.

Focus and Benefits

The focus of this book is to teach you how to use C++ to enhance your Visual Basic development efforts. However, with the knowledge you will gain after completing this book, you should be able to create many different types of solutions using Visual Basic and C++.

The main benefit you will realize from this book is a solid knowledge of the C++ programming language as well as a good understanding of the internal workings of the Windows operating system(s). This knowledge can then be built upon with other books and learning resources.

Style of Presentation

With apologies to my various English teachers over the years, this book is written in the first person. Why? Because I think technical books written in the first person are much easier to read and follow than books that are not. I've tried to write the chapters of this book as if I were speaking to you in person. I hope you find the content easier to understand this way.

Prerequisites

For this book to be effective, you should have a good handle on Visual Basic syntax. This is because I use Visual Basic to explain the language elements of C++. You don't need to have any prior knowledge of C or C++, but familiarity with the Win32 API is a plus. There will be some advanced Visual Basic code used to explain some concepts in a few of the chapters, but I will go through them in detail when we get there.

Finally, you will also need Visual C++ 6.0 Introductory Edition (included on the CD-ROM that accompanies this book) or higher (Professional and Enterprise Editions), if you wish to work through the code samples on your own. All of the sample code I use throughout this book may be found on the book's accompanying Web site at http://www.apress.com.

Other than that you just need some willpower and hunger for knowledge!

CHAPTER 1

Why C++? (And Why with Visual Basic)

PITCHERS ARE IMPORTANT MEMBERS OF A BASEBALL TEAM even though they generally don't hit the ball very well. But the fact that most pitchers aren't good at bat doesn't seem to bother anyone because pitchers aren't expected to be good batters (even though all of the other players on the team are). All that pitchers are expected to do is strike out the batters on the other team.

Pitchers are specialists, and because they are specialists, everyone expects them to do only one thing well—pitch. Now imagine a pitcher who not only can pitch well, but also is able to hit the ball well. How much more valuable is this pitcher to his team than a pitcher who offers nothing once his team is up to bat? Considerably more.

Now imagine a Visual Basic programmer. Using only Visual Basic and the Windows application program interface (API), a Visual Basic programmer can build many types of robust Windows applications. However, there are some application requirements that are impossible, impractical, or inefficient to implement using Visual Basic alone. In order to meet these requirements, most Visual Basic programmers either have to find a third-party tool to complete the work (which often doesn't do exactly what they want it to do), or get help from a programmer who is willing to write a "VB-friendly" library that implements the requirements in a language such as Delphi or C++. Not a very pretty picture is it? And yet as Visual Basic programmers, we have all been in a similar situation.

Now imagine a Visual Basic programmer who is able, by himself, to implement these types of requirements using C++, and then integrate them into his Visual Basic application. How much more valuable will he be than a developer who relies on outside assistance in order to implement these types of requirements? Just like the pitcher who can also hit the ball well, a lot more.

Don't get me wrong. I am not discounting the power of Visual Basic as a stand-alone tool. Visual Basic is a powerful programming language for building Windows applications all by itself. However, couple the strengths of Visual Basic with the strengths of C++ and you have an even more powerful tool for developing Windows applications than with Visual Basic or C++ alone.

Why Visual Basic Was Created

Before Microsoft created the Visual Basic programming language, writing a Windows application was difficult. In fact, developing even the simplest user interface could take weeks or even months using C, which was the predominant language for Windows development at that time. Oddly enough, as difficult as it was to implement a Windows application, at higher levels, the Windows architecture was pretty simple. First, a Window was created. Second, the window had a *message loop* function attached to it. The purpose of this function was to handle messages from the operating system. Then, each time something interesting happened to the Window (such as clicking the mouse on it or the user resizing it), the operating system called on this function that enabled the Window to react to the action. If this message loop function was written in Visual Basic, it might have looked something like this:

```
'Message function for our window
'This function gets called by the operating system
'when any actions happen to our window.
Public Function HandleWindowEvent(EventType As String) as Long
If EventType = "MouseClick" Then
    Call Form_Click()
Else If EventType = "MouseDoubleClick" Then
    Call Form_DoubleClick()

<Other 'Else If' statements ommited for readability>


End If
End Sub
```

Simply stated, the operating system was responsible for monitoring and reporting events, and the message loop function for the application was responsible for deciding what to do given each different type of event. But as I implied earlier, the devil was in the details and without a solid knowledge of C, you didn't stand a chance of writing applications for the Windows operating system. Fortunately, around the time Windows 3.0 was released, Visual Basic was brought onto the scene with the single intention of making it easier to write Windows applications. Granted, the first two incarnations of Visual Basic, Version 1.0 and Version 2.0, were not robust or feature-rich, but they did enable a developer to write a Windows application in a significantly shorter amount of time than previously possible, and with significantly less knowledge of the internal workings of Windows. Even companies outside of Microsoft started to realize the power and ease of Visual Basic, and started writing add-on components for Visual Basic as their sole business function.

Add-ons, which were known as *custom controls* or *VBXs*, rapidly became a huge market and indirectly contributed to the fast growth of the Visual Basic programming community. Because each add-on component essentially extended the Visual Basic development environment by encapsulating some tedious, difficult, or even impossible tasks in an easy-to-use component. These add-on components were usually written in C.

As time went on, Windows evolved into a 32-bit operating system and as such, Microsoft added 32-bit capabilities to Visual Basic 4.0. When the Internet "Gold Rush" hit, Microsoft created a new technology called ActiveX (which had actually been around under a different name for years—but we won't go there), and wanted it to be the technology of the Internet. The problem was that creating an ActiveX control was a terribly difficult assignment. Enter Visual Basic again. With Version 5.0 Microsoft gave Visual Basic developers the ability to create ActiveX controls. Again, Microsoft used Visual Basic to make a difficult task very easy.

By the release of Version 5.0, Visual Basic was becoming a formidable programming language in the Windows world and was starting to be taken seriously by other programming language camps such as Delphi, PowerBuilder, and even the almighty C++—camps that had previously considered Visual Basic to be a "toy" language. The fact that with Visual Basic you could now write ActiveX controls and still write robust Windows applications within a relatively short period of time forced people to stop and take notice.

However, one problem with the new features and capabilities of Visual Basic was that some developers were starting to go to the opposite extreme with Visual Basic and force it to do things it had never been intended to do. Similar to a carpenter who loves his saw so much that he tries to hammer nails with it, many Visual Basic developers were coming up with some pretty interesting, unstable, and dangerous uses of Visual Basic. There is a tool for every job, and for 90 percent of graphical user interface (GUI) development—and application development in general for that matter—there is no better tool than Visual Basic. However, it is that other 10 percent that requires a little more thought.

I read an article in a popular Visual Basic magazine not too long ago that described how to intercept the Visual Basic compile process and add inline assembly code into it. This scared me to death because I was sure that there would be Visual Basic programmers out there implementing this technique before too long, not having any idea of the dangers of using it. I am not trying to knock the author of this article because I believe the intention of his article was to educate the reader about Visual Basic's compiler. (In fact, he even pointed out the fact that this technique was completely unsupported by Microsoft and that it would not work with future releases of Visual Basic.) However, this article made me realize something. The mere fact that this article had been published in such a widely distributed magazine meant that Visual Basic programmers were hungry for anything that would enable them to expand the boundaries of their programming ability with Visual Basic. They wanted to go to the next step.

The Next Step

I applaud the efforts and accomplishments of the Visual Basic programmers pushing the boundaries of the tool's capabilities. In fact, I consider myself a long-time member of this group. I wrote a non-apartment model, multi-threaded application using Visual Basic 5.0 just because I read an article that said that not only could it not be done, but also that it *should* not be done. It's our nature as artistic people to want to bend the rules and find new and interesting ways of doing things, and again, I encourage this type of growth experience.

I simply believe that there is a better and more effective method of pushing the boundaries of Visual Basic programming, which is to use C++ to extend Visual Basic as opposed to hacking up the language. Using C++ to implement advanced features into your Visual Basic applications is safer than digging into Visual Basic, and it is forward compatible. For example, the multi-threaded application I developed ran well under Visual Basic 5.0, but when I tried to get it run under Visual Basic 6.0, it crashed and burned.

Microsoft makes no bones about it; Visual Basic is a closed environment. What this means to the Visual Basic hacker is, if you happen to discover some undocumented functionality or a way to break a Visual Basic "rule," chances are that by the next revision of Visual Basic, it will not work.

Conclusion

In this chapter we have seen a bit of the history of Visual Basic as well as why it has become the de facto standard for creating Windows applications. We have also seen that there are some tasks that are either very difficult or impossible to accomplish in Visual Basic alone, being much better suited for a C++ implementation. I hope that I have convinced you that Visual C++ should be your weapon of choice when implementing advanced functionality that is not available in Visual Basic into your applications. So, if you are ready to add C++ to your programming toolbox then, Hooray! Let's do it.

CHAPTER 2

Where Do We Start?

OKAY, NOW THAT WE HAVE ESTABLISHED THAT Visual C++ is a valuable tool to add to our programming toolbox, where are we going to start in the learning process? Because we already know how to use Visual Basic, I will use Visual Basic as a point of reference throughout this book. And because you already know programming logic such as loops and decision trees (select-case, if-then-else, do-while, and so on) I will only detail the syntactical differences between Visual C++ and Visual Basic.

However, our first order of business is to become comfortable with this new environment, C++. So, first we will look at the Visual C++ development environment, Visual Studio, which is where we will write all of our source code and compile our projects. Then we will examine the C++ runtime environment. And, after that we'll check out the Visual C++ debugging environment—the most awesome debugger in existence today. Again, we'll compare each of these areas to the parallel area in Visual Basic in order to expose commonalities and explore any differences.

Visual Studio

Visual Studio is a robust development tool; in fact it is the single most impressive piece of software I have ever used. Figure 2-1 shows the Visual Studio environment, open and with no project selected. On the surface, it looks quite similar to Visual Basic. However, it contains many advanced features that Visual Basic does not have, or need, for that matter. Because it would be impossible to detail all of the features in Visual Studio and still cover the necessary content of this book, I will only explain the features that are applicable to the subject matter being covered. (For an explanation of each Visual Studio feature, check out the Visual Studio manual.)

In order to get a good feel for the Visual Studio development environment, let's create a new project. After opening Visual Studio, select File ➜ New. You will see the window shown in Figure 2-2.

As you can see, you have a choice of creating many different types of projects in Visual Studio just as you do in Visual Basic. Let's choose the "Win32 console application" as our project type. A *console application* is simply a DOS-style application, meaning that it runs at a DOS prompt and has no windows. PING and NET USE are examples of console applications. Okay, now enter the name **ex02_1** in

Figure 2-1. The Visual Studio development environment

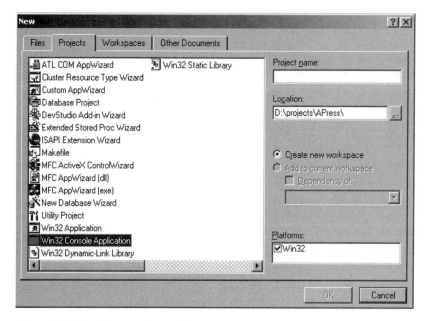

Figure 2-2. The New project window

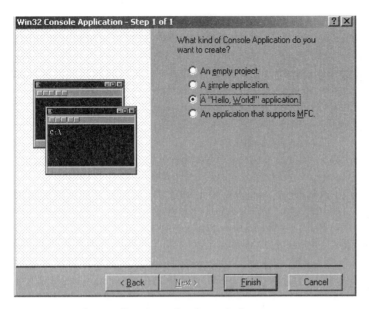

Figure 2-3. The application selection window

the Project name textbox. If you don't like the default folder location in the Location box, feel free to change it. (This is the location where all of your project files will be stored.) Once you are finished, press OK; you will see the screen pictured in Figure 2-3.

> **NOTE:** *When you create a new project in Visual Studio, a .dsp file is created. This file contains information about your particular project and is tied to a .dsw file, a workspace file. This is analogous to the relationship between a .vbp file and a .vbg file in Visual Basic. In other words, a workspace file can encompass many project files. By opening a single .dsw file, Visual Studio will automatically open all of its related .dsp files. Generally speaking, when you are creating a new project you will choose the option 'Create new workspace' unless you are creating a group of projects that need to work together, in which case you would choose to 'Add to current workspace' as your project creation option. It is important to remember that in Visual Studio a .dsp has to be a member of some workspace or you will not be able to open it.*

Select the "Hello World" application type and click Finish. You will see an information box that tells you about the project files that are going to be created. Select OK. You should now have a project open that looks similar to the one shown in Figure 2-4.

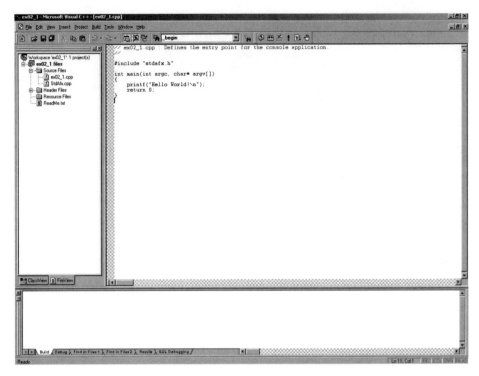

Figure 2-4. The ex02_1 *project*

Let's go ahead and build the executable file so that we can get our mandatory technical book "Hello World" application out of the way. Select Build ➜ Build ex02_1.ex and you should see the window shown in Figure 2-5 at the bottom of the development environment.

The messages in this window tell us that the files have been successfully compiled and linked. That's great news, assuming you know what *compiling* and *linking* are. (If you have no idea what compiling and linking are, the messages probably don't mean much to you at all. Don't worry; compiling and linking are covered in detail in the next chapter.)

Figure 2-5. The Visual Studio "Build Output" window

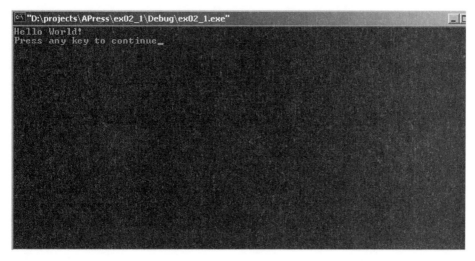

Figure 2-6. ex02_1.exe *at runtime*

The messages also tell us that an executable file has been created. Let's run it and see what it looks like. To run our newly created file, select Build → Execute ex02_1.exe. You should see the DOS-style console window, as shown in Figure 2-6.

Pretty cool, huh?! You just wrote your first application using C++ and didn't even have to write any code. But how is this possible? Obviously, the computer had to execute some code to draw the window on the screen and to write the words "Hello World" within it. Where is that code and how did it get wherever it is? Although we didn't write the code to make those things happen, someone did—Microsoft, in the form of the C/C++ runtime library.

C++ Runtime Environment

One of the biggest knocks on Visual Basic has always been the fact that executables require a sizeable runtime library to translate its instructions into machine code at runtime. Even with the ability to compile native executables with Visual Basic (since Version 5.0), the dependency on the runtime is still very real.

"Hold on! I don't even know what a runtime is," you say? Well, a *runtime* is a set of support files that either directly or indirectly allow an application to run. Its functionality is usually exposed as a Dynamic Link Library (DLL) or other type of library. The runtime for Visual Basic is encapsulated in the file MSVBVM60.DLL (which stands for *Microsoft Visual Basic Virtual Machine 6.0*). Consider the following Visual Basic code snippet:

```
Dim lngLen As Long
Dim strName As String

strName = "Bill Gates"
lngLen = InStr(1, strName, "G")

MsgBox CStr(lngLen)
```

The Visual Basic *InStr* function, from the previous code snippet, is part of the Visual Basic runtime. When you call InStr, Visual Basic forwards the call to a function in the Visual Basic runtime DLL (MSVBVM60.DLL). That function searches for the string that you passed as a parameter to InStr and returns the position of the first occurrence it finds to Visual Basic. That value is then given to you by Visual Basic as the return value of the InStr function. Let's take a look at how this works:

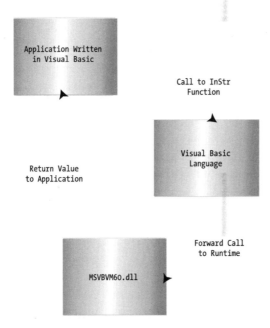

In fact, any of the built-in functions that you call in your Visual Basic code are all forwarded to the MSVBVM60.DLL in this manner. Below is a partial /EXPORTS listing from MSVBVM60.DLL, using *Dumpbin.exe* (a tool that ships with Visual Studio). It tells many things about a file including which functions it exports, or exposes, to other applications.

```
Dump of file C:\WINNT\system32\msvbvm60.dll

File Type: DLL

  Section contains the following exports for MSVBVM60.DLL
    ordinal hint RVA       name
<Section ommited>
      630  213 000E922C rtcInStr
      709  215 000F7D69 rtcInStrRev
      596  216 000E0CF2 rtcMsgBox
<Section ommited>
```

Those exported function names may look familiar. As a matter of fact, they look identical to Visual Basic built-in function names except that they have *rtc* in front of them. (What "rtc" stands for is still anybody's guess as the meaning is still undocumented—Runtime Call, perhaps?). This explains why MSVBVM60.DLL is required at runtime for any application that is compiled with Visual Basic 6.0.

So why don't applications written in other languages have this restriction of being dependant on a separate runtime library placed on them? Actually, they do. Most any programming language you use will have some type of runtime dependency. Even Java, the supposedly totally portable language, has a runtime called the *Java Virtual Machine*. The Java compiler generates byte-code from the Java source code, which is a step between machine code and Java source code, and creates what is called a *.class file*. The Java Virtual Machine interprets the .class file at runtime and translates it into the native machine code of the processor that is on that machine. This is frighteningly similar to the way Visual Basic runs applications that it has compiled to p-code, but that is a topic for another book.

You may be wondering whether Visual C++ has a runtime. The answer is yes, it does, but I will go into even further detail in the next chapter, in which I discuss dynamic and static linking. It is encapsulated into the file MSVCRT.DLL (Microsoft Visual C++ Runtime), which should be in your system directory.

So why then would people complain about Visual Basic having to ship a runtime library, but say nothing of Visual C++'s same requirement? First of all, the Visual Basic runtime is six times larger in file size than its Visual C++ counterpart. Second, MSCVRT.DLL is used by many parts of the Windows operating system (or at least core applications that ship with the OS), so there is a good chance that every machine running Windows has a copy of this file. Aside from these differences, the execution environment of Visual Basic and Visual C++ are very similar.

Visual C++ Debugging Environment

The Visual Studio debugger is the most incredible programming tool I have ever seen. It is without a doubt the most advanced and feature-rich debugger in existence today. Not only does it give you complete access to your application at runtime, but also it enables you to trace through all of your function calls, even into the runtime library calls. You can also view memory, registers, and threads. Unfortunately (or fortunately), you may be unimpressed by some of these features simply because Visual Basic has had them in its debugger for some time, such as the ability to make "on-the-fly" code changes and the ability to view the contents of a variable at execution time.

All right then, let's take the Visual Studio debugger for a test drive. First, open the project we created earlier (ex02_1) by selecting File ➔ Open Workspace. Choose ex02_1.dsw and click the Open button. At this point you should have the project open for editing. In the Workspace window, select the File View as pictured in Figure 2-7.

Again from the workspace window, double-click ex02_1.cpp. This action should open the file for editing.

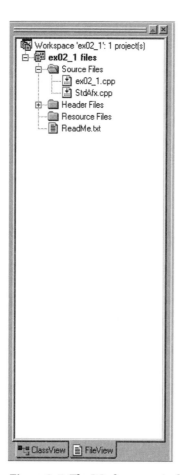

Figure 2-7. The Workspace window in File View mode

To begin the debug process, press the F11 key (which is a shortcut to selecting Build → Start Debug → Step Into). You should see a yellow arrow pointing to the first line of executable code in the ex02_1.cpp file as shown in Figure 2-8.

If you continue to press F11 a few times, you will see some pretty scary looking code. What is it? Well my friend, you are now inside the C++ runtime library, and *it* is the C++ runtime function *printf. printf* is a function that writes a character to the screen. It is very similar to calling Debug.Print in Visual Basic. Don't get too worried about the code you are stepping through; the point of this exercise is to show you that there is a plethora of information available to you through the Visual Studio debugger.

In the View → Debug Windows menu, there are several debug windows at your disposal that contain useful information (and some not so useful, depending on what you're trying to do). I pictured a few of them here. It should be pretty self-explanatory as to their individual function, but I will detail them a bit just in case.

The *Memory* window, shown in Figure 2-9, enables you to see the contents of a specific memory address. This is useful for examining variables that are not easily represented as a string or a number. Some examples might be a byte array or something of that nature.

The *Registers* window (Figure 2-10) shows the contents of the central processing unit's (CPU) registers. (We will not be using this window.)

The *Callstack* window is just like the Callstack window in Visual Basic—it shows you where the current execution point is, and where it will return.

The *Disassembly* window shows the assembly language instructions that are executed for each line of C++ code that you write.

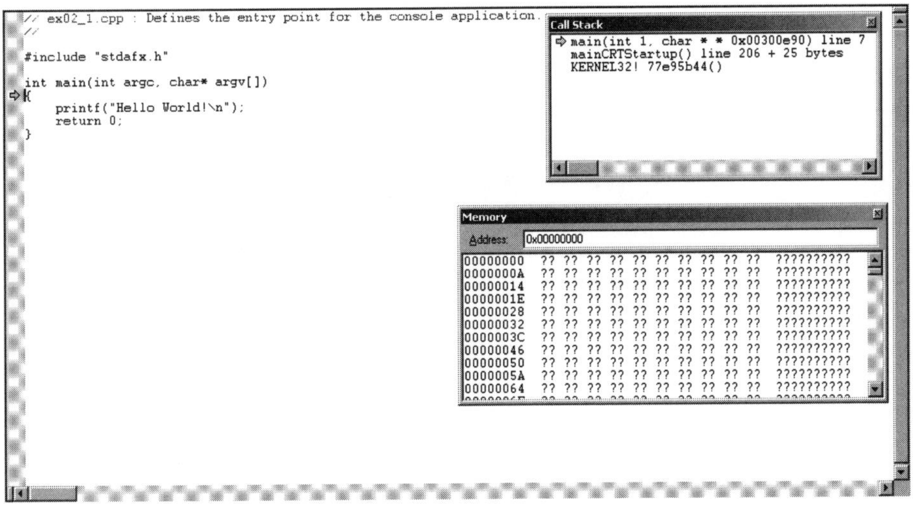

Figure 2-8. Debugging ex02_1.cpp

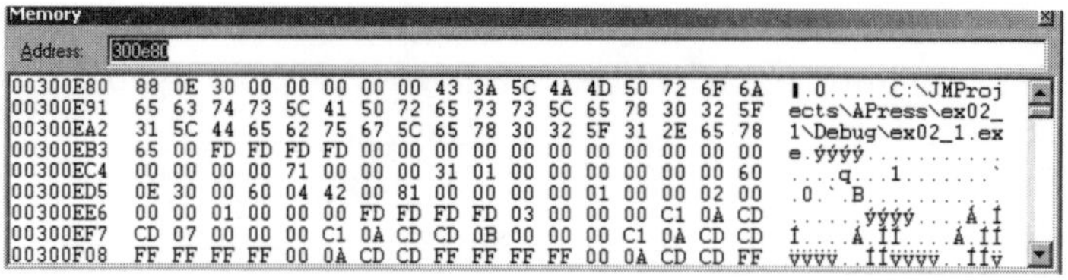

Figure 2-9. The Memory window

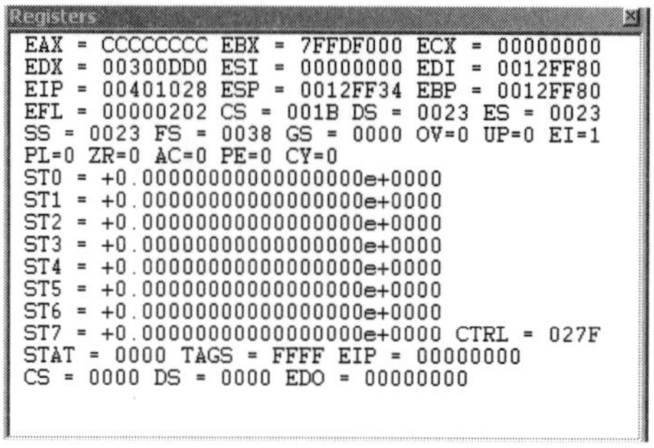

Figure 2-10. The Registers window

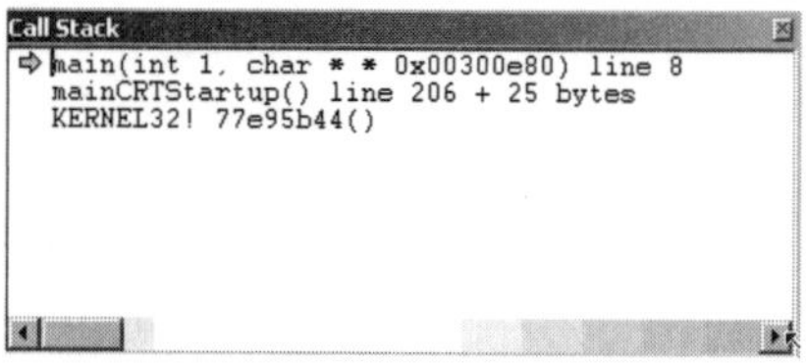

Figure 2-11. The Callstack window

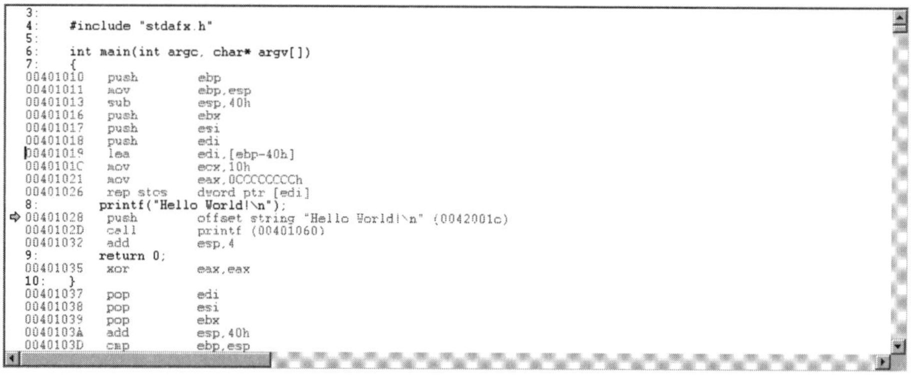

Figure 2-12. The Disassembly window

As we use the various debug windows in our example programs, I will describe their use in more detail.

Conclusion

This chapter provided a brief introduction to the Visual Studio development environment as well as a description of some differences between the way Visual Basic and C++ operate as programming languages. The next step on our journey is to actually learn about how programs are created by the compiler and linker—you might want to have a cup of coffee or some Jolt Cola before diving in!

CHAPTER 3

How Do You Do That Voodoo That You Do?

WHEN I SAW C++ SOURCE CODE FOR THE FIRST TIME, I became convinced that anyone able to write applications using this frightening language, which is full of curly brackets and pound signs, must have surely sold his soul to the devil. For, how else could a person use such an evil-looking tool for good? To go from the neat and clean syntax of Visual Basic to this complicated-looking language seemed an impossible task. However, my real aversion to C++ stemmed from the fact that at the time I did not understand that all programming languages served basically the same purpose: to enable programmers to give commands to a computer chip in a language both the programmer and the computer chip understand.

Imagine for a moment two English-speaking people are sitting at a restaurant table. One says to the other, "I am going to get another drink. I will be back in a minute." The second person replies, "Okay. I'll wait here."

What has really happened here? The first person communicated to the second person that he will leave for a short period of time in order to get some liquid refreshment. The second person communicated to the first person that he understood the first person's command and that he, the second person, will not leave until the first person returns. Simple enough?

Now suppose that these same two people are speaking a language other than English. First of all, the conversation will sound very different from the English conversation. For example, the number of syllables spoken may differ from the previous conversation, as most languages cannot be directly translated on a word-for-word basis. Suppose that in this particular foreign language the English word *drink* expands to six or seven words.

This is exactly why different languages exist for writing computer programs. Some programming languages express certain ideas and complete certain tasks better than other languages. For instance, assume a programming language exists that does not have a concept of numeric values. This particular language would probably not be the language of choice for writing a calculator program. Does this mean that this language is no good? Absolutely not. Perhaps this language is suitable for artificial intelligence, or graphics rendering, or some other task. If only one language was perfect for all programming tasks, there would eventually only be one programming language. But the fact is, any computer programming language's source code is ultimately be reduced to a set of machine instructions that can be understood by the computer chip on which they are going to run. The usefulness of any programming language is based on its ability to represent those low-level machine instructions as high-level syntax and programming logic.

While the example of the two diners is a simple one, the point it makes is important. All languages accomplish the same task: communicating information. Be assured that any application that is running on an Intel Pentium III processor is nothing more than a series of Intel Pentium III processor machine instructions, regardless of the programming language used to write it. In order to communicate with an Intel Pentium III processor, you have to speak in the language it understands. If you can't speak that language directly, you had better get a translator!

Compiling

Most likely you have heard the term *compiling*. In fact, when you build an executable with Visual Basic, the progress bar at the top of the development environment even says *Compiling. . . .* So then, what is it?

In Computer Science terminology, *compile* simply means to translate a program from source code into machine language. A compiler is really just a translator. Going back to our previous example of the two people in the restaurant, imagine now that one of the diners speaks English and the other one speaks a different language. It is apparent that they will have a communication problem unless they find a translator that can speak and understand both languages. For Visual Basic programs, that translator is the *Visual Basic compiler* and for C++ programs it is the *Visual C++ compiler*. Consider the following Visual Basic code snippet:

```
Dim i As Integer

Do While i < 50
    i = i + I
Loop
```

When this code is run through the Visual Basic compiler, it is converted into machine instructions, which are stored in an .obj file. The contents of the .obj file are shown in Figure 3-1.

Just as this set of instructions looks like garbage to us, our Visual Basic code looks like garbage to the computer chip.

So how does our source code actually get turned into machine instructions? Again, it depends on the language and environment that you are using. If you compile with Visual Basic then the compile process follows these steps:

```
0003a0  6F 73 6F 66 74 20 56 69  73 75 61 6C 20 53 74 75  osoft Visual Stu
0003b0  64 69 6F 5C 56 43 39 38  5C 41 54 4C 5C 49 4E 43  dio\VC98\ATL\INC
0003c0  4C 55 44 45 22 20 2D 54  50 20 2D 58 00 73 72 63  LUDE" -TP -X.src
0003d0  00 44 3A 5C 70 72 6F 6A  65 63 74 73 5C 41 50 72  .D:\projects\APr
0003e0  65 73 73 5C 63 68 61 70  74 65 72 33 5C 65 78 33  ess\chapter3\ex3
0003f0  5F 30 31 5C 65 78 33 5F  30 31 5C 65 78 33 5F 30  _01\ex3_01\ex3_0
000400  31 2E 63 70 70 00 70 64  62 00 44 3A 5C 70 72 6F  1.cpp.pdb.D:\pro
000410  6A 65 63 74 73 5C 41 50  72 65 73 73 5C 63 68 61  jects\APress\cha
000420  70 74 65 72 33 5C 65 78  33 5F 30 31 5C 65 78 33  pter3\ex3_01\ex3
000430  5F 30 31 5C 44 65 62 75  67 5C 76 63 36 30 2E 70  _01\Debug\vc60.p
000440  64 62 00 00 00 77 10 55  8B EC 83 EC 44 53 56 57  db...w.U....DSVW
000450  8D 7D BC B9 11 00 00 00  B8 CC CC CC CC F3 AB C7  .}..............
000460  45 FC 00 00 00 00 83 7D  FC 32 7D 0B 8B 45 FC 83  E......}.2}..E..
000470  C0 01 89 45 FC EB EF 33  C0 5F 5E 5B 8B E5 5D C3  ...E...3._^[..].
000480  0E 00 00 00 00 00 18 00  00 00 02 00 1F 00 00 00  ................
000490  04 00 25 00 00 00 06 00  2E 00 00 00 07 00 30 00  ..%...........0.
0004a0  00 00 0A 00 32 00 00 00  0B 00 2A 00 0B 10 00 00  ....2.....*.....
0004b0  00 00 00 00 00 00 00 00  00 00 39 00 00 00 18 00  ..........9.....
0004c0  00 00 32 00 00 00 43 10  00 00 00 00 00 00 00 00  ..2...C.........
0004d0  01 04 6D 61 69 6E 1C 00  12 10 44 00 00 00 40 00  ..main....D...@.
0004e0  00 00 04 00 00 00 0C 00  00 00 00 00 00 00 00 00  ................
0004f0  00 00 00 00 0F 00 06 10  08 00 00 00 74 00 00 00  ............t...
000500  04 61 72 67 63 0F 00 06  10 0C 00 00 00 41 10 00  .argc........A..
000510  00 04 61 72 67 76 0C 00  06 10 FC FF FF FF 74 00  ..argv........t.
000520  00 00 01 69 02 00 06 00  20 00 00 00 0E 00 00 00  ...i............
000530  0B 00 24 00 00 00 0E 00  00 00 0A 00 02 00 00 00  ..$.............
000540  46 00 16 00 F3 40 39 38  03 00 00 00 38 64 3A 5C  F...@98....8d:\
000550  70 72 6F 6A 65 63 74 73  5C 61 70 72 65 73 73 5C  projects\apress\
000560  63 68 61 70 74 65 72 33  5C 65 78 33 5F 30 31 5C  chapter3\ex3_01\
000570  65 78 33 5F 30 31 5C 64  65 62 75 67 5C 76 63 36  ex3_01\debug\vc6
000580  30 2E 70 64 62 F3 F2 F1  2E 66 69 6C 65 00 00 00  0.pdb....file...
000590  00 00 00 00 FE FF 00 00  67 03 44 3A 5C 70 72 6F  ........g.D:\pro
0005a0  6A 65 63 74 73 5C 41 50  72 65 73 73 5C 63 68 61  jects\APress\cha
0005b0  70 74 65 72 33 5C 65 78  33 5F 30 31 5C 65 78 33  pter3\ex3_01\ex3
0005c0  5F 30 31 5C 65 78 33 5F  30 31 2E 63 70 70 00 00  _01\ex3_01.cpp..
0005d0  40 63 6F 6D 70 2E 69 64  E8 1F 0B 00 FF FF 00 00  @comp.id........
0005e0  03 00 2E 64 72 65 63 74  76 65 00 00 00 00 01 00  ...drectve......
0005f0  00 00 03 02 38 00 00 00  00 00 00 00 00 00 00 00  ....8...........
000600  00 00 00 00 00 00 00 00  00 00 00 00 00 00 00 00  ................
000610  00 00 00 00 00 00 00 00  2E 64 65 62 75 67 24 53  .........debug$S
000620  00 00 00 00 02 00 00 00  03 02 33 03 00 00 00 00  ..........3.....
000630  00 00 00 00 00 00 00 00  00 00 00 00 00 00 00 00  ................
000640  00 00 00 00 00 00 00 00  00 00 00 00 00 00 2E 74  ...............t
```

Figure 3-1. The contents of the .obj file in Visual Studio

1. Visual Basic converts your source code into an intermediate library language that is the equivalent of C code.

2. This intermediate library is then fed to `C2.exe`, which is an old Microsoft C compiler specially designed to work with Visual Basic. You can verify that Visual Basic uses `C2.exe` by looking at the Windows Task Manager during the build process, as shown in Figure 3-2.

3. C2.exe produces an `.obj` file from the intermediate library. (This `.obj` file is what you saw as the machine instructions in Figure 3-1.)

If you compile with Visual C++, the compile process is as follows:

1. The source code file is sent to `CL.exe`, which is the C++ compiler.

2. `CL.exe` produces an `.obj` file from the source code.

Pretty cool huh? Well that's all well and good, but we all know that you can't run an `.obj` file. So where does the `.exe` file come from? That, my friend, is where the linker comes into play.

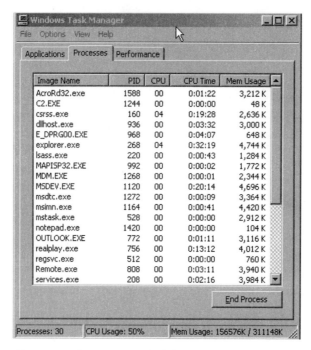

Figure 3-2. C2.exe is invoked during the compile process.

Linking

Now that we know how our source code is turned into machine language (or an .obj file), we now must learn how our .obj files get turned into an .exe file.

First, let me point out that for each source file you write, an .obj file will be created. Let's say you create a Visual Basic project with one .frm file and two .bas files—how many .obj files will be created after compiling? (This is not a trick question by the way.) The answer is three: one for each source file created. The linker's job then is to connect all of the .obj files into an .exe.

Simple, right?

Well, not exactly. It would be except for the fact that when we write code, we sometimes call functions that exist in other modules. For instance, let's say that you have a function in one of your .bas modules called CheckSpelling, and it is called from your .frm file. When the compiler encounters the call to CheckSpelling in your .frm file, it will have no idea where the function Check-Spelling is because the compiler only looks at one file at a time. If that function has not been encountered previously in that file, then the compiler will have no idea what to do. The compiler will essentially leave that part of the .obj file blank and write a special line in the .obj file that instructs the linker to find out where CheckSpelling is (fix-up) and add it to that part of the .obj file before it creates the .exe. The linker then comes in and looks at all of the .obj files, looking for these special instructions. When it finds the missing functions in each .obj file, it fills in the blank areas of the `.obj` file with the correct code as if the function had existed in that module when it was compiled. Now please understand that this explanation is extremely simplified, but for our purposes it will suit us just fine.

In order to further explain this topic, let's digress for a moment. Suppose there is a new service available to consumers called "At Home Grocery Shopping" that works like this: A shopper first creates a grocery list with each item desired listed on a separate piece of paper. Each page specifies the aisle and shelf on which a grocery item can be found. Second, each page is faxed to the "At Home Grocery Shopping" shopping service. Then lastly, the groceries show up at your door ready for consumption.

We can use this scenario to describe the way a linker works. First, you create a grocery list (source code), which indicates the aisle and shelf for each item. Second, you fax each page of the list to the service (the `.obj` files). Last, the groceries show up at your door (the `.exe` is created).

Assume that on my grocery list I have an entry for "Olga Dogs," but I am not sure which aisle and shelf this item is on. What will happen when the shopping service encounters this item? Well, the shopping service will go and look for an item that has this name, find the item (fix-up), and add the location of the item, aisle, and shelf to my list. Now if that store doesn't carry Olga Dogs, or they are referred to as a different name (such as OlgaDogs@12FAYZZ), the shopping service (linker) will return the error, "Grocery Item Not Found" ("LINK ERROR 2001: Unresolved External Symbol").

You will become familiar with this error as we go along. But what does this mean? It means that I won't be having Olga Dogs for supper (and that we won't get an `.exe` either). You see, although the shopping service will still deliver my groceries even if it can't find an item, the linker will not create an `.exe` unless it can resolve all the function names (symbols) it encounters. If you are not completely comfortable with this whole process, don't worry! We will beat this concept of linking to death throughout the rest of the book.

C Preprocessor

If you've ever seen C++ code, you have probably seen a *preprocessor directive*. Preprocessor directives are any lines that start with a pound sign (#), such as `#define` ("pound def"), `#include` ("pound include"), and so on.

What are they? These preprocessor directives are special instructions to a tool called *the C preprocessor*. (From here on the C preprocessor will be referred to as just the *preprocessor*.) The preprocessor is the first tool to run in the compile process. Its job is very much like the groundskeeper for a football stadium. The groundskeeper is responsible for having the field ready for the big game on Sunday. His responsibilities include drawing the yard lines on the field with chalk, painting the team logo in the end zones ("Chiefs not Chefs," "Great koogaly-moogaly!"), and so on. Basically, the groundskeeper has to prepare the field for play before anything else can happen. While the preprocessor doesn't do any of the aforementioned tasks specifically, it does "prepare the field" in the context of program compilation. However, in order to fully understand how this works we must look at the preprocessor directives and their uses.

#include

The #include directive is probably the most often used directive in C++ programming. It has a simple purpose: It copies code from other files into your source code. Consider the following C++ source code files named myfile.cpp and myfile.h.

Contents of myfile.cpp:

```
001:    //This is the C++ source code file myfile.cpp
002:    #include <stdio.h>
003:    #include "myfile.h"

004:    //Other code to run the program
005:    //End of myfile.cpp
```

Contents of myfile.h:

```
001:    //This is the C++ header file myfile.h
002:    //Useful stuff goes here
003:    //End of myfile.h
```

Note that in these sample listings, the numbers on the left of the line are simply line numbers I put in to make it easier to follow the code. (They have nothing to do with the source code and do not appear in the actual source code files.)You may also be wondering why we have one file with a .h extension and one with a .cpp extension. I hate to disappoint you, but it's a pretty boring explanation: .cpp files are the files where your C++ source code—such as functions and other program code—will reside. But so are .h files. .h files (or *header* files) are simply a matter of organization and convenience. Although they have a different extension than .cpp files (C++ source code files) they contain C++ source code and will always get #included into a .cpp file. Thus the reason .h, or header files, are called header files: they go at the head of a .cpp file.

Line 003 of myfile.cpp contains the line #include "myfile.h". This preprocessor directive tells the preprocessor to open the file "myfile.h", copy the contents, and paste it into myfile.cpp in the place previously occupied by the line #include "myfile.h" (Line 003).

Now you may also be wondering why Line 002 of myfile.cpp has angle brackets around the #include file name and Line 003 has double quotes around it. Simple. In C++ there are "standard" header files, such as the header files for the operating system API and the C++ standard library (which I'll discuss in the next chapter). These standard header files usually reside in the folder pointed to by the INCLUDE environment variable (this variable should be set by the installation program when you install Visual C++). By enclosing a header file name in angle brackets in a #include directive, you tell the preprocessor to start searching for the file listed in the #include directive in this folder. If the header file name is enclosed in double quotes, the processor starts searching for the file in the current directory and then goes to the INCLUDE path. If the file is still not found, the normal search path for the operating system is followed. That's the only difference. We will discuss stdio.h later in this book. For now just know that its contents will also be copied into myfile.cpp because of Line 002 of myfile.cpp (#include <stdio.h>).

That pretty much sums up the #include directive, so let's move on to another heavily used preprocessor directive: #define.

#define

The #define directive has many uses, including declaring constants, defining macros, and controlling compilation. When used to declare a constant, the #define directive is used to accomplish the same result as the Const keyword in Visual Basic. Let's look at an example:

```
#define    MAGIC_NUMBER    7
```

When the preprocessor runs, it will replace all occurrences of the word MAGIC_NUMBER with the number 7. Understand, you will never see the source file after the preprocessor has modified it, but to clear the point let's see what it would look like if we could.

Contents of main.cpp before the preprocessor:

```
//This is the C++ source code file main.cpp
#include "myfile.h"

int main(int argv, char *argc[])
{
    int x = MAGIC_NUMBER;

    return x;
}

//End of myfile.cpp
```

Contents of `main.h`:

```
//This is the C++ header file main.h
#define    MAGIC_NUMBER    7
//End of myfile.h
```

Contents of `main.cpp` after the preprocessor:

```
//This is the C++ source code file main.cpp
//This is the C++ header file main.h
#define    MAGIC_NUMBER    7
//End of myfile.h

int main(int argv, char *argc[])
{
    int x = 7;
    return x;
}


//End of myfile.cpp
```

You can see that the post-preprocessor version of `main.cpp` contains the entire contents of the file `main.h` as well as the original contents of `main.cpp` with one exception: the text `MAGIC_NUMBER` has been replaced with the number 7 for each occurrence in both files. Apparently, the preprocessor has done its job and done it well. In actuality, this modified version of `main.cpp` is what is sent to the compiler.

However, the #define directive has many uses other than just defining constants. First of all it can be used to create conditions for compilation, as shown in the following code listing:

```
001:    #define LUCKY_SEVEN

002:    #ifdef LUCKY_SEVEN
003:        #define    MAGIC_NUMBER    7
004:    #else
005:        #define      MAGIC_NUMBER    1
006:    #endif
```

In the first line we declare that `LUCKY_SEVEN` is defined, which is roughly equivalent to creating Boolean variable named `luckySeven` and setting its value to true. In line 002 the preprocessor decides which lines to process based on the value of `LUCKY_SEVEN`. Line 002 would be roughly equivalent to the statement, If `luckySeven` = True Then…. So if `LUCKY_SEVEN` has been #defined previously in the source code, the preprocessor will go to Line 003. If it has not been defined previously, the preprocessor will go to Line 005. This concept is called *Conditional Compilation*, because the compiler only compiles what the preprocessor gives to it, and these directives control the output of the preprocessor.

Another use of the #define directive, is to create *Macros*. Macros are very much like functions except for the fact that they don't get type checked at compile time. Consider the following code:

```
001:    #define        DOUBLE(x)        (x + x)
002:    //other program code
003:    int a = DOUBLE(4);
004    int b = 16 / DOUBLE(a);
```

After the preprocessor runs, the code will be expanded to look like this:

```
001:    #define        DOUBLE(x)        (x + x)
002:    //other program code
003:    int a = (4 + 4);
004:    int b = 16 / (a + a);
```

Line 001 #defines the macro DOUBLE (x), which takes one argument: x. The end of Line 001 tells the preprocessor to replace all occurrences of the text DOUBLE (x), with x + x, or the parameter passed to DOUBLE (x) added to the parameter passed to DOUBLE (x) just like what happened on Line 003.

Macros are very useful, but there are a few caveats. The first caveat has already been mentioned: there is no type checking, which means that I could pass the letter "a" as the parameter for DOUBLE or any other value. This will produce unexpected results at best. Having this "non-type checking" freedom can seem like a benefit in some cases, but is usually better implemented using other language facilities, which I will discuss later in this book.

The other problem is that when macros are "expanded" (or processed by the preprocessor), they are expanded exactly as the #define tells them to. Look at Line 001 in the pre-preprocessor code. There are parentheses around the text x + x. This may not seem important, but if they were not there, Line 004 in the second example would look like the following after expansion:

```
004:    int b = 16 / a + a;
```

which reads, "take the result of 16 divided by *a* and add a to it," which is going to give a much different result than the correct listing:

```
004:    int b = 16 / (a + a);
```

which reads, "take 16 and divide it by the result of *a* plus *a*."

These types of bugs can be nightmarish to find. As a general rule, if your macro is difficult to work with as a macro, it shouldn't be a macro.

Other Directives

The directives used for conditional compilation are #if, #ifdef, #undef, #elif, #else, and #endif, some of which you have already seen. They work exactly like the If, ElseIf, Else, End If keywords in Visual Basic except for #ifdef and #undef. They essentially check for a condition or reset a previously #defined expression as in the following:

```
001:    #define LUCKY_SEVEN

002:    #ifdef LUCKY_SEVEN
003:        #define    MAGIC_NUMBER    7
004:    #else
005:        #define        MAGIC_NUMBER    1
006:    #endif
007:    #undef    LUCKY_SEVEN

008:    #ifdef LUCKY_SEVEN
009        #define    STILL_THERE
010:    #endif
```

In this example the text (also called a *token*), LUCKY_SEVEN, is defined in Line 001. So the #ifdef LUCKY_SEVEN in Line 002 evaluates to true, and as such the pre-processor will process Line 003. However, the same expression on Line 008 will evaluate to false because the symbol LUCKY_SEVEN was #undef-ed on Line 007. Therefore, the preprocessor will skip Line 009 during its process. There is also a #ifndef, which is the same as #ifdef except that it checks for the absence of a definition as in the following:

```
#ifndef    LUCKY_SEVEN
//Do something here if LUCKY_SEVEN has not been defined
#endif
```

The #error directive tells the preprocessor to raise a compile error as in the following:

```
#if TIME > 5PM
    #error Time to go home!
#endif
```

So that if you try to compile this file after 5 P.M., the compiler will give you the error Time to go home! This directive is rarely used except to check the version of the operating system and version of the development environment. There are several other directives that we will cover later on in this book.

Now that we know about the compiling, linking, and preprocessing processes, we are almost ready to dive into the C++ language itself. There is, however, one more important area that we must cover before we go on. Let's see now, what was it? Um… I can't remember what it was. Oh yes, memory!

Memory

These days, the subject of memory has become very convoluted. We have random access memory (RAM), read-only memory (ROM), Physical Memory, Virtual Memory, and so on. Fortunately for us application developers, we only care about one type of memory: our process's virtual memory address space. We don't care where our memory is. We only care that it is there—somewhere.

This definitely needs some explanation, but first I must make sure we are on the same page (no pun intended) when it comes to our understanding of what our process's *virtual memory address space* really is. As a supplement to the following primer, I highly suggest reading Tutorial 2 from *Dan Appleman's Win32 API Puzzle Book and Tutorial for Visual Basic Programmers* (Apress, 1999) and Chapter 15 of *Dan Appleman's Visual Basic Programmers Guide to the Win32 API* (Sams, 1999). I suggest these texts because they should be a required part of every professional Visual Basic programmer's library. Both of these sections give a wonderful description of Windows memory management as well as memory management and theory in general.

Process Address Space

A process's address space is a lot like a Bingo card from the game of the same name. Yes, Bingo. You see, in the game, each player is given a card with a 5 by 5 grid on it. Each cell in the grid contains a number between 1 and 100. Across the top, in each cell is one letter from the word *Bingo* listed from left to right as shown in Figure 3-3.

A "caller" chooses different combinations of numbers and letters from the word *Bingo*. (For example, B-42, N-76, and so on.) The object of the game is to get a line of cells in a row, either across, down, or diagonally. When you want to refer to a cell, you call it by the column heading letter and cell number as such: the third row down in the first column is B-85. The fourth row down in the third column is N-22, and so on.

Okay, so what could this possibly have to do with the process address spaces? Well, nothing really except that it shows the concept of *virtual memory*. You see, in Bingo, each player's card will have different numbers in each of the cells so that on the card pictured in Figure 3-3, the second row down of the fourth column is

B	I	N	G	O
68	52	61	82	29
42	20	59	5	55
85	86	93	41	33
14	27	22	90	23
8	53	19	71	7

Figure 3-3. A typical Bingo playing card

G-5. On another card it might be G-27, or G-40. Each player's card has the same size, number and location of squares—but the contents of those squares are different.

This is exactly the same way that process address spaces work. Each process (under 32-bit Windows) receives a 4GB linear address space that is totally private. What does it mean to have a 4GB linear address space? Essentially it means that an application has access to any address in the range of 0x00000000 and 0xFFFFFFFF, which make up its 4GB of address space. Let's say I create a variable *x* that is of type *integer* and is stored at memory address 0x00FC8924 in my process's address space. Now assume that another application also creates a variable *x* of type *integer* and stores it at memory address 0x00FC8924 in its address space. If I change the value of *x* in my process, should the value also change for the other application? No. The reason is simple. Just as G-5 was the second row down of the fourth column on my card and may have been the third row down of the fourth column on another card, my process's address 0x00FC8924 is in no way related to the address 0x00FC8924 in any other process space. In fact, the address 0x00FC8924 may contain garbage in that other process's address space. In other words, everything is relative. The name of an address in a process address space (such as 0x00FC8924) has nothing to do with its physical location in memory.

Well, you may be thinking, if all of a process's addresses are virtual, who keeps track of where stuff is really stored? Windows. You see one of the most important jobs that an operating system has is memory management. The beauty of this is that you don't have to know where stuff is really stored. The variable x at virtual address 0x00FC8924 in my application might be stored on the hard drive while your variable x at virtual address 0x00FC8924 might be stored in RAM—it doesn't really matter. All we care about is that when we reference variable x, the right value shows up. Now if you are just dying to know about the underlying mechanics of virtual memory, then be my guest to dig deeper. However, throughout this book we assume that it all works the way the folks in Redmond, Washington, say it does.

Allocating and Initializing Memory

One huge difference between Visual Basic and C++ is *memory manipulation.* When you declare a variable in Visual Basic, many things happen that you never know about. Consider the following code:

```
Dim iNum As Integer
MsgBox CStr(iNum)
```

What value will appear in the message box? 0, right? Yep. Now this may seem absolutely normal but when you think about it, it really isn't. The reason I say that this isn't normal is because you never told Visual Basic what value to store in iNum. So why did Visual Basic put 0 in it? Well Visual Basic always initializes numeric variables to 0. In fact, you have no choice in the matter. Let's look at the following code:

```
001:    Dim iNum As Integer
002:    Dim iCounter As Integer
003:    iNum = 0
004:    For iCounter = iNum To 5000
005:        'Do Something useful
006:    Next iCounter
```

When Visual Basic encounters Line 001, it will request a place to store the variable iNum. It will then set iNum equal to the value 0. The same is true with Line 002.

When Line 003 is run, Visual Basic will change the value of iNum from 0 to 0 (no this is not a typo—it doesn't check to see if the variable already contains zero). Now notice that step one in this process was for Visual Basic to request one of those 4 billion addresses (0x00000000 through 0xFFFFFFFF) in the process's address space in which to store the variable iNum. Then it set the value of iNum to 0. What if the step that set the value of iNum to 0 had been skipped? What would iNum have equaled? We don't know. It could have been 28000,13, –185, or any legal value within the storage capacity of an integer. The reason for this is because once a variable is "Dim-ed" (or allocated), it contains the value that existed at that address before it was allocated. If iNum had not been set to 0 by Visual Basic, iNum would be what is known as an *un-initialized* variable.

Visual Basic essentially does in two steps for us what we perceive to be one. Asking the operating system for a place to store a variable is called *variable declaration*, or *allocation*. (Just in case you're curious why Visual Basic uses Dim for variable declaration, it is short for *Dimension*, which means "to allocate.") All this means is that we have a real live variable that exists at some memory address in our process's address space. Explicitly setting the initial value of a variable is called *variable initialization*.

This begs the question, "Why would Visual Basic do this for us?" To protect us from ourselves. Most of the time you will want a variable to start at 0 as in our previous code example. Imagine we forgot to put in Line 003. In Visual Basic it wouldn't matter because Visual Basic automatically sets iNum to 0 for us (And most of us count on Visual Basic to do this for us. I challenge you to find Visual Basic code that has the line 'i = 0' before i is ever used.) However, in C++ (as in most other languages), if we had omitted Line 003, the code would most assuredly result in a very difficult-to-find bug. Why? Because in our For-Next loop we assume that we are looping from 0 to 5000. But if iNum was initially equal to 521,452 (because we forgot to initialize it to 0 before our loop), we would never even enter our loop and this would most likely cause problems in our program.

Remember that each one of the 4GB of addresses in your process space have something in them. It may be garbage or just some previous value, but there is something there. Think of it as driving up to a fast-food drive-through window and ordering a "mystery" combo meal. This meal is called a "mystery" combo because you don't know what is in it, and each one ordered will be different. I order one and get a cheeseburger, French fries, and a soda. You order one and get a hot-dog, baked potato, and a chocolate milkshake. This is because we have ordered an un-initialized combo meal. It could contain anything, and worse yet, we can't complain about it because we never specified what we wanted our meal to contain. Now suppose I order a "mystery" combo meal and specify that I want it to contain a cheeseburger, French fries, and a Coke. I have now initialized my combo meal and won't get any unwanted surprises. This concept is very important to understand as we progress. Again, memory always contains something, either garbage or values that were put there intentionally. If you're still a little confused about the whole process address space issue, don't worry: we will definitely be re-visiting this topic throughout the course of this book.

Conclusion

This chapter attempted to both de-mystify and introduce some elements of C++ at the same time. The key point to remember from this chapter is that C++ is just a programming language like Visual Basic. It includes some elements that do not have a parallel element in Visual Basic, but they are not that difficult to grasp— you should now be comfortable with the process of compiling, linking, and pre-processing. It is time to start learning the actual syntax of C++. This is where it is going to start getting fun.

CHAPTER 4

C++ 101

WELL, IT'S INEVITABLE. IF WE ARE GOING TO DO anything useful with C++ we are going to have to learn the syntax of the language. Because you already know Visual Basic, it seems logical to use this knowledge as a crutch for learning C++, which is what we will do throughout this chapter.

As you start to learn C++ it is important to remember that you already know how to program—you just don't know the syntax of C++. Think of the process as learning how to drive a new type of car for the first time. You already know how to drive; you just have to learn where the trunk release is and how to set the clock in the new car and you're as good as you were in your old car.

Data and Variables

Regardless of the language in which it was written, every computer program contains some amount of data. Even if the program is only to write the words "Hello World," the fact that a program runs on a computer is proof that the program contains data. Thus, it is a good idea to start our learning of the C++ language by examining the available C++ data types, their Visual Basic equivalents (where applicable), and their storage capacity, which is summarized in Table 4-1.

You can see that there are many different data types available in C++. Also notice that in most cases they map directly to Visual Basic types.

> **NOTE:** *The* void *data type in C++ is special in that it has no value. It is used to show that there is an absence of value. The void type is usually used as the return type of a function to denote that the function does not return a value, or as the only item in a parameter list for a function that takes no arguments.*

Declaring Variables

Knowing the data types available in C++ is one thing, but we also need to know how to declare variables in order to make use of these data types. The syntax for variable declaration is in the form:

```
DataType VariableName [= InitialValue];
```

Table 4-1. C++ Data Types

NAME	SIZE (BYTES)	VISUAL BASIC EQUIVALENT	RANGE
short	2	Integer	−32,768 to 32,767
unsigned short	2	N/A	0 to 65,535
bool	1	Boolean	**true or false
int	*4	Long	−2,147,483,648 to 2,147,483,647
unsigned int	*4	Long	0 to 4,294,967,295
long	4	Long	−2,147,483,648 to 2,147,483,647
unsigned long	4	Long	0 to 4,294,967,295
char	1	N/A	−128 to 127
unsigned char	1	Byte	0 to 255
enum	*4	Long	Same as int
float	4	Single	3.4E +/- 38 (7 digits)
double	8	Double	1.7E +/- 308 (15 digits)
long double	10	N/A	1.2E +/- 4932 (19 digits)
void	0	N/A	Used to show an absence of value

* Assumes Win32 platform.

** In C++ the value *true* equates to any non-zero value, while in Visual Basic the value *True* equates to 1. In both cases *false* equates to 0.

An example declaration is as follows:

```
int x = 0;
```

This statement assigns the value 0 to the variable x. In fact, any of the numeric data types in C++ (which include short, int, long, float and double) can be initialized in this way. Now you may have noticed that the keyword unsigned appears before some of the types in our data type chart. This is because C++ supports the idea of unsigned numbers. An *unsigned number* is simply a number whose value cannot be less than zero. Unsigned numbers are useful for several applications, such as representing binary data. (In contrast, Visual Basic has only one unsigned data type, Byte, which covers the range 0 to 255.) For example, if I wanted to assign the number 14 to x in my code, I would write the following assignment statement:

```
unsigned int x = 14;
```

The numeric data types are straight forward, but there are several data types that require a little more explanation as to how they are used. We'll look at those now.

The char Data Type

The char data type is quite flexible. It can be used for its namesake and hold a single character with an assignment such as the following:

```
char myChar = 'a';
```

Notice the use of single quotes surrounding the initializing value of a. When you want to assign a single character to a variable of type char, you must always surround it with single quotes. You may assume that because we told our program to store the character a in memory that it did. Well, actually it didn't. Don't assume that we have a renegade variable here; it is just that a computer is not able to store characters—only numbers.

So what does get stored as the value of myChar? The number 61, which just happens to be the hexadecimal equivalent of the number 97, which just happens to be the ASCII (American Standard Code for Information Interchange) value for the character a.

Make sense? Good. Now don't let this confuse you. The key thing to remember is that all of the data in a computer is stored as numbers. It is the context in which we use those numbers that generates meaning. Think of the saying, "One man's trash is another man's treasure." To someone just looking at the memory stored in our program, the number 61 doesn't mean anything. But, because we know that 61 is the ASCII representation of a character, to us it means a lot. Just remember that all data interpretation is relative to its intended use. (This concept will start to make more sense when we cover the printf() function later in this chapter.)

The char[] Data Type

The char[] data type is not a unique data type; it is just an array of char, or basically a string of characters. We could use this data type to store any character string that is too large for the type char. (In other words, a string that is more than one character long.) Following is an example usage of type char[]:

```
char myChars[255];
```

This declaration is pretty much identical to the following declaration in Visual Basic:

```
Dim myChars As String * 255;
```

Both of these declarations allocate space for 255 characters. They cannot grow in size later in the program in which they are used, which is limiting in most cases. Where this type of declaration is useful is in a situation where you know the maximum length of a string. However, there is another way to declare a char[ ], shown here:

```
char myChars[] = "Hello";
```

This declaration is identical to the following:

```
char myChars[6] = "Hello";
```

In other words, when a char[] is set to a string with no size specified, the compiler counts the number of characters in the string and automatically sets the char[ ] to that size plus one. Why plus one? The extra space is needed to hold the *NULL terminator* (which I cover in the next chapter). What is interesting about char[ ] is that you can access any of the members of the array directly by using standard array notation. For example, the following statement references the 'e' in "Hello":

```
myChars[1]
```

Why [1]? Because unlike the schizophrenic Visual Basic (which has arrays starting at one and zero), arrays in C++ are always 0-based. The first element of an array is at index 0, such that myChars[0],from our previous example, is equal to the letter 'H' in "Hello."

The enum Data Type

The enum data type is the identical cousin of the enum construct in Visual Basic. To declare an enumeration we use the following syntax:

```
enum RETURN_VALUES
{
    RET_OK,
    RET_FAILED,
    RET_UNDEFINED
};
```

Now, just as in the Visual Basic version of enum, if no specific value is set for an element, all of the elements are incremented in order of appearance starting at zero. For example, in our previous declaration, RET_OK equals 0, RET_FAILED equals 1 and RET_UNDEFINED equals 2. If any member is set with a value then the next member that does not have a value gets incremented based on that number. Consider the following alteration to our enum:

```
enum RETURN_VALUES
{
    RET_OK,
    RET_FAILED = 100,
    RET_UNDEFINED
};
```

In this version of our enum, RET_OK equals 0, RET_FAILED equals 100, and RET_UNDEFINED equals 101. This works exactly as in Visual Basic.

> **NOTE:** *While* enums *allow for assigning some values and not others, for the sake of readability it is generally better to assign all of the values in an* enum *or assign none at all.*

User Defined Types

Although the pre-defined types in C++ are useful, sometimes you just need to create your own custom type. In Visual Basic we do this with a User Defined Type (UDT) as shown here:

```
Private Type MyType
    lngNum1 As Long
    lngNum2 As Long
End Type
```

We can then use it in code like this:

```
Private Sub Form_Load()

Dim t As MyType

t.lngNum1 = 1
t.lngNum2 = 2

End Sub
```

This creates a flexible way of representing custom data types and data relationships. It should be no surprise that C++ also has the ability to express UDTs. In C++, a struct is used to do this. The syntax for creating a struct is as follows:

```
struct myStruct
{
    int num1;
    int num2;
};
```

We can then use it like so:

```
struct myStruct x;
x.num1 = 1;
x.num2 = 2;
```

Notice that it is similar to the Visual Basic version except that we have to prefix our variable declaration with the keyword struct in C++.

Standard Library Functions

Visual Basic makes it easy to become spoiled by the number of things that are done for us by the development environment and the language itself. The fact that all of Visual Basic's language facilities are at our fingertips as soon as we open a new project is not only useful but also subversively amazing. We don't have to worry about where Visual Basic keeps the MsgBox() function or where the InStr() function lives. We just call them up as we need to and they magically appear.

In C++ however, this is not the case. We get nothing by default; we have to ask for anything we want. The way to ask for things in C++ is to use the #include directive. Remember that #include is used to bring another file (usually a header file) into our program. If we want to print to the screen from our program, we have to either write a function to do so, or we have to #include a header file that links to or contains a function that does screen output. There is no function in the C++ language itself that prints to the screen. Now, anyone with any previous exposure to C++ will probably disagree with me and say that there are in fact functions in C++ that print to the screen. And, they'd be right—sort of. Let me explain.

In C++ there is an entity known as the *Standard C++ Library*, which is a set of header files that link to the C++ runtime library. Every implementation of the C++ compiler ships with these header files and the runtime library. These header files are the C++ programmers interface into the C++ runtime library. The Standard C++ Library is a set of language support files that make using the language easier and more efficient. They are a part of the American National Standards Institute (ANSI) C++ standard but are not an official part of the language.

Whether or not the Standard C++ Runtime Library is part of the C++ language is only a matter of semantics, because the fact of the matter is that this library contains the functions that all C++ programmers use to write C++ programs. You may be wondering why I brought up this whole discussion if it is just about semantics. Here's why: Let's suppose that the C++ runtime has a function named printToScreen() and I write C++ source code that uses that function. I would expect that when I compiled my program that the compiler would find that function in the standard C++ library, but it doesn't. Remember from Chapter 3 that the linker only knows about things that are on its "to do" list, which comes in the form of function prototypes and declarations. In my source code I never told the linker anything about the printToScreen() function. I just used it in my code. This is no good because the linker has to take my call to that function and convert to a function pointer that points to the real implementation of printToScreen(), but in this case there is no declaration for the linker to resolve with. Therefore, if I want to use the printToScreen() function, I have to #include the header file that contains the declaration of that function.

There are roughly 50 header files in the Standard C++ Library, which correlate directly to the C++ runtime library. These headers are divided into logical opera-

NOTE: *Due to the vastness of the Standard C++ Library, I will not attempt to detail each one here. I will instead explain the use of each function that we use in our example programs. Microsoft has done a good job of documenting and providing example uses of each function in the C++ runtime library. I suggest that you poke around through each header file and look up the usage of the various functions. You can also search by functionality in the help file. It is also worth noting that in Windows programming, many of the C++ Runtime Library functions have more efficient counterparts available through the Win32API. However, it is useful to know the common C++ Runtime Library functions since you will be writing C++ code.*

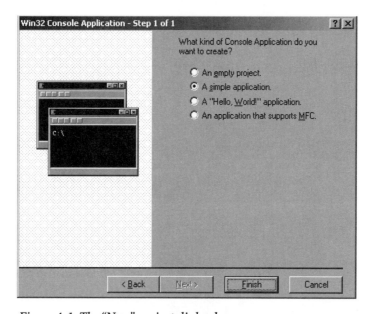

tional units. For example, the Standard C++ Library file, `<stdio.h>`, defines the standard input/output functions available from the C++ runtime library. Ultimately, if you want to use one of the functions in the runtime, you have to include the proper header file.

Program Structure

Okay, now that we have some understanding of the basic elements of C++, let's try to put them to use in an application.

C++ programs are structured pretty much like Visual Basic programs. They consist of code modules that contain functions, variables, and constants (which should all be familiar terms). There are, however, a few elements of C++ that will be completely foreign to most Visual Basic programmers. Not to worry—by the end of this book they will be as familiar as "Option Explicit" is to you today. I am a firm believer in learning by example, so, let's write a simple C++ program and then examine each part of it in detail in order to learn the different components that make up a C++ program.

To start, open Visual Studio and select File → New. Then select "Win32 console application" as our project type. In the Project Name field of the New Project dialog box, enter *ex01_ch4*. When prompted for the type of project, select "A simple application." as shown in Figure 4-1.

After clicking OK, your development environment should look similar to the environment shown in Figure 4-2.

Figure 4-1. The "New" project dialog box

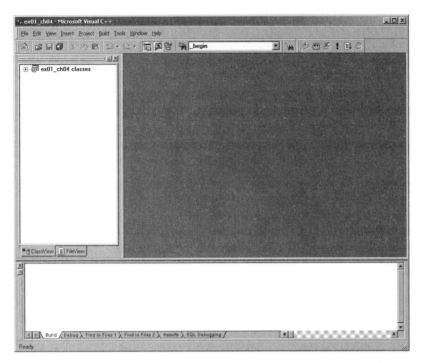

Figure 4-2. The Visual Studio development environment with ex01_ch04 loaded

Notice that there are two views available for the project: Class View and File View. These choices are available by selecting one of the aforementioned tabs at the bottom of the Workspace window on the left side of the development environment (assuming you haven't moved it), as shown in Figure 4-3.

We want to select File View as our view. This enables us to see all of the files in our project grouped by type. Let's open the Source Files node on the treeview control in the File View window. You should see two files in the node: ex01_ch4.cpp and stdafx.cpp. The contents of the file should display in your development environment's code window. Now, add the following code to your open file so that it looks like the code listed here:

```
// ex01_ch4.cpp : Defines the entry point for the console application.
//

#include "stdafx.h"
//variable declarations
int iPublicVar = 0;

int main(int argc, char* argv[])
{
    changeVar();
```

```
        printf("iPublicVar == %d.\n",iPublicVar);
        printf("The sum of 5 and 4 is %d.\n",addNums(5,4));
        changeVar();
        printf("iPublicVar == %d.\n",iPublicVar);
        changeVar();
        printf("iPublicVar == %d.\n",iPublicVar);
        return 0;
}

//function to add numbers
int addNums(int iNum1, int iNum2)
{
        int iSum = 0;
        iSum = iNum1 + iNum2;
        return iSum;
}

//sub to change a variable.
void changeVar()
{
        iPublicVar++;
}
```

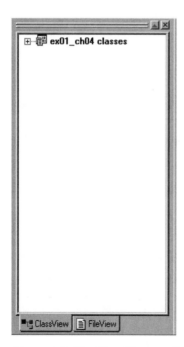

Figure 4-3. The Class View and File View tabs

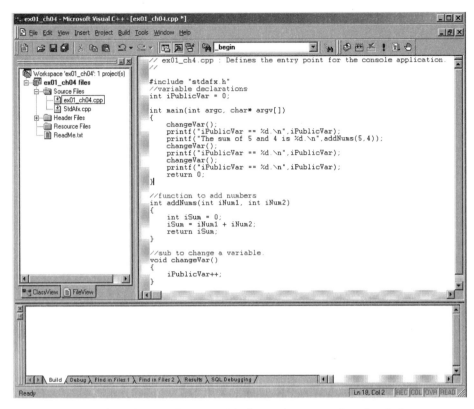

```
// ex01_ch4.cpp : Defines the entry point for the console application.
//

#include "stdafx.h"
//variable declarations
int iPublicVar = 0;

int main(int argc, char* argv[])
{
    changeVar();
    printf("iPublicVar == %d.\n",iPublicVar);
    printf("The sum of 5 and 4 is %d.\n",addNums(5,4));
    changeVar();
    printf("iPublicVar == %d.\n",iPublicVar);
    changeVar();
    printf("iPublicVar == %d.\n",iPublicVar);
    return 0;
}

//function to add numbers
int addNums(int iNum1, int iNum2)
{
    int iSum = 0;
    iSum = iNum1 + iNum2;
    return iSum;
}

//sub to change a variable.
void changeVar()
{
    iPublicVar++;
}
```

Figure 4-4. Visual Studio in File View with the project ex01_ch04 *loaded*

Your development environment should now look like the environment shown in Figure 4-4.

Remember from Chapter 3 that the #include preprocessor directive copies the contents of one file into another at compile time. Well, guess what the first line of code in our program does. Yep, #includes stdafx.h. The reason we do this is because we want to include the contents of stdafx.h in our source code file before it gets compiled. (Makes sense, right?)

Generally, header files contain variable declarations, constant definitions, or preprocessor directives (including #include; yes you can have nested #includes). One of the most common elements found in a header file is a function prototype. *Function prototyping* is the first one of those "foreign concepts" I mentioned earlier in this chapter, so let me explain. In Visual Basic we always use Option Explicit, which forces us to declare variables in our program before we use them. C++ takes this idea one step further by requiring function prototypes in our program before we use them. But, before we can go too far I must explain how a C++ function is organized. The form of a C++ function is as follows:

```
returnValueType functionName([arguments]){functionBody}
```

This is in contrast to a Visual Basic function, which takes the following form:

```
[Public or Private] Function functionName([arguments]) ReturnValueType
```

Let's look at two examples of a function prototype:

```
int addNums(int iNum1,int iNum2); //first function prototype
void changeVar(); //second function prototype
```

These are both examples of function prototypes. You may notice that the prototypes don't contain any executable code. So then, what is the point of having a function prototype? If you remember from Chapter 3, we said that when the compiler runs, it generates an error if it hits an unrecognized symbol (such as an undefined variable or function). The way we define a symbol is by either defining a variable or writing a function prototype. What a prototype does is tell the compiler that there is a function matching its description somewhere in the program. Once this is done, the compiler is satisfied. The next step is for the linker to go and actually find the executable code that implements the function prototype and put it into the program.

Think of this process as similar to having a credit card. You may have a credit card (function declaration) in your possession, which suggests that you will be able to pay for a purchase. However, when you go to the counter the cashier (the linker) will check with the credit card company to verify that you have available credit for your purchases (function's implementation). If she finds that you do (the implementation is found), you can take your purchases and go (your program gets linked into an .exe). On the other hand, if your credit card is rejected (no function implementation is found), you will not be able to purchase your items (your program will not be linked into an .exe).

Now, let's look at our header file, `stdafx.h`, after you've added the function prototypes for the functions added earlier to the file ex01-ch4.cpp:

```
//    stdafx.h : include file for standard system include files,
//    or project specific include files that are used frequently, but
//    are changed infrequently
//

#if !defined(AFX_STDAFX_H__7AC25963_B4D4_11D3_BC89_901151C10000__INCLUDED_)
#define AFX_STDAFX_H__7AC25963_B4D4_11D3_BC89_901151C10000__INCLUDED_

#if _MSC_VER > 1000
#pragma once
```

```
#endif // _MSC_VER > 1000

#define WIN32_LEAN_AND_MEAN     // Exclude rarely-used stuff from Windows headers

#include <stdio.h>

//function prototypes
int addNums(int iNum1,int iNum2);
void changeVar();

// TODO: reference additional headers your program requires here

//{{AFX_INSERT_LOCATION}}
// Microsoft Visual C++ will insert additional declarations immediately before the
previous line.

#endif // !defined(AFX_STDAFX_H__7AC25963_B4D4_11D3_BC89_901151C10000__INCLUDED_)
```

You can see the function prototypes for our two functions, addNums() and changeVar(). We also defined one public variable, iPublicVar, whose initial value is set to 0. Because we #included stdafx.h in our source code file, ex01_ch4.cpp, our function prototypes are recognized before the compiler runs into our function calls in our program.

> **NOTE:** *The order of the function prototypes and function calls is important. The function prototype must appear before any call to the function that it represents. It is for this reason that function prototypes usually live in header files that get* #included *into a source file where the actual function is called.*

Continuing on with our program, we see the line after our #include is the actual entry point of our application. We know this because of the fact that it is the definition of the function main(). Let's look at it:

```
int main(int argc, char* argv[])
```

We know from our previous definition of a C++ function that the left most symbol, int, indicates that our function will have a return value type of int. And that the next symbol, reading from right to left, is our function's name; main. The next two sets of declarations, int argc and char* argv[], are our programs arguments. The first argument tells us the number of arguments that were passed to our program, while the second argument is an array of char* that actually contains the arguments. We will leave this discussion until after we have discussed pointers, but suffice it to say that with these two parameters we can accept any number of arguments from the command line.

Curly Braces { }

In case you're not familiar with the term, *scope* identifies a certain section of code as being a cohesive unit. In other words, anything defined in that particular scope is visible to all other elements of that scope. If a variable is declared inside of a function, it is said to have *Function Scope*. If a variable is declared in a public code module not contained within a function, it is said to have *Global Scope*. When a scope is exited (such as a function returning), all items declared in that scope (such as variables) disappear as well. In C++ you can create scope by using curly braces ({ }).

If you declare a variable after a curly brace, it will only be in scope until the closing curly brace is encountered. In some cases a curly brace is optional, as in an *if* statement, but I find it much more clear to always enclose a related group of statements together in a set of curly braces. (See "The if Statement" later in this chapter for more information on *if* statements.)

Semi-Colon ;

The next line in our program is a call to changeVar() followed by a semi-colon. A semi-colon in C++ is used to terminate a statement. This is exactly the same as in Visual Basic, except that Visual Basic uses an *end of line* character to terminate a statement.

So does that mean that every line of code in C++ will be terminated with a semi-colon? No. Consider the following:

```
#define CALL_CHANGE_VAR        changeVar()
```

This line of code sets CALL_CHANGE_VAR as an alias for the text "changeVar()." So why doesn't this line need to be terminated with a semi-colon? This line is not an executable statement. Remember from Chapter 3 that #define is a preprocessor directive, not a compiler directive. Before our program compiles, the preprocessor will go through our source code and replace all occurrences of CALL_CHANGE_VAR with the text "changeVar()." I would use this in code as follows:

```
{
//Other program statements here
CALL_CHANGE_VAR;
//Other program statements here
}
```

Now after the preprocessor runs, this code fragment would look like this:

```
{
//Other program statements here
changeVar();
//Other program statements here
}
```

Just as in Visual Basic, in C++ there is no requirement that a statement be on a single line. Consider the following statement:

```
int x = 2 + 2;
```

I could have just as easily (and correctly) written it as:

```
int x
=
2
+
2;
```

An equivalent statement in Visual Basic would look like this:

```
Dim x As Integer
x _
= _
2 _
+ _
2
```

As you can see, C++ does not require a "line continuation character" (like Visual Basic does) to continue a program statement to the next line. Use this technique judiciously, however, as it can make the source code more difficult to read.

printf()

Our next program statement:

```
printf("iPublicVar == %d.\n",iPublicVar);
```

makes use of the Standard C++ Library function, printf(). This function is used to print to the standard output device (which is usually a computer monitor's screen). The function prototype for this function is in the stdio.h header file, which we #included in our program inside of our header file, stdafx.h. The printf() prototype looks like this:

```
int printf(const char *, ...);
```

Now, if we dissect this prototype, we can see that printf() returns a value of type int (which indicates the number of characters written to the screen, or a negative number if there was an error). You may notice that the arguments section of our function prototype look a bit odd. This is because we have just encountered two new C++ language elements, one of which is the *ellipsis* (the three periods next to each other in the place of the functions second parameter). An ellipsis is simply a matter of notation that tells the compiler that this function will accept any number and type of arguments. The compiler then disables typechecking for the additional parameters (because there is nothing to check against).

This is considered bad programming practice in most cases. However, there are some functions that necessitate using the ellipsis. I will not go into the specifics of implementing a function that uses an ellipsis, but you will probably see them from time to time. For example, printf() is one of those functions that makes legitimate use of the ellipsis. To see why, let's continue examining our call to printf():

```
printf("iPublicVar == %d.\n",iPublicVar);
```

The first parameter we pass to printf() in the previous code is an ordinary string literal. There is, however, something that looks a little odd contained within that ordinary string literal. First, you may have noticed a %d in the place where we want our variable's (iPublicVar) value to be displayed. Then at the end of our string literal you may also have seen a \n. This brings to the surface two more new C++ language features: format specifiers and escape sequences. First let's examine the area of format specifiers.

Format Specifiers

The f in printf() stands for *format*, which means printf(), prints a formatted string. In fact, printf() is somewhat similar to the Format function in Visual Basic. However, to achieve the effect of our call to printf() with Visual Basic, we have to use concatenation. Let's see how this looks:

```
Dim strMessage As String
Dim lngPublicVar As Long

Public Sub Main
lngPublicVar = 5
    Print "lngPublicVar = " & lngPublicVar & "." & vbCrLf
End Sub
```

> **NOTE:** Concatenation *is the process of joining various string literals and variables together to form one string.*

With these few lines of code we concatenate the variable `lngPublicVar` to the string literal `"lngPublicVar = "`. We also add a `vbCrLf` to the end of the line to ensure that we send a carriage return/line feed to the screen. `printf()` produces the same result, but using *format specifiers* instead. `printf()` actually takes the format specifiers from our string literal and replaces them with the values of the variables passed in to the ellipsis parameter. Remember, because we are not restricted by the number of arguments we can pass to `printf()`, we could actually use `printf()` as follows:

```
printf("iPublicVar == %d.%d%d\n",iPublicVar,iPublicVar,iPublicVar);
```

This would produce the following output (assuming that `iPublicVar` equals 5):

```
"iPublicVar == 5.55"
```

You may be wondering why I put a `%d` as the format specifier. Well, `%d` tells `printf()` to interpret the variable passed to it as a decimal number (hence, `d` for decimal).

> **NOTE:** *There are many other format specifiers available in C++. All of the C++ format specifiers and their respective meanings and uses are available in the online documentation provided with Visual Studio 6.0. We will be seeing some of the additional format specifiers used throughout the rest of the book though.*

Escape Sequences

Much like the format specifiers we just looked at, escape sequences tell C++ functions how to format output. In the above example of printf:

```
printf("iPublicVar == %d.%d%d\n",iPublicVar,iPublicVar,iPublicVar);
```

The \n after the three %d format specifiers is the "newline" escape sequence. It tells the printf function to force the output device to place a newline (or carriage return) in the place the \n escape sequence occupies. There are many escape sequences available in C++. They are all listed with their meanings and uses in the Visual Studio Help File. The next line in our program:

```
printf("The sum of 5 and 4 is %d.\n",addNums(5,4));
```

makes another call to printf(), but instead of passing a variable as the second parameter, we pass the results of a function call, addNums(5,4). This may seem strange, but the statements in the second parameter position of a call to printf() are always fully evaluated before being passed to the actual call, printf(). For example, our function, addNums(), evaluates to the sum of the parameters passed to it. For all intents and purposes, printf() doesn't know the difference between a function in its parameter list and an actual hard coded value. As far as printf() is concerned, the following two calls are identical:

```
printf("The sum of 5 and 4 is %d.\n",addNums(5,4));
printf("The sum of 5 and 4 is %d.\n",9);
```

Most of the rest of the code in our program is just a repeat of earlier calls with one exception:

```
    return 0;
}
```

The keyword *return* is used to exit a function. In this case we tell the program to exit the function main() and return a value of 0. To exit a function that does not return a value, you just call return with no value as such:

```
return;
```

Figure 4-5 shows the output of our program.

Granted, this example is fairly useless as an application, but it explains the structure of a C++ program pretty well.

Operators

In order to benefit from C++ we are going to perform various operations on our data, so it's important that you learn about some of the operators available in C++. I listed the most relevant C++ operators, their Visual Basic equivalents (where applicable), and a description of the functionality they provide in Table 4-2. A complete list of C++ operators is available in the C+ help file.

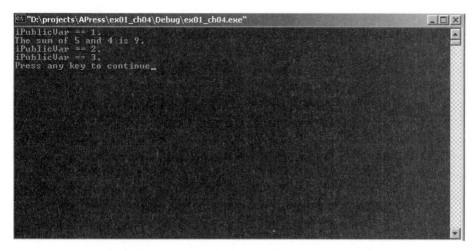

Figure 4-5. The output of ex01_ch04.exe

Table 4-2. C++ Operators

C++ OPERATOR	VB EQUIVALENT	DESCRIPTION
+	+	Addition
-	-	Subtraction
*	*	Multiplication
/	/	Division
%	%	Remainder from a division (modulus)
++	N/A	Increment operator
--	N/A	Decrement operator
=	=	Assignment
==	=	Equality
!=	<>	Inequality
>	>	Greater than
<	<	Less than
>=	>=	Greater than or equal to
<=	<=	Less than or equal to
&	And	Bitwise AND
&&	N/A	Logical AND
|	Or	Bitwise Or
||	N/A	Logical Or
~	Not	Bitwise Not (complement)
!	N/A	Logical Not
+=	N/A	Addition and assignment
-=	N/A	Subtraction and assignment
*=	N/A	Multiplication and assignment
/=	N/A	Division and assignment

In order to get a better feel for the operators in C++ let's build a small program that will use a variety of the operators as well as some of the logic control structures such as for-loops and select-case. Don't expect to learn too much about good programming practice from this application, just use it to learn about the use of the C++ operators. Again, I am only reviewing a few of the most commonly used operators.

Open a new console application project in Visual Studio and copy the contents of the source file *ex02_ch4* and the header file *stdafx.h,* which are listed here. (This project is also located on the Web site that accompanies this book at www.apress.com.)

The contents of the file ex2_ch4.cpp are

```cpp
// ex02_ch4.cpp : Defines the entry point for the console application.
//

#include "stdafx.h"

int i1 = 0;

int main(int argc, char* argv[])
{

    //increment i1 by 5
    printf("Begin for-loop with (i1 == %d)...\n",i1);
    for (int a = 0; a < 5; a++)
    {
        printf("i1 == %d.\n",i1++);
    }
    printf("End for-loop with (i1 == %d)...\n\n",i1);



    //decrement it back down to 0
    printf("Begin do-while-loop with (i1 == %d)...\n",i1);
    do
    {
        printf("i1 == %d.\n",i1--);
    }while (i1 > 0);
    printf("End do-while-loop with (i1 == %d)...\n\n",i1);

    //increment i1 by 5
    printf("Begin for-loop with (i1 == %d)...\n",i1);
    for (int b = 0; b < 5; b++)
    {
        printf("i1 == %d.\n",++i1);
```

```
    }
    printf("End for-loop with (i1 == %d)...\n\n",i1);

    //increment i1 by multiples of 5
    printf("Begin for-loop with (i1 == %d)...\n",i1);
    for (int c = 0; c < 5; c++)
    {
        printf("(i1 += 5) == %d.\n",(i1 += 5));
    }
    printf("End for-loop with (i1 == %d)...\n\n",i1);

    //bitwise and logical operations
    printf("Begin logical and bitwise operations with (i1 == %d)...\n",i1);
    printf("(i1 & 2) == %d\n",i1 & 2); //bitwise
    printf("(i1 && 2) == %d\n",i1 && 2); //logical
    printf("(i1 | 2) == %d\n",i1 | 2); //bitwise
    printf("(i1 || 2) == %d\n",i1 || 2); //logical
    printf("(!i1) == %d\n",!i1); //logical
    printf("(~i1) == %d\n",~i1); //bitwise
    printf("End logical and bitwise operations with (i1 == %d)...\n",i1);

    return 0;
}
```

The contents of the file stdafx.h are

```
// stdafx.h : include file for standard system include files,
//    or project specific include files that are used frequently, but
//    are changed infrequently
//

#if!defined(AFX_STDAFX_H__ED10E577_1CBD_4B53_8CB3_FC5D51278B80__INCLUDED_)
#define AFX_STDAFX_H__ED10E577_1CBD_4B53_8CB3_FC5D51278B80__INCLUDED_

#if _MSC_VER > 1000
#pragma once
#endif // _MSC_VER > 1000

#define WIN32_LEAN_AND_MEAN    // Exclude rarely-used stuff from
#include <stdio.h>

//{{AFX_INSERT_LOCATION}}
// Microsoft Visual C++ will insert additional declarations immediately before the
previous line.
#endif // !defined(AFX_STDAFX_H__ED10E577_1CBD_4B53_8CB3_FC5D51278B80__INCLUDED_)
```

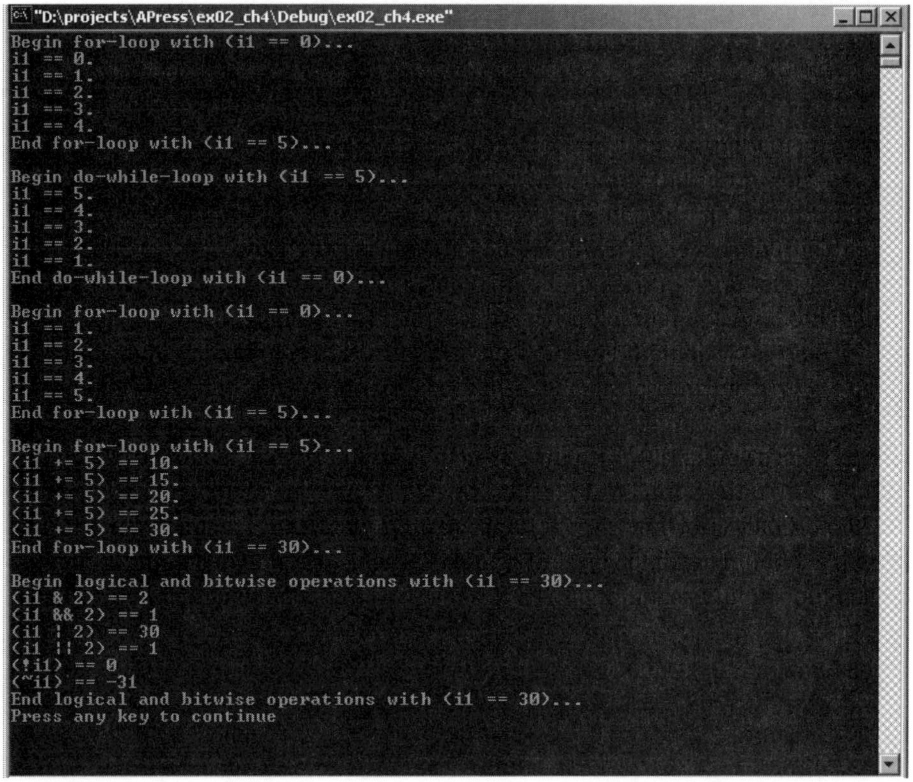

```
"D:\projects\APress\ex02_ch4\Debug\ex02_ch4.exe"                    _ □ ×
Begin for-loop with (i1 == 0)...
i1 == 0.
i1 == 1.
i1 == 2.
i1 == 3.
i1 == 4.
End for-loop with (i1 == 5)...

Begin do-while-loop with (i1 == 5)...
i1 == 5.
i1 == 4.
i1 == 3.
i1 == 2.
i1 == 1.
End do-while-loop with (i1 == 0)...

Begin for-loop with (i1 == 0)...
i1 == 1.
i1 == 2.
i1 == 3.
i1 == 4.
i1 == 5.
End for-loop with (i1 == 5)...

Begin for-loop with (i1 == 5)...
(i1 += 5) == 10.
(i1 += 5) == 15.
(i1 += 5) == 20.
(i1 += 5) == 25.
(i1 += 5) == 30.
End for-loop with (i1 == 30)...

Begin logical and bitwise operations with (i1 == 30)...
(i1 & 2) == 2
(i1 && 2) == 1
(i1 | 2) == 30
(i1 || 2) == 1
(!i1) == 0
(~i1) == -31
End logical and bitwise operations with (i1 == 30)...
Press any key to continue
```

Figure 4-6. ex02_ch4.exe

Figure 4-6 displays the output from the program when it is run.

There certainly is a lot going on in this little program. First and foremost there are a lot of mathematical operations. Now I won't spend time going over the obvious operations such as addition and subtraction, but I will briefly explain the operators that do not have a Visual Basic equivalent.

The ++ and -- Operators

The origin of the name for the C++ programming language comes from the ++ operator. The ++ operator is a unary operator that increments the variable that it precedes or follows. The C programming language was an improvement to the proprietary Bell Labs programming language "B". (*B* presumably stands for *Bell*.) And C++ was an improvement on the C programming language. Therefore, C++ should theoretically be called "D." However, the inventors of C++, being the jokesters they are, decided to increment the C programming language by calling it C++.

There is an important point to be made about the placement of the ++ opera-tor. If the ++ operator comes before the operand, such as:

```
x = ++i;
```

the value i will be incremented before its current value is assigned to x. This is called a *prefix operator*. The postfix version of the ++ operator (or one that comes after the operand) is used as in the following:

```
x = i++;
```

In this case, x will be assigned the current value of i before it is incremented. This is an important difference to note, as you can see from the example. Our first for-loop (we will discuss the for-loop statement later in this chapter) starts at 0 and ends with 4 by using the postfix version of the ++ operator. However, the sec-ond for-loop using the same exact logic and data, prints the values 1 through 5 because the ++ operator is a prefix.

Following is the C++ operation followed by the equivalent Visual Basic code necessary to accomplish the same output.

The C++ version (postfix) is

```
x = i++;
```

The Visual Basic version (postfix) is

```
x = i
i = i + 1
```

The C++ version (prefix) is

```
x = ++i;
```

The Visual Basic version (prefix) is

```
i = i + 1
x = i
```

The - and -- operators follow the same exact principles as the + and ++ oper-ators, but for subtraction.

Binary Operators

You may not realize that Visual Basic does not have any boolean operators. Daft you say? Well it's true (no pun intended). To prove my case let's do a test.

In Boolean logic, "Not 1" should equal 0 (or false). However, if I run this statement in Visual Basic, I get the result of –2. The reason is that Visual Basic does only bitwise operations. In most cases this doesn't make a difference, but you do need to be careful. Consider the following Visual Basic code:

```
Option Explicit

Private Sub Form_Load()

'Check the return value of the function
If Not GetVal Then
    MsgBox "Function failed."
Else
    MsgBox "Function succeded."
End If

End Sub

Public Function GetVal()

'Return what most API functions will return as 'true'
GetVal = 1

End Function
```

Following the logic of this code, you can see that we are checking the return value from our call to GetVal() and continuing or terminating our program based on what that return value is. Now, because our version of GetVal() always returns 1 (or true, as any non-zero value is true according to Boolean logic), we would expect the following statement:

```
If Not GetVal()
```

to always evaluate to true (or "not false"). However, in this code example it does not. If you run this code, you will see that our *if* statement evaluates to false (or "Not true"). Let's examine why this happens.

Our GetVal() function returns 1, which is binary 00000001. When we apply the *Not* operator to the return value of 1, we are not doing a logical Not, but a bitwise Not operation. The bitwise Not of the binary value 00000001 equates to

11111110, which equates to the decimal value (-2). The value of *True* in Visual Basic is equal to decimal (-1). And because (-1) and (-2) are not equal, our *if* statement will always fail.

> **TIP:** *If you don't understand bitwise operations, run, don't walk, and learn basic binary mathematics. It will prove invaluable in your understanding of computer programming and computers in general.*

The reason that I point this out is that most application program interface (API) functions use 1 as their return value to indicate *True* and 0 to indicate *False*. Imagine what would happen if GetVal() was an API function. This could lead to some very hard to find bugs. Let's look at a more realistic example of how this could happen:

```
Option Explicit

Public Declare Function SetWindowText Lib "user32" Alias "SetWindowTextA" (ByVal
hwnd As Long, ByVal lpString As String) As Long

Public Sub main()

'Variable to catch the return value of the API call
Dim lngRetVal As Long

Load Form1

'Call SetWindowText to change the text in our window
lngRetVal = SetWindowText(Form1.hwnd, "My Title has Been Changed")

'Check the return value of SetWindowText
If Not lngRetVal Then
    'SetWindowText returned false
    MsgBox "Error: Could not change the window's title."
Else
    'SetWindowText returned true so....
    'Continue with the program
End If

Form1.Show

End Sub
```

This simple example shows a very real bug. The return value of SetWindowText is documented to be "non-zero on success," which means that SetWindowText is successful if it returns any value other than zero. Now when Visual Basic evaluates an expression such as:

```
Dim x As Integer

x = 1

If x Then
```

it will evaluate the *if* statement as true. This is because in this grammar, Visual Basic is only checking for the absence of zero. However, the following statements would evaluate as false:

```
Dim x As Integer

x = 1

If x = True Then
```

This is because Visual Basic will now compare x (1) and *True* (-1) and (correctly) return the fact that they are not equal; such that:

```
(1 = (1 = True)) = False
```

Fear not. There is a simple solution to this problem. Always assign values that are logically either true or false to a Boolean variable. Take our previous code for example. If we had made the small change noted here in bold, our program would run correctly:

```
Option Explicit

Public Declare Function SetWindowText Lib "user32" Alias "SetWindowTextA" (ByVal hwnd As Long, ByVal lpString As String) As Long

Public Sub Main()

'Variable to catch the return value of the API call
Dim lngRetVal As Boolean 'Changed from Long to Boolean

Load Form1

'Call SetWindowText to change the text in our window
```

```
lngRetVal = SetWindowText(Form1.hwnd, "My Title has Been Changed")

'Check the return value of SetWindowText
If Not lngRetVal Then
    'SetWindowText returned false
    MsgBox "Error: Could not change the window's title."
Else
    'SetWindowText returned true so....
    'Continue with the program
End If

Form1.Show

End Sub
```

The reason is that Visual Basic coerces any non-zero value to true upon assignment to a Boolean type variable. We could accomplish the same thing by putting the CBool function around our lngRetVal variable when it was dim-ed as a Long. Here's the bottom line: in C++ you should always use the Boolean operators for comparison unless you actually need to perform a bitwise operation. For instance, if I wanted to compare the return value of a function for success I would do the following:

```
if (!SetWindowLong(hWnd, "My App"));
```

This statement uses the logical *Not* operator, which will give us the desired effect of checking for success or failure. However, the following would not:

```
if (~SetWindowLong(hWnd, "My App"));
```

Using this form of the *Not* operator would put us in the same boat that we were in with Visual Basic.

Assignment and Equality Operators

The last group of operators that I discuss is the assignment and equality operators. One of the most frequent bugs I used to create in my early C++ programs was a very innocent looking one:

```
if (var = condition)
{
    //Do something interesting
}
```

Looks pretty innocent, right? (Forget that we don't know the exact syntax of an *if* statement yet.)

Here is the equivalent code in Visual Basic:

```
If var = condition Then
'Do something interesting...
End If
```

Do you see the problem yet? No? Let's look at the C++ version a little closer. It appears at first glance that I am asking if the value var is equal to the value condition. However, what I am really asking is, if the return value of the statement var = condition is true or false. You see, in Visual Basic the equals sign means both assignment and equality. It uses the context of the call to decide which operation to use. In C++, however, the symbol "=" means to assign the value on the right side of the equals sign to the storage location on the left.

So the question still remains, "What does var = condition really equal?" Let's look at the following example:

```
printf("%d\n",i1 = 10);
printf("%d\n",i1 = 5);
printf("%d\n",i1 = 3);
```

This program will produce the values 10, 5, and 3, respectively. The answer to our question is: the return value of an assignment operation is always the value on the right hand side. Assuming that i1 is equal to zero at this point in time, the following statement will return 0 (or false):

```
i1 = 0;
```

You should be able to see the possibility for hard to find bugs here. If you had built a conditional statement based on this statement being true, you'd be in big trouble.

Here's a simple trick to alleviate this kind of bug when you are checking for a constant value. Always put your constant value on the left side of the equals sign as such:

```
0 = i1;
```

This way, if you accidentally put in the assignment operator by mistake, your program won't even compile. The reason is that you can't assign a value to a constant.

Okay, so how do we check for equality? With the == operator. Here is the correct version of our previous statement:

```
0 == i1;
```

That's it. Just put an extra equal sign next to the old one and we're done.

Assignment and … Operators

The other types of operators that are new in C++ are the "two-for-one" operators, such as +=. These operators do two operations in one shot. Consider the following statement:

```
x += 10;
```

To see what this statement is doing, let's look at an equivalent Visual Basic statement:

```
x = x + 10
```

Pretty simple, right? All that these types of operators do is combine two operations into one. Refer to Table 4-2 and the sample program, ex2_ch4, for more uses of these operators.

Loops and Control Statements

C++ has loop and control facilities just like Visual Basic, although the syntax is different. We'll go through each type of these logic control structures and their respective use.

The if Statement

The *if* statement is probably the most widely used control statement of any programming language. Regardless of the programming language implementing it, they all work pretty much the same. In Visual Basic, an *if* statement looks like this:

```
If x = y Then
    'Do something
End If
```

All of the statements between If and End If are executed if the conditional statement is True. The same *if* statement in C++ looks like this:

```
If (x == y)
    //do something;
```

Now this is where the stylistic approach to programming comes into play. I feel that the previous line is a little unclear. I would, and always do, write my if statements with a set of curly braces surrounding the conditional statements as follows:

```
if (x == y)
{
    //do something;
}
```

By using the curly braces I am creating a scope for the *if* statement. I feel that this makes the code easier to read.

For Loop

The C++ for-loop construct is pretty much identical in function to the Visual Basic version. To get a feel for the similarities and differences in the two let's look at an example.

The Visual Basic version is

```
Dim i As Long
For i = 0 To 100
    'something interesting here
Next i
```

The C++ version is

```
for (int i = 0;i < 100;i++)
{
    //Something interesting here.
}
```

You already know what the Visual Basic version does so I'll jump right into the description of the C++ section. The first line starts with our declaration of the for loop. We do this by using the keyword *for*. Now just as in the Visual Basic for-loop, we must give a starting value for the loop. We use the statement int i = 0 to accomplish this. Notice that unlike in Visual Basic, in the C++ version we can actually declare and initialize the iterating variable (in this case *i*) right inside the first parameter of the for-loop. Consequently, the variable i will have scope only in the for loop. Now all of the arguments of the for loop are separated by a semi-colon. The actual definition of the for-loop arguments are as follows:

```
for (iterting variable;conditional statement;action[s])
```

We satisfied the first parameter with our declaration and initialization of the variable i. Our *conditional* statement is

```
i < 100
```

which means "while i is less than 100," but I am sure you have already figured that out. Our final parameter is our *action* clause, which we have denoted as

```
i++
```

This simply means that each time the loop iterates the value of i will be incremented by one. Now we aren't tied to just iterating based on i increasing by one. I could have just as easily written a loop as follows:

```
for (int i = 0;i < 100;i+=5)
{
    //Loop statements here
}
```

This is identical to the following for-loop in Visual Basic:

```
For I = 0 To 100 Step 5
    'Loop statements
Next I
```

Do-While Loop

The do-while-loop is similar to the Visual Basic version, just as was the for-loop construct. Let's look at an example of these two constructs in the aforementioned languages.

The Visual Basic version is

```
Do
    'Statements Here
    If x > 10 Then
        Exit Do
    End If
Loop While True
```

The C++ version is

```
do
{
    if (x > 10)
{
    break;
    }
}while (true)
```

Notice the use of the keyword, *break*. This keyword essentially tells the program to "break"-out of the loop. There is also a *continue* keyword that could be used in the place of *break*. The difference in the two is that *break* actually starts executing the next line after the loop statement, but *continue* causes the program to ignore the statements after the continue keyword and begin the next iteration of the loop immediately. Break is the equivalent of the *Exit* keyword in Visual Basic. Consider the following Visual Basic code:

```
Dim x As Integer

Do
    If x > 10 Then
    Exit Do
    End If
    x = x + 1
Loop

For x = 0 To 100
    If x > 10 Then
    Exit For
    End If
    x = x + 1
Next
```

Both the *Exit Do* and *Exit For* are used to exit loops. In C++, it is not necessary to explicitly state which structure you are breaking out of.

Switch-Case

Although the *switch* keyword may not look familiar to you, it is the first cousin of the *Select-Case* construct in Visual Basic. The switch-case construct takes the following form:

```
switch (condition)
{
    case case[n]:
        [break];
    case case[n + 1]:
        [break];
}
```

To continue our previous compare and contrast format, let's look at the control structure in both languages.

The Visual Basic version is

```
Dim I As Long

I = 10

Select Case I
    Case I = 1
        'Do something
    Case I = 3,4,5
        'Do something
    Case 10
        ' Do something great
    Case Else
        ' Default Action
End Select
```

The C++ version is

```
int I = 0;

switch (I)
{
    case 1:
        //Do something
        break;
    case 3:
    case 4:
    case 5:
        break;
    case 10:
        //Do something great
    default:
        //default action
}
```

Notice that the structure of the statement is pretty much the same as the Visual Basic version, with a couple of exceptions. The first exception is that unlike in Visual Basic, in C++ we must explicitly break out of the *switch* statement by using the *break* keyword. Second, we can check several conditions by simply listing them with no break between them as we did with 3, 4, and 5. The third and last exception is that we use the keyword *default* as our "catch-all" condition as opposed to the *Case Else* that is used in Visual Basic.

Comments

I saved this topic for last in this chapter because it is an important one. In C++ it is extremely important to write comments in your code, because there are so many ways to represent the same operations and manipulations of a program's data. Believe me, I have spent hours and hours trying to understand other programmers' uncommented, cryptic code only to find out that the time spent could have been reduced to nothing had the code included even one comment. (I'll leave you and your conscience to deal with the matter from here.)

Following are two ways to specify comments in C++:

```
//This is a comment line. It works just like VB.
```

```
/* This is the C-style comment block. Unlike VB
even the comments here are blocked. Nothing will be
interpreted as code until the closing tag is encountered
like this */
```

And that's it. Either start a line with the // symbol to comment only that line (this works just like the apostrophe in Visual Basic), or use the /* */ pair to enclose a group of comments (I wish that Visual Basic had an equivalent for this one!).

Conclusion

Although far from all-inclusive, this chapter should have given you a good induction into the basics of C++. I suggest supplementing this chapter with the first few chapters of the definitive C++ guide, *The C++ Programming Language* by Bjarne Stroustrup, the inventor of C++ (2000, Addison-Wesley). It is available from any good technical book source. Other than that, get ready to attack the C++ language.

In the next few chapters we will continue our journey into the world of C++ by learning about pointers, classes, and templates. We will also pick up additional techniques and insights regarding the things we have already learned as we go along. Are we having fun yet?!

CHAPTER 5

It's Not Polite
to Point

POINTERS ARE WITHOUT A DOUBT THE BIGGEST REASON non-C++ programmers fear C++. In fact, most people I know who have tried to learn C++ and quit, have quit because of pointers. Now don't get me wrong, pointers are an advanced computing concept. Nevertheless, once you have mastered pointers, you will have conquered the steepest part of the C++ learning curve.

I devoted an entire chapter to this one subject (which should give some indication of its importance), but don't let this scare you. Although pointers are tricky at first, I provide a lot of examples in this chapter to really drive home the concept of pointers, so don't give up on me. Let's do it!

What Is a Pointer?

Before we can discuss pointers in any depth, a definition of a pointer is needed.

A *pointer* is a variable that holds the address of another variable or the address of a location in memory. This in itself may not seem very useful, but you will see that pointers are extremely powerful when used properly. So how do you declare a pointer variable? You use the *pointer operator* (*) as follows:

```
int *p = 0;
```

The previous line of code creates a pointer that points to the memory address 0x00000000 in the process's address space. If you try to access the data pointed to by this pointer, you would most assuredly get a memory exception because you are restricted from accessing the lower 4MB of the process's memory of which 0x00000000 is a part. In fact, any time you try to access a memory address that is either restricted by the operating system or outside of the range of your process's address space, you will get a memory access violation. It is for this reason that a pointer should always point to a valid variable's address.

> **NOTE:** *There are times when you will want to create a pointer that points to the memory address* 0x00000000 *(also called a* Null *pointer). But generally you will want your pointers to point to a valid variable's address.*

So how do you find out what a variable's address is so that you can set your pointer equal to it? Use the *address of* operator (&). Consider the following code snippet:

```
int i = 0;
int *p_i = &i;
```

In the first line you declare a variable i of type int and set its initial value to 0. Next, you declare a variable of type *pointer* to int and set its initial value to the address of i by using the address of operator. You are essentially telling the program to find the memory location at which the variable i resides and putting that address in the pointer variable p_i. There is one important detail that should be mentioned here—pointers are typed. This means you must tell the compiler what type of variable you will be pointing to. If you change the code listing to read this way:

```
char i = 0;
int *p_i = &i;
```

the compiler will tell you that you can't use an int pointer (p_i) to point to a variable of type char. There is a pointer that can point to any type called a *void* pointer. (I discuss void pointers later in this chapter when I talk about the malloc function.) Here, let's go ahead and break down the variable declarations to get a better understanding of what is going on when a pointer is created.

```
int i = 0;
```

In the previous line of code you are telling the compiler to create an integer variable with an initial value of 0.

In the following line, you are telling the compiler that you want a variable that can hold the address of an integer variable:

```
int *p_i = &i;
```

Notice how the pointer operator (*) is next to the p_i in the declaration. This is simply stylistic. The same declaration could also be written like this:

```
int* p_i = &i;
```

The placement of the pointer operator is not important. Some C++ programmers feel that it is more clear to write int* (as to say an *int pointer*) than int *, but it just depends on your personal preference. What is important is that you put the pointer operator in front of the variable in your declaration. It is also important to remember to initialize your pointers. What do you think would happen if you declared the pointer variable as follows:

```
int *p_i;
```

Nothing good, that's for sure. Remember that all variables contain some data when they are created—this includes pointers. Because pointers actually point to some memory address (valid or not), it is extremely important that they contain NULL (0) or a valid variable's address at all times. In the previous line of code, you don't know what the pointer is pointing to. It could be zero, an invalid memory address, or worse, a valid memory address that you may unwittingly corrupt. With pointers, what you don't know *will* hurt you. Remember: *Always* initialize pointers.

A Pointer Example

To get a better feel for how pointers work, let's go through a sample application that uses them and discuss each part of that application. Open the project *ex01_ch5*, which can be found on the Web site that accompanies this book (www.apress.com), or create a new console application project with the same name and copy the following code into the ex01_ch5.cpp source code file:

```
// ex01_ch5.cpp : Defines the entry point for the console application.
//

#include "stdafx.h"
#include <stdio.h>

int main(int argc, char* argv[])
{
        //Variable of type 'int'
        int i = 0;

        //Variable of type 'pointer to int' -- initialized to
        //the address of i
        int *p_i = &i;

        //Loop 5 times; printing the value of i,the de-referenced
        //value of p_i and the value of p_i each time
```

```
    for (i = 0; i < 5; i++)
    {
    printf("i == %d \t *p_i == %d \t p_i == %x\n", i, *p_i, p_i);
    }

    return 0;
}
```

Figure 5-1 shows the output of the program when it is run.

There are some important details to note in this short program. Let's look at the following line:

```
int *p_i = &i;
```

With this line of code you are doing two things. First, you are declaring a variable of type `pointer to int`. Second, you are initializing it with the address of the variable i. This is important to note because from this point on i and *p_i will return the same value, but i and p_i will not. Let me explain. When you declare a variable, you use the pointer operator (*) because, when used in a variable declaration, the character * means that the variable is a pointer. However, when used in contexts other than declarations, the character * has other meanings. For example, in Chapter 4, you saw that the character * can mean multiplication as in the following code snippet:

```
x * y;
```

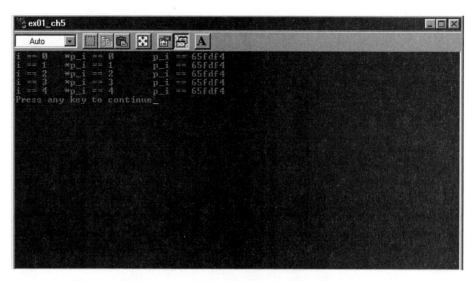

Figure 5-1. The result of the sample program, ex01_ch5, when it is run

The character * can also represent the indirection operator (*) as in:

```
//Assume that x has been declared as a pointer and is pointing to a //valid
address.
*x = 0;
```

This simply means that the program needs to find the value at the address stored in x and change it to 0. For example, if you assume that x is a variable of type pointer to int whose value is set to the address of y, and that y is a variable of type int as indicated by the declaration

```
int *x = &y
```

then the following two lines of code are identical in function:

```
*x = 0;
y = 0;
```

and *x and y are at the same address.

To explain further, imagine that I have ten envelopes on my desk. The envelopes are numbered from 1 through 10. Written on the first envelope is the number 1, written on the second envelope is the number 2, and so on. Inside each envelope is either some amount of money or a slip of paper that contains the number of another envelope. Table 5-1 lists the contents of each envelope.

Now imagine that there are ten people in my office, and I tell each of them to choose an envelope with the understanding that if there is money in the envelope, they can use it in whatever way they see fit. And, if their envelope contains a slip of paper with another envelope's number on it, the money in the envelope

Table 5-1. Envelope Contents Chart

ENVELOPE NUMBER	ENVELOPE CONTENTS
1	$200.00
2	A slip of paper with the number 3 on it.
3	$10.00
4	A slip of paper with the number 5 on it.
5	$50.00
6	A slip of paper with the number 1 on it.
7	A slip of paper with the number 8 on it.
8	$800.00
9	A slip of paper with the number 1 on it.
10	A slip of paper with the number 8 on it.

listed on the slip of paper is theirs to use as they wish. However, in no case is any-one allowed to physically remove any envelope from my desk; they can only open the envelope and remove its contents in part or whole.

Now let's suppose that the person who chose envelope number 1 takes $100 from his envelope to buy a new pair of shoes. This would leave $100 in envelope number 1. And suppose that while he goes to buy his shoes, the person with enve-lope number 6 opens his envelope and sees that it contains a slip of paper with the number 1 on it. The owner of envelope number 6 (who now knows that he is to open envelope number 1 to retrieve his money) opens envelope number 1 and sees that there is $100 inside. He then takes $50 to buy some new CDs at the record store, which leaves $50 in envelope number 1. While he's away, the first person who chose envelope number 1 returns with his shoe purchase. He opens envelope number 1 expecting to find the $100 he left in it, but much to his dis-may, there is only $50 in the envelope because the owner of envelope number 6 took the other $50.

This is exactly how pointers work—envelope 6 is essentially a pointer to enve-lope number 1). This also illustrates why it is important to make sure you know what your pointer is pointing to. Although you can use two different names to refer to a value (such as *x and y), remember that they do reside at the same phys-ical location in memory.

Let's now return to the example. Consider the following code block:

```
for (i = 0; i < 5; i++)
{
 printf("i == %d \t *p_i == %d \t p_i == %x\n", i, *p_i, p_i);
}
```

This is a loop that writes the value of i, the value of *p_i, de-referenced using the *indirection operator* (*), and the value of p_i. (Remember from Chapter 4 that printf uses format specifiers in place of actual values, and then replaces those format specifiers with the list of variables supplied in a comma-delimited format after the closing double parenthesis.) Let's examine the call to printf:

```
printf("i == %d \t *p_i == %d \t p_i == %x\n", i, *p_i, p_i);
```

When the program runs, it replaces the first %d listed in the format string with the first variable in the list, i, which is equal to 0 during the first iteration of the for loop. The second %d in the format string is replaced with the value of *p_i, which is equal to 0 during the first iteration of the for loop as well. The third %d listed in the format string is replaced with the value of p_i, which is equal to the memory address of the variable i (which was 0x0012FF7C when I ran the program on my machine; it will most likely be different when you run the program on your machine).

Variable	Memory Address	Valve
i	12ff7c	1
p_i	0x12ff40	0x12ff7c
*p_i	0x12ff7c	1

Figure 5-2. The variables i and p_i in memory

The second iteration of the loop increments the variable i by one (this is due to the i++ in the for declaration), so naturally you expect that the second time through the loop, the value of i will be increased to 1, and it is. However, the value that replaces the second %d, *p_i, is now equal to 1 as well. How did this happen? You didn't increment *p_i, right? Actually you did. Remember that once a pointer is set to the address of a variable, it is actually pointing to the same physical memory location as the variable itself. When you set p_i equal to the address of i with the line:

```
int *p_i = &i;
```

you made *p_i a synonym for i. Figure 5-2 shows the variables i and p_i, their addresses in memory and their values in memory, respectively.

The key element to remember from this section is that once you set a pointer to the address of a variable, any modifications made to the pointer are actually made to your variable, so be careful.

Allocating Memory for Pointers

As mentioned earlier in this chapter, one of the ways to initialize a pointer is to directly assign the address of a variable using the *address of* operator when you declare the pointer. This is the best way to create a pointer to ensure that it has the proper address stored in it. However, there are times when you will need to create a pointer without knowing the address of the variable that you want to store. It is for this type of situation that the malloc function was created.

malloc()

malloc is declared in the header file, malloc.h, which is part of the C++ runtime library. Therefore, if you want to use malloc in your programs, you will have to #include malloc.h in them. The purpose of malloc is to find a valid memory address in the current process space, allocate a block of memory (based on the size in bytes passed as a parameter to malloc), and assign the starting address of the memory block to a pointer as follows:

```
#include <malloc.h>

int main(int argc, char* argv[])
{
    int *i = (int *)malloc(sizeof(int *));
    return 0;
}
```

In the previous code listing, you are declaring a variable of type pointer to int as you did before:

```
int *i = (int *)malloc(sizeof(int *));
```

But notice the (int *) directly in front of the call to malloc. Somewhat odd, don't you think? Well, not really. This is called a *typecast*. The function malloc returns a *void pointer*, which means that it is a pointer of no particular type (not to be confused with a *Null pointer*, which is a pointer that points to the memory address 0x00000000). I said previously that pointers are typed with respect to the type of variable that they will point to except for void pointers. This is exactly what I was talking about. A void pointer points to a valid memory address in the process space just as any other pointer would, but without regard to type. It is, in some ways, similar to a variant in Visual Basic. A related concept in Visual Basic would look like this:

```
"Variable of type Integer
Dim intNum1 As Integer

"Variable of type Variant
Dim varNum2 As Variant

varNum2 = 9

intNum = Cint(varNum2)
```

The difference in Visual Basic is that a typecast is not necessary because Visual Basic is very loosely typed. This means that Visual Basic will coerce different types of variables to be compatible with each other, even if you don't necessarily want it to (which can be good or bad depending on the situation), whereas C++ will not. The C++ compiler will warn you when you try to assign different types to each other, even in non-pointer assignments, as in the following:

```
short sNum1 = 0;
long lNum2 = 2;

sNum1 = lNum2
```

Now you know how the typecast works to coerce the return value of `malloc` to some certain type, so the only part of the call left to explain is the parameter passed to `malloc`. Notice the use of the *sizeof operator* in the code listing. This function is almost identical to the *LenB* function in Visual Basic. It returns the number of bytes occupied by the variable passed in as the parameter to `sizeof`. The only difference between `sizeof` and `LenB` is that you can't pass a variable type as the parameter to `LenB`, but you can with `sizeof`. Essentially, what you are doing in the following line of code,

```
int *i = (int *)malloc(sizeof(int *));
```

is creating a variable of type `pointer to int`, casting the return value of the `malloc` function to an `int *`, and passing the `sizeof()` function as the parameter to `malloc` using `int *` as its parameter value. All this really means is that you are creating a memory block of 4 bytes (the size of an `int` pointer) and storing that address in the pointer `i`. Hang in there; it will all start to make sense very soon.

free()

An important point that should be made here is that any call to `malloc()` must be matched with a call to `free()`. The reason is that any memory created with `malloc()` can only be reused if it is freed using the `free()` function. (In Chapter 6, you will delve into more efficient ways to manage memory.)

Strings and Char Pointers

Up to this point, you have dealt only with pointers that point to variables of type `int` and have been presented with a brief discussion of void pointers. But there are pointers for all kinds of variable types. This section focuses on strings and char pointers—user-defined types (called *structs* or *classes* in C++) are covered later in this book.

Strings

Strings are one of the most difficult entities to represent in a computer because strings are variable by nature. For instance, a variable of type int is 4 bytes (32 bits) on an Intel X86 processor. This never changes. So when a pointer points to an int, it knows that when you reference the stored value, you are accessing the address of the pointer and the 3 bytes following it for a total of 4 bytes (the size of an int variable). The same is true of any other variable type except for string pointers. The reason string pointers are different is because the length of the string they point to is unknown.

So how do you get around this problem? Read on.

Char Pointers

String pointers (actually called *char pointers*) are read starting from the address stored in the pointer until a NULL character (the binary value 0, which is the same as the Visual Basic constant vbNullChar) is found. This is, in fact, the infamous *NULL terminated string* so often referred to in the WIN32 application programming interface (API). Moreover, almost all API calls that take or return a string parameter use Null terminated strings. Let's look at the following code listing example (ex02_ch5 on the Web site that accompanies this book):

```
#include "stdafx.h"
#include <stdio.h>

int main(int argc, char* argv[])
{
    char *lpString = "Hello C++";

    printf("%s\n",lpString);

    return 0;
}
```

Let's examine the line:

```
char *lpString = "Hello C++";
```

As with the pointer to int variable declarations discussed earlier in this chapter, you declare the pointer to char variable by using the pointer operator.

The difference in this declaration and the previous one is that you set the pointer equal to the string "Hello C++". As a result, in memory somewhere, there is a set of bytes that hold the characters that make up this string. To get a better idea of how char pointers work, let's look at the memory window while the program is running. You do this by pressing F10 while in the development environment. This will set the program into debug mode. Each time you press F10, you will advance by one line in the program. This is the same as debugging using F8 in Visual Basic. Continue to press F10 until the following line is reached:

```
printf("%s\n",lpString);
```

Now select View ➔ Debug Windows ➔ Memory. A window that contains a block of memory addresses will open. Hold the mouse over the lpString variable and look at its address (see Figure 5-3). Type its address into the Address box of the Memory window. The result should be similar to the content in Figure 5-4.

You can see that the actual pointer's value is the same as the location of the first character in the string "Hello C++." Notice that the numbers listed to the left of the string are the ASCII character codes of the characters in the string. Now look at the character after the last + in the string. It looks like a period, but it's really a NULL character (the Memory window provides a period for all unprintable characters, such as NULLs). Now look at the numbers to the left of the string again, you will see the pattern {48 65 6C 6C 6F 20 43 2B 2B 00}. The 48 represents an uppercase H, the 65 represents the lowercase e, and so on until you reach the consecutive 2Bs, which represent the ++ in the string. Now look at the last number in the list, 00. This is the Null terminator (or Null character). This Null terminator tells the program that this is the end of the string pointed to by the variable lpString.

Simple right? Don't feel too discouraged if it hasn't hit home quite yet. The best way to learn this concept is to practice using it. I encourage you to open a

```
#include "stdafx.h"
#include <stdio.h>

int main(int argc, char* argv[])
{
        char *lpString = "Hello C++";

        printf("%s\n",lpString);
                      ┌─────────────────────────────────┐
                      │ lpString = 0x00420020 "Hello C++" │
        return 0;     └─────────────────────────────────┘
}
```

Figure 5-3. Obtaining the address of the lpString variable

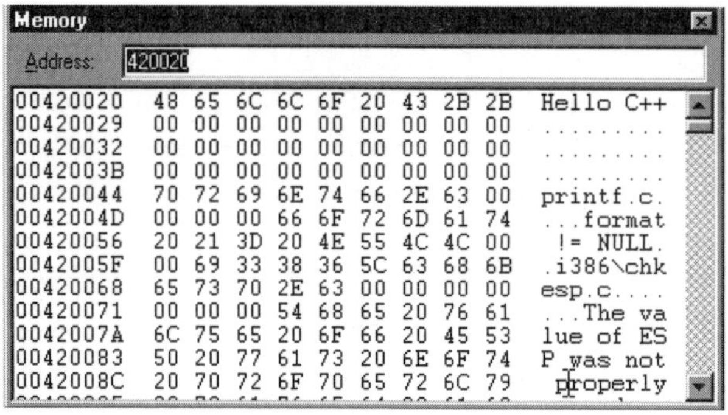

Figure 5-4. The Memory window

project and give it a try. You may cause a few exceptions here and there, but you will understand how it works.

Another interesting characteristic about char pointers is that you can actually address them as a char array. In other words, if the lpString variable had been declared as

```
char lpString[] = "Hello C++";
```

by referring to lpString[2] in my code, I am actually referring to the letter *l* in "Hello C++." So, after adding the following block of code to my program:

```
for (unsigned int i = 0; i < strlen(lpString); i++)
    {
        printf("%c\n",lpString[i]);
    }
```

the output shown in Figure 5-5 is produced.

I am essentially treating the variable lpString as a char array. Notice in the call to printf that I use the format character %c (which means char) as opposed to %s (which means string) in the previous call. The reason I do this is, when I use lpString[2] as the parameter to printf, I pass the value 72 (which is the ASCII code for the lowercase letter l) as the replacement for the %c format code. However, if I had passed lpString as the parameter to printf, I would be passing the address of the beginning of the string "Hello C++." This would be recognized as the character that represents the ASCII code of the first byte of the address of lpString. The odds are 254 to 1 that this will not be the character that I am trying to print.

Similarly, if I use %s as the format code and pass lpString[2] to it, I still would not get the expected result. However, in this case the result would be much worse; the printf function would try to interpret the character value as a pointer and would probably cause a memory access violation. The reason is that %s uses the

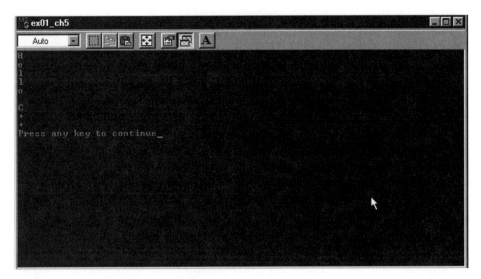

Figure 5-5. The "Hello World" output

passed value as a pointer to a string, and 72 (which is the value of lpString[2]) is not an accessible memory address.

Conclusion

To really master the concepts presented in this chapter, you should practice them. But don't worry, once you understand them, you will be unstoppable. Chapter 6 covers pointers to user-defined types and classes, which build on concepts you have already learned. In fact, they are probably a little easier to use.

CHAPTER 6

Classes

YOU'RE STILL HERE! THAT'S GREAT NEWS. IF YOU'VE made it this far, the rest of this book is going to be a snap. The steepest part of the learning curve for Visual Basic programmers trying to learn C++ is learning the actual language syntax of C++ and its usage. So, if you've made it to this chapter, then you have done that. Congratulations!

In this chapter, we explore the subject of C++ classes. If you're an accomplished Visual Basic programmer, you've already used classes extensively in your Visual Basic applications. However, if you haven't been practicing "good" Object-Oriented Programming (OOP) techniques (which includes using classes to encapsulate your data elements and business rules), the first part of this chapter will review basic object-oriented techniques and ideologies. If you are comfortable with the notion of using classes and have used them in Visual Basic with success, then feel free to skip this section. However, I have found that it never hurts to hear one more person's explanation of OOP and its benefits.

Class Dismissed

Unfortunately, many developers dismiss classes as something that might be useful for a large scale project that is being done by some big company with lots of money to spend on developers and designers and . . . well, you know how the story goes. However, in truth, using classes is the right choice for most applications, and if you're not using classes in your applications, then you're not taking advantage of the power of an OOP paradigm. This may sound a little pragmatic (and it probably is), but it is true that most applications imitate a real-life process or activity in one way or another. And modeling those real-life activities using classes makes sense. Let me present my case.

In most linear non-object-oriented applications, data elements and business rules are represented as public variables and functions in one or more code modules. These business rules and data elements are compiled into binary executable files and used as a whole unit. This in itself is fine, providing that your data elements and business rules never change, and you never want to reuse code. (If you never need to change business rules, you should write a book titled *How to Get Users to Tell You What They Really Want in an Application in 21 Days*). However, classes provide a very powerful mechanism for separating data elements and business rules into logical reusable units.

A Class-y Example

Let's suppose for a moment that you have been contracted to write an application for a shoe company, and that you need to have this application up and running in under a month. You've been given a set of requirements by the user, which details the required functionality that the application needs to provide. Many programmers would laugh if you told them that the first thing you were going to do was sit down and design the classes for this application based on the user's requirements instead of jumping straight into writing source code. However, this step of designing classes is important because it forces you to understand the user's business in such a way that you can model their real-life entities and operations with source code.

Suppose that the first class that you create based on the user's requirements is called a Shoe class. In order to create this class, you must understand the elements of a shoe and which business rules apply to it, if any. You investigate and find that the attributes of a shoe include its type, size, color, and material. You also discover that for any shoe sold, if the size is greater than 15, then 10 percent is added to its cost. This is due to the additional cost and relatively low demand of such large shoes. To continue creating this class, you need to document all of the elements that were discovered as well as any business rules that the class will need to implement, and then create a class module. (This assumes you are using Visual Basic as we are still trying to prove the usefulness of classes and not yet worrying about how to create them in C++.) The following code is the basic stub of this class and its elements, which I created with the Visual Basic Class Builder wizard add-in.

```
Option Explicit

'local variable(s) to hold property value(s)
Private mvarSize As Long 'local copy
Private mvarColor As String 'local copy
Private mvarMaterial As String 'local copy
Private mvarShoeType As String 'local copy

Public Property Let Material(ByVal vData As String)
'used when assigning a value to the property, on the left side of an assignment.
'Syntax: X.Material = 5
    mvarMaterial = vData
End Property

Public Property Get Material() As String
'used when retrieving value of a property, on the right side of an assignment.
'Syntax: Debug.Print X.Material
    Material = mvarMaterial
```

```
End Property

Public Property Let Color(ByVal vData As String)
'used when assigning a value to the property, on the left side of an assignment.
'Syntax: X.Color = 5
    mvarColor = vData
End Property

Public Property Get Color() As String
'used when retrieving value of a property, on the right side of an assignment.
'Syntax: Debug.Print X.Color
    Color = mvarColor
End Property

Public Property Let Size(ByVal vData As Long)
'used when assigning a value to the property, on the left side of an assignment.
'Syntax: X.Size = 5
    mvarSize = vData
End Property

Public Property Get Size() As Long
'used when retrieving value of a property, on the right side of an assignment.
'Syntax: Debug.Print X.Size
    Size = mvarSize
End Property

Public Property Let ShoeType(ByVal vData As String)
'used when assigning a value to the property, on the left side of an assignment.
'Syntax: X.Size = 5
    mvarShoeType = vData
End Property

Public Property Get ShoeType() As String
'used when retrieving value of a property, on the right side of an assignment.
'Syntax: Debug.Print X.Size
    ShoeType = mvarSize
End Property
```

TIP: *The Class Builder wizard is one of the few wizards that I like in Visual Basic because it saves me from having to type out each property Get and Let by hand. Granted, the naming of the parameters and variables is not exactly the way I would do it, but I think the trade-off is quite good.*

You can see that there are several properties: shoe type, size, color and material. These properties represent the physical properties of a shoe. Once the class is created, it can be used as follows:

```
Option Explicit

Public newShoe As New Shoe

Public Sub main()

newShoe.ShoeType = "Tennis"
newShoe.Color = "Red"
newShoe.Material = "Canvas"
newShoe.Size = 12

'Do something interesting with the shoe

End Sub
```

Building a shoe class may seem like a lot of work for this simple application, but if you expand this into a full application used to buy and sell shoes over the Internet, it is virtually certain this class would be used heavily. However, this shoe class is missing something. It doesn't implement the business rule that I mentioned earlier, which increases the price of shoes that are larger than size 15. To solve this problem, you need to add a function to the class that will expose this functionality for use by the application. The following function accomplishes this:

```
Public Function GetCost() As Currency

Dim curCost As Currency

'Code to find the price of the shoe in question goes here.
'Place the cost of the shoe in curCost.
'We will assume the shoe is $50.00

curCost = 50

If mvarSize > 15 Then
    'If the shoe is greater than size 15 then add 10% to the cost
    curCost = curCost + (curCost * 0.1)
End If

GetCost = curCost

End Function
```

Now, any shoe object whose size property is greater than 15 will return the increased sales price from the GetCost method.

The Payoff

You could just as easily have written the program without using classes and produced the same results. Right? Well, actually yes. In the shoe application, the class is nothing more than a logical grouping of property procedures, functions, and private variables. You may be wondering, then, why there is so much hype about object-oriented programming with classes. Well, the advantages become obvious when you need to either re-use the shoe class in another program or create, for instance, a GolfShoe class based on the Shoe class. Let's look at an example.

Say you have successfully finished the shoe application that you were hired to develop in the previous example, and you did such a good job that word of your success spread through the shoe industry. A new client comes along whose application requirements are almost identical to the previous application's except for the business rules and the type of shoes sold. In addition to selling regular shoes (as the previous customer did), this client also sells golf shoes, which has an additional property—the NumberOfSpikes property—that holds the number of spikes on a shoe. Furthermore, this client charges an additional cost for golf shoes over size 19. Regular shoe costs are still increased by 10 percent over size 15 as with the previous client.

To build the new application, you need to create a GolfShoe class that will be based on the Shoe class. This means that the GolfShoe class inherits the properties and methods of the Shoe class plus any additional properties and methods that you want to add. However, the rule for oversized shoes in the Shoe class is different from the rule that you need for the GolfShoe class. That's the beauty of classes. When you inherit from a class, you have the option of using the existing functions in the base class or overriding one or more of them with your own custom function. Let's look at the GolfShoe class:

```
Option Explicit

Private m_Shoe As New Shoe
Private m_lngNumberOfSpikes As Long

Public Property Let Color(ByVal vData As String)

m_Shoe.Color = vData

End Property

Public Property Get Color() As String
```

```vb
        Color = m_Shoe.Color

    End Property

    Public Property Let Material(ByVal vData As String)

        m_Shoe.Material = vData

    End Property

    Public Property Get Material() As String

        Material = m_Shoe.Material

    End Property

    Public Property Let Size(ByVal vData As Long)

        m_Shoe.Size = vData

    End Property

    Public Property Get Size() As Long

        Size = m_Shoe.Size

    End Property

    Public Property Let ShoeType(ByVal vData As String)

        m_Shoe.ShoeType = vData

    End Property

    Public Property Get ShoeType() As String

        ShoeType = m_Shoe.ShoeType

    End Property

    'Override the GetCost() function from our base class.
    Public Function GetCost() As Currency
```

```
Dim curCost As Currency


'Code to find the price of the shoe in question goes here.
'Place the cost of the shoe in curCost.
'We will assume the shoe is $50.00


curCost = 50


If m_Shoe.Size > 19 Then
    'If the shoe is greater than size 19 then add 10% to the cost
    curCost = curCost + (curCost * 0.1)
End If


GetCost = curCost


End Function


Public Property Let NumberOfSpikes(ByVal vData As Long)


m_lngNumberOfSpikes = vData


End Property


Public Property Get NumberOfSpikes() As Long


NumberOfSpikes = m_lngNumberOfSpikes


End Property
```

There are several things to notice about this class. It has all of the property assignments found (Let and Set) in the Shoe class. In fact, it has an identical set of functions and properties as the Shoe class with one additional property, NumberOfSpikes. The difference between the two classes is the code inside those functions, and properties are the code that is contained within those functions. In the Shoe class, the assigned values passed into the property procedures to the private variables contained therein. But in the GolfShoe class there is only one private variable assigned in this way. The rest of the GolfShoe class's properties are stored in a private copy of the Shoe class. You'll notice that in the GetCost function, the GetCost function of the private shoe class is not called. Instead, a custom version of the function GetCost is written and implements the different rule for the GolfShoe class. This is known as method overriding.

There are a few terms associated with the techniques that have just been applied with which you need to become familiar. The Shoe class is known as a *Base*

Class, meaning that other classes can use it as a base for their functionality. The act of creating a private copy of a base class (or the class that is being inherited from) internally in another class and presenting its (the class that is inheriting) functionality as if it was its own is called *containment.* This is a powerful technique, which is also known as *inheritance* (actually to be correct, the example achieves inheritance through containment). But be forewarned, this is not inheritance in its truest sense. There are two types of inheritance: *interface inheritance* and *implementation inheritance.* The example uses interface inheritance, which means that you inherit the property names and function signatures from another class, but not the code that is contained in those functions. (Actually, the example simulates this: To really have interface inheritance, you would have to use the *Implements* keyword to implement the Shoe interface.)

> **NOTE:** *I discuss interface inheritance in more detail in Chapter 7. If you're not yet familiar with this subject, I suggest reading Chapter 5 of* Creating ActiveX Components with Visual Basic *by Dan Appleman (Sams, 1998), and the first three chapters of* Essential COM *by Don Box (Addison-Wesley, 1998).*

To achieve implementation inheritance, you have to inherit the functions and properties along with their code. In Visual Basic, there is currently no facility for implementation inheritance; however, Microsoft announced that this feature will be supported in the next version of Visual Basic. The closest thing to implementation inheritance in Visual Basic today is containment. In C++, there is a facility for achieving implementation inheritance and it is, in my opinion, the most powerful aspect of C++ classes. Nevertheless, before you can delve into this subject, you need to understand how C++ classes work.

C++ Classes

Regardless of whether you skipped the previous section because you are familiar with classes in Visual Basic or learned about them for the first time here, from this point forward I assume that you are familiar with classes in Visual Basic. Now let's see how classes work in C++.

The Basics

You will need to know the syntax for creating a class, so let's look at a simple class declaration, and then examine its individual parts.

```
class Dummy
{
public:
    int GetName(void);
    int SetName(char *name);

private:
    int m_name;
};
```

This is a basic example of a class. But it is also a good example of how simple a class's structure really is. And *structure* is the operative word here. A class and a *struct* are actually the same thing. The same class declaration could have been made in the following way:

```
struct Dummy
{
public:
    int GetName(void);
    int SetName(char *name);

private:
    int m_name;
};
```

Surprisingly, I have found that few C++ programmers actually know this. There seems to be a mystique about classes, but they are really just data structures that contain functions. In fact, the only difference between classes and structs is that the members of a class are *private* by default, and the members of a struct are by default *public.*

The reason there are two similar keywords for classes is to maintain compatibility with the many lines of C code written using the struct keyword before there was such a thing as a *class.* Furthermore, C does not support the keyword class. In fact, the first version of C++ was called "C with classes."

For example, in the previous listing, notice how the public and private keywords are followed by a list of function prototypes and variable declarations. These keywords explicitly denote the visibility of the members that follow them until the next keyword is found. Such that any members declared after the private keyword are only visible to the other members of the class, whereas members following the public keyword are visible to any creator of the class. If the public or private keyword does not appear, the default visibility comes into play. Believe it or not, all of the following declarations produce the same exact class:

```
struct Dummy
{
public:
    int GetName(void);
    int SetName(char *name);

private:
    int m_name;
};



struct Dummy
{
    int GetName(void);
    int SetName(char *name);

private:
    int m_name;
};

class Dummy
{
public:
    int GetName(void);
public:
    int SetName(char *name);

private:
    int m_name;
};



class Dummy
{
public:
    int GetName(void);
    int SetName(char *name);

private:
    int m_name;
};
```

In addition to the public and protected keywords, you can also use the pro-tected keyword to denote that a member of a class is available to any class derived from that particular class, but not to the general public. (You'll read more about this later when I discuss inheritance in the Inheritance section of this Chapter7.)

Building the Class

Now that you have some idea of the basic structure of a class, let's build the Shoe class from the beginning of the chapter in C++ instead of Visual Basic. The class definition is contained in the header file ex02_ch6.h, and the implementations of the functions contained in the class are housed in the file ex02_ch6.cpp on the Web site that accompanies this book at www.apress.com. Remember that placing the declaration of the class in the header file is merely a matter of style and standards. Theoretically, you can place the definition of the class in the same file with the implementation. The following code illustrates the Shoe class written in C++:

```
// Shoe.h: interface for the Shoe class.
//
//////////////////////////////////////////////////////////////////////

#if !defined(AFX_SHOE_H__1122DF41_C79C_11D3_BC89_801F52C10000__INCLUDED_)
#define AFX_SHOE_H__1122DF41_C79C_11D3_BC89_801F52C10000__INCLUDED_

#if _MSC_VER > 1000
#pragma once
#endif // _MSC_VER > 1000

class Shoe
{
public:
    Shoe();
    Shoe(int size, char *type, char *material);
    char *GetType();
    int GetSize();
    virtual double GetCost();
    char *GetMaterial();
    void SetType(char *type);
    void SetSize(int size);
    void SetMaterial(char *material);
    virtual ~Shoe();

private:
    char *m_Material;
    char *m_Type;
```

```
        int m_Size;

};

#endif // !defined(AFX_SHOE_H__1122DF41_C79C_11D3_BC89_801F52C10000__INCLUDED_)


// Shoe.cpp: implementation of the Shoe class.
//
//////////////////////////////////////////////////////////////////////

#include "stdafx.h"
#include "Shoe.h"
#include "string.h"
#include "malloc.h"
#define MAX_STRING  255
//////////////////////////////////////////////////////////////////////
// Construction/Destruction
//////////////////////////////////////////////////////////////////////

Shoe::Shoe()
{
    m_Type = (char *)malloc(MAX_STRING);
    m_Material = (char *)malloc( MAX_STRING);

    m_Size = 10;
    strcpy(m_Type,"Tennis");
    strcpy(m_Material,"Canvas");
}

Shoe::Shoe(int size, char *type, char *material)
{
    m_Type = (char *)malloc( MAX_STRING);
    m_Material = (char *)malloc(MAX_STRING );
    m_Size = size;
    strcpy(m_Type,type);
    strcpy(m_Material,material);
}

Shoe::~Shoe()
{
    free(m_Type);
    free(m_Material);
}
```

```
double Shoe::GetCost()
{
    //get the cost from a database or somewhere.
    double dblCurrCost = 50;

    if (m_Size > 15)
    {
        //increase the cost by 10%
        dblCurrCost += dblCurrCost * .10;
    }

    return dblCurrCost;
}

char* Shoe::GetType()
{
    return m_Type;

}

char* Shoe::GetMaterial()
{
    return m_Material;

}

int Shoe::GetSize()
{
    return m_Size;
}

void Shoe::SetType(char *type)
{
    strcpy(m_Type,type);

}

void Shoe::SetMaterial(char *material)
{
    strcpy(m_Material,material);

}

void Shoe::SetSize(int size)
```

```
{
    m_Size = size;
}
```

Lucy, You Got Some 'Splainin to Do!

The previous code may seem like a rather sharp departure from the first example, but it really isn't. Let's step back for a moment, and I'll explain each part of the code.

The :: Operator

One of the first things you probably noticed about this code example is the use of the :: (class scope) operator at the beginning of most of the functions in the implementation file (ex02_ch6.cpp) found on the Web site that accompanies this book. This operator specifies that the function named on the right side of the operator is a member of the class named on the left side of the operator. The following declaration tells the compiler that this function is the implementation of the method *MyFunction,* which was prototyped in the class declaration of *MyClass:*

```
int MyClass::MyFunction(void)
{
    //Implementation of function here
}
```

Of course, this assumes that MyClass was declared similarly to the following:

```
class MyClass
{
public:
    MyFunction(void);
    //other prototypes here
};
```

To understand why you have to go to this level of specificity with your function definitions, let's consider what would happen if you added another function prototype after the Shoe class as shown here:

```
//Previous declaration of Shoe class with no change made
class Shoe
{
```

```
public:
    Shoe();
    Shoe(int size, char *type, char *material);
    char *GetType();
    int GetSize();
    virtual double GetCost();
    char *GetMaterial();
    void SetType(char *type);
    void SetSize(int size);
    void SetMaterial(char *material);
    virtual ~Shoe();

private:
    char *m_Material;
    char *m_Type;
    int m_Size;

};

//The new line added to our file.
char *GetType();
```

It may seem that this additional declaration of the GetType() function should not be allowed because there already is a GetType function prototype in the class. In fact, it is allowed because the two functions are in a different scope—one is a method of the Shoe class, the other is a global function available throughout the application. All functions are evaluated within their scope. Just as in Visual Basic, you can declare a variable strName as a global variable and have another variable named strName declared inside a function. You can also have a function named MyFunction declared globally and another one declared within a class.

The ~ Operator

Another new (and somewhat strange looking) operator is the ~ (destructor) operator. The *destructor* operator denotes a function that will be called anytime a class is being destroyed. It is identical to the Class_Terminate() function in a Visual Basic class module. Just as in the Visual Basic Class_Terminate() function, it is important to free any resources that were allocated during the lifetime of the class, in the destructor. Destructors are always prefixed with the virtual keyword, which denotes that a destructor is a virtual function. I will explain virtual functions in a moment when we discuss Inheritance.

The Shoe::Shoe Function

For every action there is an equal and opposite reaction, and such is the case with the destructor operator. It is called the *constructor*. The constructor always takes the form `ClassName::ClassName` and, as you have probably guessed, is just like the `Class_Initialize()` function in a Visual Basic class module. Curiously, in the Shoe class, there are two definitions that have this form. The reason for this is, in C++ you can have more than one constructor defined for a class as long as they each take a different number and type of parameter. For instance (no pun intended), in the Shoe class, two constructors are defined as follows:

```
Shoe::Shoe()
{
    m_Type = (char *)malloc( MAX_STRING);
    m_Material = (char *)malloc( MAX_STRING);

    m_Size = 10;
    strcpy(m_Type,"Tennis");
    strcpy(m_Material,"Canvas");
}

Shoe::Shoe(int size, char *type, char *material)
{
    m_Type = (char *)malloc( MAX_STRING);
    m_Material = (char *)malloc(MAX_STRING);
    m_Size = size;
    strcpy(m_Type,type);
    strcpy(m_Material,material);
}
```

The first constructor doesn't take any parameters, and therefore loads the private class variables (`m_Type`, `m_Size`, and `m_Material`) with some arbitrary default values. The second constructor takes three parameters and places them in the private variables instead of the default values from the parameter-less constructor. Using the constructor with parameters is equivalent to creating an instance of the class with the parameter-less constructor (also known as the default constructor), and then immediately calling the `SetMaterial()`, `SetType()`, and `SetSize()` functions with the values passed in as parameters. The ability to have these additional constructors enables a user to create classes and initialize them in one step as opposed to three, four, or five steps. Visual Basic doesn't allow this type of multiply defined constructor. You can actually do this with any function in a class. This technique is called function overloading.

Inheritance

Now that you have a handle on classes in general terms, let's dive into inheritance. The formal definition of inheritance is as follows:

inheritance: The ability to derive new classes from existing classes in object-oriented programming. A derived class ("subclass") inherits the instance variables and methods of the base class ("superclass") and may add new instance variables and methods. New methods may be defined with the same names as those in the base class in which case they override the original ones.

To recap, when a class inherits from another class, it automatically gets all of the properties and methods of the base class plus any others defined in the new "subclass." Let's look at an example by creating the GolfShoe class from the example used earlier in the chapter. But this time let's not use containment to fake inheritance, let's use inheritance directly.

```cpp
// GolfShoe.h: interface for the GolfShoe class.
//
//////////////////////////////////////////////////////////////////////

#if !defined(AFX_GOLFSHOE_H__FA134DC1_CDFF_11D3_BC89_805352C10000__INCLUDED_)
#define AFX_GOLFSHOE_H__FA134DC1_CDFF_11D3_BC89_805352C10000__INCLUDED_

#if _MSC_VER > 1000
#pragma once
#endif // _MSC_VER > 1000

#include "Shoe.h"

class GolfShoe : public Shoe
{
public:
    GolfShoe();
    virtual ~GolfShoe();

};

#endif //
!defined(AFX_GOLFSHOE_H__FA134DC1_CDFF_11D3_BC89_805352C10000__INCLUDED_)


// GolfShoe.cpp: implementation of the GolfShoe class.
//
//////////////////////////////////////////////////////////////////////
```

```
#include "stdafx.h"
#include "GolfShoe.h"

//////////////////////////////////////////////////////////////////////
// Construction/Destruction
//////////////////////////////////////////////////////////////////////

GolfShoe::GolfShoe()
{

}

GolfShoe::~GolfShoe()
{

}
```

Believe it or not, the GolfShoe class contains the functions: GetType, GetSize, and GetMaterial, even though you don't see them defined here. The reason is that the GolfShoe class has inherited them from the Shoe class. The actual syntax for inheriting from a class is the same as any other class definition except for the presence of the inheritance statement as follows:

```
class GolfShoe : public Shoe
```

This line of code tells the compiler that you are creating a class that will use the class to the right of the colon as the base for the class on the left. It should be quite obvious that the GolfShoe class is rather useless at this point because all you did was create a mirror image of the Shoe class. In order to make this class useful in an application, you need to add the functionality you added in the Visual Basic GolfShoe class. The first thing you need to do is add the special version of the GetCost function, which increases the cost of shoes over size 19. You also need to add the NumberOfSpikes property. This is what your files should look like after these alterations are made:

```
// GolfShoe.h: interface for the GolfShoe class.
//
//////////////////////////////////////////////////////////////////////

#if !defined(AFX_GOLFSHOE_H__FA134DC1_CDFF_11D3_BC89_805352C10000__INCLUDED_)
#define AFX_GOLFSHOE_H__FA134DC1_CDFF_11D3_BC89_805352C10000__INCLUDED_

#if _MSC_VER > 1000
#pragma once
```

```
#endif // _MSC_VER > 1000

#include "Shoe.h"

class GolfShoe : public Shoe
{
public:
    int SetNumberOfSpikes(int iSpikes);
    int GetNumberOfSpikes();
    GolfShoe();
    double GetCost();
    virtual ~GolfShoe();
private:
    int m_NumberOfSpikes;

};

#endif //
!defined(AFX_GOLFSHOE_H__FA134DC1_CDFF_11D3_BC89_805352C10000__INCLUDED_)


// GolfShoe.cpp: implementation of the GolfShoe class.
//
//////////////////////////////////////////////////////////////////////

#include "stdafx.h"
#include "GolfShoe.h"

//////////////////////////////////////////////////////////////////////
// Construction/Destruction
//////////////////////////////////////////////////////////////////////

GolfShoe::GolfShoe()
{
    m_NumberOfSpikes = 30;
}

GolfShoe::~GolfShoe()
{

}

int GolfShoe::GetNumberOfSpikes()
{
```

```
        return m_NumberOfSpikes;
}

int GolfShoe::SetNumberOfSpikes(int iSpikes)
{
    m_NumberOfSpikes = iSpikes;
    return m_NumberOfSpikes;
}

double GolfShoe::GetCost()
{
    //get the cost from a database or somewhere.
    double dblCurrCost = 50;

    if (GetSize() > 19)
    {
        //increase the cost by 10%
        dblCurrCost += dblCurrCost * .10;
    }

    return dblCurrCost;
}
```

Using the GolfShoe Class

You can now test your class with a small test program, but before you do, let me explain several details regarding the way to access the class member's properties and methods. When an instance of a class is declared as in the following C++ code snippet:

```
GolfShoe m_golfShoe;
```

you can access the members of the class just as you would with a Visual Basic class; by using the "." operator.

The Visual Basic version looks like this:

```
Public Sub Main()
Dim m_golfShoe As New GolfShoe
m_golfShoe.GetCost()
End Sub
The C++ Version:
int main()
{
```

```
GolfShoe m_golfShoe;
m_golfShoe.GetCost();
    return 1;
}
```

However, in many cases, you will declare the class variable as a pointer like this:

```
GolfShoe *m_golfShoe = new GolfShoe();
```

In this case, you have to use a different syntax to manipulate the object. Here is the same code listed previously, but it uses a class pointer instead of an object directly:

```
int main()
{
GolfShoe *m_golfShoe = new GolfShoe();
m_golfShoe->GetCost();
    return 1;
}
```

The -> Operator

In the example, the (pointer to member) -> operator was used instead of the . operator. This may seem rather useless, but consider the case where you want to pass an object to a function. If you have a large object (or any object for that matter), you definitely wouldn't want to pass it on the stack. You would want to pass a pointer to that object.

The new and delete Operators

The keyword *new* creates an instance of the specified class and returns a pointer to it. Therefore, you need to use a *pointer to class* variable type to capture the return value of a call to *new*. This works very much like the new operator in Visual Basic. Just as in the Visual Basic version of *new*, when you create an object using it, you need to destroy that object when you're done. In Visual Basic you use the statement:

```
Set MyObject = Nothing
```

However, in C++, you use the delete operator to free objects created with the keyword *new*. So this means that the previous example, which created a pointer to the GolfShoe class by using *new,* should actually look like the following:

```
int main()
{
GolfShoe *m_golfShoe = new GolfShoe();
m_golfShoe->GetCost();

//don't forget to free that object.
delete m_golfShoe;
    return 1;
}
```

If you forget to use the delete operator, you open the door for a *memory leak.* A memory leak occurs when you have unreferenced (or un-*delete*-ed) objects in memory. Visual Basic is very good about cleaning up these "orphaned" objects for you, but in C++ you are responsible for your own clean up. Actually, the C++ compiler will sometimes make a call to delete for an object that goes out of scope within a single function and has not had a call to delete made on it, but don't rely on the C++ compiler to watch your back. Play it safe and always call *delete* explicitly for any object created with *new.*

Don't Use malloc()

What I am about to say may surprise you, but you should always allocate memory with *new* and always free that memory with *delete.* I know that I told you to use malloc() to create memory and free() to destroy it in Chapter 5, but I only did that so you could see how malloc() works and to gain a better understanding of why you should use the *new* operator instead.

Here is a quick rundown explaining why you should use *new* and *delete* instead of *malloc* and *free.* When memory is allocated with the malloc() function, the system reserves a block of memory, which is the same size as the requested number of bytes in the call to malloc(). When you make a call to free() and pass the pointer to that previously allocated memory's starting address, the system will free that block of memory. No problem. Right? Well, sometimes. You see, whether this is okay or not depends on what it is that you are allocating space for. If you are allocating space for a built-in type (such as int, char, or long), then there are no ill effects when using malloc() and free() to allocate and de-allocate memory. However, if you are allocating space for an object, you might run into serious problems. Consider what happens when you create an object with malloc() as follows:

```
Class1 *c1 = (Class1*)malloc(sizeof(Class1));
```

You will indeed have a valid *Class1* type object. You could call its functions and utilize it in a similar way to the same class created with new, unless you had some code that had to run in the class constructor. Consider the following class definition:

```
class Class1
{
public:
Class1()
{
    m_Value = 0;
}
int GetValue(void);

private:
int m_Value;
};
```

Now assume that you create and call the class something like this:

```
Class1 *c1 = (Class1*)malloc(sizeof(Class1));
int i = c1->GetValue(); //we expect this to return 0
```

You expect that the call to c1->GetValue() will return 0 because you have the code in the constructor to do so. However, because you created the object using malloc(), the call to c1->GetValue() will return an undefined result. The reason is that malloc() doesn't call a class's constructor. And really, it shouldn't. You didn't ask malloc() to create a Class1 object for you. You just asked it to allocate space for it. And if you're thinking ahead, yep—you guessed it; free() doesn't call destructors either. Not to worry. As long as you create all objects with *new* and destroy them with *delete*, you can be assured that your constructors and destructors will be called.

Allocate Built-In Types with new

Because *new* should always be used to create objects, wouldn't it make sense to use *new* and *delete* to allocate and free all of your memory? Well, sometimes. If you are going to allocate a large chunk of memory, say larger than 1000 bytes, you should probably use the *new* operator. If memory allocation is smaller than 1000 bytes, you should probably just allocate the memory directly. Here is an example of allocating memory using both methods:

```
char temp[100]; //create the variable directly
char *temp = new char[100]; //allocate the variable using new
```

(The details of memory allocation are discussed in Chapter 7.)

There are also array versions of *new* and *delete*: *new[]* and *delete[]*. Use new[ ] when you are creating an array of a type, such as:

```
char *c = new char[1000]; //use delete[]
int *x = new int; //use delete
delete[] c;
delete x;
```

Testing It Out

Let's use all of this knowledge to write a test application and test the new class.

```cpp
// ex02_ch6.cpp : Defines the entry point for the console application.
//

#include "stdafx.h"
#include "shoe.h"
#include "golfshoe.h"
#include <stdio.h>

int main(int argc, char* argv[])
{
    Shoe *myShoe = new Shoe(14,"Boot","Leather");

    GolfShoe *myGolfShoe = new GolfShoe();

    printf("The shoe is size %d.\n",myShoe->GetSize());

    printf("The shoe is made of %s.\n",myShoe->GetMaterial());

    printf("The shoe is a %s shoe.\n",myShoe->GetType());

    printf("The shoe costs $%.2f.\n",myShoe->GetCost());

    printf("The non-member version of GetType() returns: %s.\n",GetType());

    myGolfShoe->SetMaterial("Canvas");
```

```
myGolfShoe->SetNumberOfSpikes(35);

myGolfShoe->SetSize(25);

myGolfShoe->SetType("Golf");

printf("The golf shoe is size %d.\n",myGolfShoe->GetSize());

printf("The golf shoe is made of %s.\n",myGolfShoe->GetMaterial());

printf("The golf shoe is a %s shoe.\n",myGolfShoe->GetType());

printf("The golf shoe costs $%.2f.\n",myGolfShoe->GetCost());
return 0;
}
```

This code listing produces the output shown in Figure 6-1.

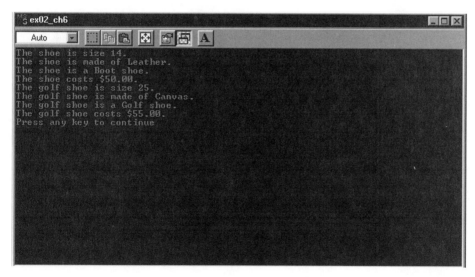

Figure 6-1. The test application at runtime

Virtual Functions

You can see that the GolfShoe class retains all of the functionality of the Shoe class, but uses the overridden functions where supplied. These overridden functions are called virtual functions. The way that virtual functions work is as follows. The compiler looks at a derived class's definition and notes any functions that are defined in the base class with the keyword virtual and then overridden in the derived class. When it finds a matching function in both classes, it puts the function from the derived class in the program, but uses the base class functions where no match is found. This enables a feature of object oriented programming, known as *polymorphism,* to take place. Polymorphism is the ability of a base class and a derived class to contain functions with the same name and parameter lists. In the case of polymorphism, the compiler must decide which version of a function to call based on the type of object that calls it. Consider the following two class definitions:

```
class A
{
public:
    A();
    virtual func1(int num1);
    virtual ~A();

};

class B : public A
{
public:
    B();
    virtual func1(int num1);
    virtual ~B();

};
```

A is a base class that defines one virtual function (besides its destructor) called func1. B is derived from A and thereby inherits A's version of func1; however, B also defines func1 with the same parameter list as A's version. This means B is implementing the func1 virtual function. The compiler will now have to check any program that uses B to verify which version of func1 to call. The following code snippet should clarify this subject:

```
#include "stdafx.h"
#include "A.h"

void polyFunc(A *p_objA);

int main(int argc, char* argv[])
{
    A *objA = new A(); //create an A class
    B *objB = new B(); //create a B class
```

```
    objA->func1(100); //call the base class version of func1
    objB->func1(100); //call the derived class version of func1
    objB->A::func1(100); //call the base class version of func1

    polyFunc(objA); //call polyFunc passing an A class
    polyFunc(objB); //call polyFunc passing a B class

    return 0;
}

void polyFunc(A *p_objA)
{
    p_objA->func1(100);
}
```

You can see that we create two objects, one A and one B. We then call func1 for each object. This works as expected: the call on the object objA causes the message box shown in Figure 6-2 to appear, while the call to objB causes the message box shown in Figure 6-3 to appear.

Now look at the following call:

```
objB->A::func1(100); //call the base class version of func1
```

With this call I am forcing the compiler to use A's version of func1 by naming the class and then the function explicitly, even though I call the function through a B pointer. This technique can be used on any derived class. However, it cannot be used inversely you can not safely call a derived class from a base class pointer.

The next two calls are simply used to show how effective polymorphism can be. I call a function, polyFunc, which takes a parameter of type A, and pass it both classes in consecutive calls. The right version of func1 is called for each passed class because while the parameter is of type A, the compiler checks what type of object was actually passed to the function. Declaring the parameter for func1 as type A causes the compiler to ensure that only objects that derive from A are passed to the function. It does not cause the function to interpret each passed object as being of type A.

Figure 6-2. The Base Class Called message box

Figure 6-3. The Derived Class Called message box

Conclusion

This was a relatively long chapter, but an important one for understanding C++ classes. Classes will be used in examples from this point forward, so you will be able to see them used in more practical situations. If you still feel unsure about how classes are used, try reading the beginning of this chapter again.

In the next chapter, we explore C++ templates, which should prove to be as interesting as classes on many levels because templates are just special types of classes. Hang in there. If you understand most of what has been presented, then you're doing great. (If not, don't worry—you'll catch on.)

CHAPTER 7

Templates

TEMPLATES MAY NOT BE WIDELY USED IN MOST C++ programs, but the implementation of the Component Object Model (COM) and the Active Template Library (ATL) are based heavily on them. In this chapter I cover template classes thoroughly enough for you to get a good understanding of how they work internally as well as how to use them. Don't let the syntax of templates scare you off because it may be a little weird looking. Just remember that everything else in C++ looked weird the first time you saw it. Okay, let's get started.

Understanding Templates

A template is a *parameterized class*, which essentially means that a template is a normal class except for the fact that various parameters are passed to it at instantiation time. Consider the following code listing for the template class, *Bucket*:

```
// Bucket.h: interface for the Bucket class.
//
/////////////////////////////////////////////////////////////////////

#if!defined(AFX_BUCKET_H__CE21A7CB_D174_11D3_BC89_B02152C10000__INCLUDED_)
#define AFX_BUCKET_H__CE21A7CB_D174_11D3_BC89_B02152C10000__INCLUDED_

#if _MSC_VER > 1000
#pragma once
#endif // _MSC_VER > 1000

template <class T>
class Bucket
{
public:
    Bucket()
    {
        m_Key = 0;
        m_itemCount = 0;
    }
```

```
        ~Bucket(){}

public:
    int AddItem(T* item)      //This function adds an item to the collection
    {
        m_Items[m_Key] = item;
        m_itemCount++;
        return m_Key++;
    }


    T* GetItem(int key)          //This function retrieves an item from the
collection
    {
        //m_itemCount--;
        return m_Items[key];
    }

    int GetCount()
    {
        return m_itemCount;
    }

private:
    T *m_Items[1024];
    int m_Key;
    int m_itemCount;

};


#endif // !defined(AFX_BUCKET_H__CE21A7CB_D174_11D3_BC89_B02152C10000__INCLUDED_)
```

It looks similar to any other class definition, with a few notable exceptions. Look at the following line of code:

```
template <class T>
```

What does this statement do? It establishes the fact that this is a template class, which takes one parameter, T, of type class. And what exactly does it mean to say that a class takes a parameter of type class? Well, it may help to re-examine how a function works as we answer that question.

Consider the following lines of code:

```
int DoSomething(int numIn)
{
return 1;
}
```

Now, you should easily recognize this as a function that takes one argument of type int. Based on our existing knowledge, we know that the value of numIn (our function DoSomething's argument) will be determined at the time the function is called when the caller supplies a value for our function's argument. For example:

```
int x = 12;
DoSomething(x);
```

will call the function DoSomething and pass the value 12 as the parameter *x*. DoSomething will then use the value of x to do something internally.

A template class works very much the same way. A template class receives a parameter (or parameters) at compile time and then uses the parameter(s) at compile time to affect the creation of its internal members.

Let's break down the template class Bucket so we can get a better feel for what a template class is all about:

```
template <class T>
class Bucket
```

These are the first two lines of our template class definition for *Bucket*. There is nothing special here, just the declaration that the template class Bucket is going to take a parameter of type class. You may notice that the implementations of our functions (Constructors and Destructors, too) are in the Bucket class header file (Bucket.h) instead of in their own separate implementation file (Bucket.cpp), as we saw with non-template classes. The reason is because a template class requires the class declaration and the class definition to both be available at the same time in order for compilation and linking to take place. The easiest way to make that happen is to put each function's definition inside its declaration.

> **NOTE:** *You are free to put the implementation (or definition) of your class's member functions inside the declarations all the time. However, it is generally better to separate the two as to allow for readability and separation of interface from implementation. (For more detail on the concept of interface/implementation separation, see Chapter 12.)*

Now, let's look at the next few lines in the class:

```
public:
    Bucket()
    {
        m_Key = 0;
        m_itemCount = 0;
    }


    ~Bucket(){}
```

There's nothing special going on here(just our regular class constructor and destructor. Again, note the constructor implementation inside of its declaration.

The next section gets more interesting:

```
public:
int AddItem(T* item)
{
    m_Items[m_Key] = item;
    m_itemCount++;
return m_Key++;
}
```

Here we can see that the member function AddItem uses a pointer to the variable T of type class (which was passed in to our template class) as the type of its parameter. Consider the following code:

```
//Declare Class1 without defining it
class Class1;

Bucket<Class1> b_c1;
```

Assuming this declaration, the Bucket member function AddItem would in essence be compiled as the following:

```
int AddItem(Class1* item)
{
        m_Items[m_Key] = item;
        m_itemCount++;
return m_Key++;
}
```

Notice that the variable *T* has been replaced by the type name `Class1`. If our declaration had been made as follows:

```
//Declare Class1 without defining it
class Class1;

Bucket<int> b_c1;
```

`AddItem` would wind up looking like this:

```
int AddItem(int* item)
{
        m_Items[m_Key] = item;
        m_itemCount++;
return m_Key++;
}
```

Make sense? Good.

It is important to understand that a template class is just like any other class. The closest Visual Basic analogy would be to use the Variant type in Visual Basic; for instance:

```
Option Explicit
Public colHolder As New Collection

Public Sub Main()
'Allocate our user defined class (assume that CVarPasser is defined in its own
Visual Basic class file.
Dim a As New CVarPasser
a.Name = "Dave"
VarPasser (d)
End Sub

Public Function VarPasser(varParam As Variant) As Long
colHolder.Add varParam
End Function
```

The function `VarPasser` takes a parameter of any valid type and adds it to a collection. No type checking occurs here. A single block of code is used regardless of the type of variant passed to the function.

The big difference between this approach and that of templates is that with templates the parameter types are set at compile time instead of runtime. Perhaps some hypothetical Visual Basic code will help make this subject more clear.

(Note: The following code is not legal Visual Basic code; it is here to show what a template would look like in Visual Basic if templates were legal in Visual Basic.)

```
Public Function VarPasser(varParam As ClassName) As Long
Dim varTemp As varParam
    Set varTemp = new varParam

    varTemp.Name = "joe"
End Function
```

For the purpose of this example, we pretend that Visual Basic can accept a *type name* (such as String or Integer) as a parameter. Now, if we called our function VarPasser like this:

```
VarPasser(String)
```

the body of VarPasser would be modified to look like this at compile time:

```
Public Function VarPasser(varParam As ClassName) As Long
Dim varTemp As String
    Set varTemp = new String

    varTemp.Name = "joe"
End Function
```

If we called our function like this:

```
VarPasser(MyCustomStringClass)
```

the body of VarPasser would look like this:

```
Public Function VarPasser(varParam As ClassName) As Long
Dim varTemp As MyCustomStringClass
    Set varTemp = new MyCustomStringClass

    varTemp.Name = "joe"
End Function
```

Again, this is *fake* Visual Basic code. Please do not try this at home. I know that this topic may seem confusing, but it really isn't. Just remember that the only difference in a function's parameters and a template's parameters is that a function's parameters will be used as a value for some *type* in the function body, while a template's parameters will be used as the *type* for some value in the function body.

Multiple Template Parameters

Just as a function can take more than one parameter, so can a template class. Consider the following template class definition:

```
template <class T,int I>
class cl
{
public:
    T m_cl[I];

};
```

In this class definition, we can see that there are two parameters: *T* and *I*. We are using the parameter I to denote the number of T classes that should be in the array m_cl. This can prove to be very useful in many cases, especially for container classes. We can also deduce from this example, that a template can take different types of parameters. We are not restricted to class type variables.

Using a Template Class

Talking about template classes is all well and good, but let's look at an example of how we would actually use a template class in practice. Here we will create two instances of our template class *Bucket*, and fill them with different types of classes. Following are the contents of our program's files, which can all be found at this book's companion Web site (www.apress.com) in the project *ex01_ch7 files*.

The Bucket.h File

```
/////////////////////////////////////////////////////////////////////
// Bucket.h: interface for the Bucket class.
/////////////////////////////////////////////////////////////////////

#if !defined(AFX_BUCKET_H__CE21A7CB_D174_11D3_BC89_B02152C10000__INCLUDED_)
#define AFX_BUCKET_H__CE21A7CB_D174_11D3_BC89_B02152C10000__INCLUDED_

#if _MSC_VER > 1000
#pragma once
```

```cpp
#endif // _MSC_VER > 1000

template <class T>
class Bucket
{
public:
    Bucket()
    {
        m_Key = 0;
        m_itemCount = 0;
    }

    ~Bucket(){}

public:
    //This function adds an item to the collection
int AddItem(T* item)    {
        m_Items[m_Key] = item;
        m_itemCount++;
        return m_Key++;
    }

    //This function retrieves an item from the collection
T* GetItem(int key)    {
        //m_itemCount--;
        return m_Items[key];
    }

    int GetCount()
    {
        return m_itemCount;
    }

private:
    T *m_Items[1024];
    int m_Key;
    int m_itemCount;

};


#endif // !defined(AFX_BUCKET_H__CE21A7CB_D174_11D3_BC89_B02152C10000__INCLUDED_)
```

The ex01_ch7.cpp File

```
//////////////////////////////////////////////////////////////////////////
// ex01_ch7.cpp : Defines the entry point for the console application.
//////////////////////////////////////////////////////////////////////////

#include "stdafx.h"
#include "bucket.h"
#include "class1.h"
#include "class2.h"

int main(int argc, char* argv[])
{
    //Declare our Bucket classes
    Bucket<Class1> b_c1;
    Bucket<Class2> b_c2;

    //Declare 5 instances of Class1
    Class1 c1_1;
    Class1 c1_2;
    Class1 c1_3;
    Class1 c1_4;
    Class1 c1_5;

    //Declare 1 instance of Class2
    Class2 c2;

    //Variables to hold the keys in the collection
    int key_c1[5];
    int key_c2;

    //Add the items to Class1 the Bucket
    key_c1[0] = b_c1.AddItem(&c1_1);
    key_c1[1] = b_c1.AddItem(&c1_2);
    key_c1[2] = b_c1.AddItem(&c1_3);
    key_c1[3] = b_c1.AddItem(&c1_4);
    key_c1[4] = b_c1.AddItem(&c1_5);

    //Add the items to the Class2 Bucket
    key_c2 = b_c2.AddItem(&c2);

    //Call a Class1 member function through the Bucket pointer
```

```
        b_c1.GetItem(key_c1[0])->SetNumber(1);

        //Call a Class1 member function through the Bucket pointer
        b_c2.GetItem(key_c2)->SetNumber(2);

        printf("b_c1 has %d items in it.\n",b_c1.GetCount());
        printf("b_c2 has %d items in it.\n",b_c2.GetCount());

        printf("%d\n",b_c1.GetItem(key_c1[0])->GetNumber());
        printf("%d\n",b_c2.GetItem(key_c2)->GetNumber());

        return 0;
}
```

The Class1.h File

```
// Class1.h: interface for the Class1 class.
//
//////////////////////////////////////////////////////////////////////

#if !defined(AFX_CLASS1_H__CE21A7CF_D174_11D3_BC89_B02152C10000__INCLUDED_)
#define AFX_CLASS1_H__CE21A7CF_D174_11D3_BC89_B02152C10000__INCLUDED_

#if _MSC_VER > 1000
#pragma once
#endif // _MSC_VER > 1000

class Class1
{
public:
    Class1::Class1()
    {
    }

    virtual ~Class1()
    {
    }

    void SetNumber(DWORD number)
    {
        m_Number = number;
    }
```

```
    DWORD GetNumber()
    {
        return m_Number;
    }

private:
    DWORD m_Number;

};

#endif // !defined(AFX_CLASS1_H__CE21A7CF_D174_11D3_BC89_B02152C10000__INCLUDED_)
```

The Class2.h File

```
// Class2.h: interface for the Class2 class.
//
//////////////////////////////////////////////////////////////////////

#if !defined(AFX_CLASS2_H__CE21A7D0_D174_11D3_BC89_B02152C10000__INCLUDED_)
#define AFX_CLASS2_H__CE21A7D0_D174_11D3_BC89_B02152C10000__INCLUDED_

#if _MSC_VER > 1000
#pragma once
#endif // _MSC_VER > 1000

class Class2
{
public:
Class2::Class2()
{
}
virtual ~Class2()
{
}
void SetNumber(DWORD number)
{
    m_Number = number;
}
DWORD GetNumber()
{
    return m_Number;
}
```

```
private:
DWORD m_Number;

};


#endif //defined(AFX_CLASS2_H__CE21A7D0_D174_11D3_BC89_B02152C10000__INCLUDED_)
```

The output from the program when it is run is shown in Figure 7-1.

Our two *item* classes (or classes that get put in the Bucket) are Class1 and Class2, which are defined in their respective header files. I put the function definitions inside their function declarations (which reside in the header files) to conserve space in the printed text. Again, I defined the functions of the *Bucket* class inside the Bucket.h header file.

Notice that by using our template class we now have the ability to call a member function of an item class through a Bucket variable as shown here:

```
b_c1.GetItem(key_c1[0])->SetNumber(1);
```

Although this syntax may look strange, it is very powerful in practice. In this single statement we are referencing the Class1 object at array element 0 (with the bolded part of this statement):

b_c1.GetItem(key_c1[0])->SetNumber(1);

Figure 7-1. The program output

and then immediately using that pointer to call `Class1`'s `SetNumber` member function as shown here (again, the bolded part of the statement is what accomplishes this):

```
b_c1.GetItem(key_c1[0])->SetNumber(1);
```

This technique could be used to add a loop to our program, which would iterate through our collection of Class1 objects and call a function of those objects like this:

```
for (int i = 0;i < b_c1.GetCount() - 1;i++)
{
    printf("%d\n",b_c1.GetItem(i)->GetNumber());
}
```

Imagine that I had a set of classes that were all inherited from the same base class. I could create a function that would accept a parameter of that base class type, and then manipulate all of those sub-classes without even knowing what sub-type they were. (We'll see where this is leading later on in this book.)

Conclusion

In this chapter I introduced the topic of templates. If you're still hungry for more in-depth coverage of templates, go grab your copy of *The C++ Programming Language* by Bjarne Stroustrup (Addison-Wesley, 2000) that I recommended earlier. However, my purpose in this chapter was to familiarize you with the way templates work, as a preparation for the *Active Template Library*, which I discuss later in this book. However, next we are going to use all of this knowledge we have acquired thus far and create a full working application using C++.

CHAPTER 8
Putting It All Together

Oᴋᴀʏ, ɴᴏᴡ ᴡʜᴀᴛ?

Well, first things first. Congratulations, you have now made it through all of the major language elements of C++, which is no easy feat, I might add. From this point on we will use that knowledge to build components to add to our Visual Basic development efforts. But before we begin that endeavor, in this chapter we will take our cumulative C++ skills and build a real live C++ application. This application will incorporate almost all of the skills learned so far in this book, as well as a few new tricks and techniques. I also try to challenge you to fix some small inefficiencies and errors in the application.

All of the files for this project are located on the Web site that accompanies this book at www.apress.com.

The Application Requirements

Our goal is to write an application that will enable a user to take a file and *break* it into several smaller pieces, and then reassemble those pieces back into the complete file. Such an application is useful to be able to distribute a file that cannot fit onto one single storage medium such as a floppy disk, or to create a segmented file download from the Internet.

Now understand that there are many freely available applications available that perform this task and more. So try not to focus on the functionality of our application (or the lack there-of), but instead try to remember that we are using this application to apply the skills we have learned in C++ to a real application.

The Application Design

Because we already know the requirements for our application, we can go ahead and concentrate on the design and implementation of our program's technical components. (In fact, we aren't going to spend much time on design, as this exercise is implementation-oriented.)

The first thing that stands out about this application is that it is going to deal with files in one form or another. Therefore, it makes sense to create a generic file class that encapsulates the basic operations we want to perform on a file. This generic file class will also serve as a base for other specialized file classes.

The GenericFile Class

I created just such a file class and named it *GenericFile*. The contents of the header file, *GenericFile.h*, which contains the *GenericFile* class declaration, is listed here:

```
// GenericFile.h: interface for the GenericFile class.
//
//////////////////////////////////////////////////////////////////////

#if !defined(
      AFX_GENERICFILE_H__FCE1D62C_1AC7_4D4E_8224_CE81A0D54F7B__INCLUDED_)
#define
AFX_GENERICFILE_H__FCE1D62C_1AC7_4D4E_8224_CE81A0D54F7B__INCLUDED_

#if _MSC_VER > 1000
#pragma once
#endif // _MSC_VER > 1000

#include <windows.h>
#include <stdio.h>

class GenericFile
{
public:
    //Enumeration of file open options
    enum GF_OPEN_MODE
    {
        OPEN_READ_ONLY = GENERIC_READ,
        OPEN_WRITE_ONLY = GENERIC_WRITE,
        OPEN_READ_WRITE = GENERIC_READ | GENERIC_WRITE
    };

public:
    //Construction and destruction
    //Constructor - if no path is specified then the
    //current directory is appended to the file name
  GenericFile(char *lpfileName);
    GenericFile();  //Default constructor
    virtual ~GenericFile();  //Default destructor

    char* GetFileName();    //Retrieves the name of the file
    virtual int GetFileSize();  //Returns the size of the file
```

```
    //Stores the name of the file
    virtual int SetFileName(char *lpfileName);
    //Opens the file
    virtual int Open(char *lpFileName,GF_OPEN_MODE gfo_mode);
    //Opens the file
    virtual int Open(
                        GF_OPEN_MODE gfo_mode =
                        GF_OPEN_MODE::OPEN_READ_WRITE);
    int Close();  //Closes the handle to the file
    //Reads from the file into a user passed variable
     virtual int Read(unsigned char *buff,
                                    int maxNum);
    //Writes the passed in buffer to the file
    virtual int Write(const unsigned char* buff,
                                    int maxNum);

protected:
    HANDLE m_handle;  //Variable to hold the internal file handle
    char m_fileName[MAX_PATH]; //Buffer to hold the file path and name
};

#endif // !defined(
AFX_GENERICFILE_H__FCE1D62C_1AC7_4D4E_8224_CE81A0D54F7B__INCLUDED_)
```

This class declaration should look fairly similar to the class declarations we have seen and used in previous chapters. But to become more familiar with our class declaration, let's go through it section by section.

First, you can see that we have #included windows.h and stdio.h. We must include these files in order to have access to the WIN 32 application program interface (API) functions and constants as well as the C runtime functions. (More on this later in this chapter.) Next, notice the public *enum,* GF_OPEN_MODE. The members of this enum are mapped directly to the WIN32 API file access flags, as we are going to use the WIN32 API file functions in our class. Next, we have the declarations of our two constructors for the class. The first constructor takes a parameter of type char*, while the second constructor (the default constructor) takes no parameters at all.

> **NOTE:** *It is not necessary to give names to the parameters in a function prototype or class constructor prototype. The reason is that in the function prototype or class constructor prototype, the compiler only needs the type of a parameter, not its name. In fact, if a name is given it is ignored by the*

> *compiler. The name of a parameter is only important in the function or class constructor implementation. However, using descriptive names for your parameters makes an easy way to document your code for other programmer's use. For instance, using* lpName *as the name for a parameter of type* char* *that holds a "Name" as a value, is much more descriptive than just putting the parameter type, such as* int. *The bottom line is: even though naming parameters in your function prototypes isn't required, you should, just for its value as a source of code documentation.*

The next section of our class declaration contains the member function prototypes. These functions perform the most common file manipulation routines that we will require for our application. There is one interesting new feature in the two prototypes for the virtual function Open(), and that is that these two prototypes make use of default parameter values as shown here:

```
virtual int Open(char* ,
    GF_OPEN_MODE gfOpenMode = GF_OPEN_MODE::OPEN_READ_WRITE);
virtual int Open(
    GF_OPEN_MODE gfOpenMode = GF_OPEN_MODE::OPEN_READ_WRITE);
```

A default parameter tells the compiler that if no value is passed for the parameter, use the default value of GF_OPEN_MODE::OPEN_READ_WRITE, which we supplied in our declaration. Notice that we use the scope resolution operator (::) to access the OPEN_READ_WRITE member of our class's GF_OPEN_MODE enumeration. In Visual Basic default parameter values are exposed as *Optional parameters* as in the following function declaration:

```
Public Function Open(Optional gfOpenMode As _
GF_OPEN_MODE = OPEN_READ_WRITE) As Long
```

The last element we see in our class declaration is two protected member variables, m_handle and m_filename. m_fileName is used to hold the name of the class's internal file name, and m_handle is used to hold the internal file's handle. We have just finished the declaration (or interface) of our GenericFile class.

Next we must implement the interface of our GenericFile class by writing definitions for our class's declared members. We will do this in the file *GenericFile.cpp* listed here.

The GenericFile Implementation File is

```cpp
// GenericFile.cpp: implementation of the GenericFile class.
//
//////////////////////////////////////////////////////////////////////

#include "GenericFile.h"

//////////////////////////////////////////////////////////////////////
// Construction/Destruction
//////////////////////////////////////////////////////////////////////

GenericFile::GenericFile()
{
    //initialize the file handle to NULL
    m_handle = NULL;
    m_fileName[0] = NULL;
}

GenericFile::GenericFile(char *lpfileName)
{
    //variable to hold our position in the m_fileName buffer
    int iOffset = 0;

    //check to be sure that lpFileName is valid
    if (!lpfileName)
    {
    m_fileName[0] = NULL0;
        return;
    }

    //check for a path in the string
    if (!strstr(lpfileName,"\\"))
    {
        //copy the path into the buffer
        iOffset = GetCurrentDirectory(MAX_PATH,m_fileName);

        //add the extra backslash
        strcpy(&m_fileName[iOffset++],"\\");
    }

    //copy the file name to the path if it didn't exist
    strcpy(&m_fileName[iOffset],lpfileName);
```

```
            //initialize the file handle to NULL
            m_handle = NULL;
        }


        GenericFile::~GenericFile()   //Destructor
        {
            //close the file handle if it's open
            if (m_handle)
            {
                CloseHandle(m_handle);
            }
        }



        /////////////////////////////////////////////////////////////////////
        //Member Function Implementations
        /////////////////////////////////////////////////////////////////////

        int GenericFile::Open(GF_OPEN_MODE gfo_mode) //Opens the file
        {
            //check that our member file name pointer is valid
            if (!m_fileName[0])
            {
                return 0;
            }

            //Create or Open the file
            m_handle = CreateFile(m_fileName,gfo_mode,NULL,NULL,
                                            OPEN_ALWAYS,NULL,NULL);

            //if the file could not be opened, find out why
            if (m_handle == INVALID_HANDLE_VALUE)
            {
                printf("GetLastError returned %d\n",GetLastError());
            }

            //return true if a file was created
            return ((m_handle != NULL) && (m_handle != INVALID_HANDLE_VALUE));
        }

        int GenericFile::Open(char *lpFileName,
                                        GF_OPEN_MODE gfo_mode)  //Opens the file
        {
            //variable to hold the offset into our buffer
```

```
    int iOffset = 0;

    //make sure the file name points to something
    if (!lpFileName)
    {
        return 0;
    }

    //check for a path in the name.
    if (!strstr(lpFileName,"\\"))
    {
        //if no path is found then load the buffer
        //with the current directory
        iOffset = GetCurrentDirectory(MAX_PATH,m_fileName);
        //add the extra backslash
        strcpy(&m_fileName[iOffset++],"\\");
    }

    //append the file name to the buffer
    strcpy(&m_fileName[iOffset],lpFileName);

    //Check for the existence of a file path and name
    m_handle = CreateFile(lpFileName,gfo_mode,
                              NULL,NULL,OPEN_ALWAYS,NULL,NULL);

    //if the file could not be opened, find out why
    if (m_handle == INVALID_HANDLE_VALUE)
    {
        printf("GetLastError returned %d\n",GetLastError());
    }

    //return true if a file was created
    return ((m_handle != NULL) && (m_handle != INVALID_HANDLE_VALUE));
}
//Store the path and name of the file
int GenericFile::SetFileName(char *lpfileName)
{
    //variable to hold our position in the m_fileName buffer
    int iOffset = 0;

    //make sure that lpFileName points to something
    if (!lpfileName)
    {
        return 0;
```

```
        }

        //check for a path in the string
        if (!strstr(lpfileName,"\\"))
        {
            //copy the path into the buffer
            iOffset = GetCurrentDirectory(MAX_PATH,m_fileName);

            //add the extra backslash
            strcpy(&m_fileName[iOffset++],"\\");
        }

        //return the length of the file name.
        return strlen(strcpy(&m_fileName[iOffset],lpfileName));
}
int GenericFile::Close()
{
    if (m_handle)
    {
        //close the handle
        CloseHandle(m_handle);
    }

    return !(m_handle = 0);
}


int GenericFile::GetFileSize()
{
    if (!m_handle)
    {
        return 0;
    }

    //return the size of the file.
    return (::GetFileSize(m_handle,NULL));

}


char *GenericFile::GetFileName()
{
    if (m_fileName)
    {
        //return the name of the file
```

```
        return strdup(m_fileName);
    }
    return 0;
}


int GenericFile::Read(unsigned char *buff,int maxNum)
{
    DWORD numRead = 0;

    //read in the specified number of bytes
    if (ReadFile(m_handle,buff,maxNum,&numRead,NULL))
    {
        //return the number read
        return numRead;
    }

    //return false
    return 0;
}

int GenericFile::Write(const unsigned char* buff,int maxNum)
{
    DWORD numWritten = 0;

    //if all goes well then return the number of bytes written
    if (WriteFile(m_handle,buff,maxNum,&numWritten,NULL))
    {
        return numWritten;
    }

    //return false
    return 0;
}
```

I will now go through each class member's implementation and briefly describe what each does. Our first member implementation is our default constructor's. It looks like this:

```
GenericFile::GenericFile()
{
    //initialize the file handle to NULL
    m_handle = NULL;
    m_fileName[0] = NULL;
}
```

You can see that all we do here is initialize our private member variables m_handle and m_filename to NULL. m_handle holds the handle to our class's file once it is opened. The reason we initialize it to NULL is because when we check to see if m_handle is a valid file handle in our class's other member functions, we do so by checking that m_handle contains a non-NULL value. And because we definitely don't want to operate on a bogus file handle (which we might do if m_handle contained a non-NULL value), we must be sure to set m_handle to NULL as soon as our class is instantiated (which is exactly what we have done in the previous code). The same logic holds true for m_fileName.

The next member we implement is our custom class constructor, which takes a char* as a parameter:

```
GenericFile::GenericFile(char *lpfileName)
{
    //variable to hold our position in the m_fileName buffer
    int iOffset = 0;

//check to be sure that lpFileName is valid
    if (!lpFileName)
    {
    m_fileName[0] = NULL;

        return;
    }
    //check for a path in the string
    if (!strstr(lpfileName,"\\"))
    {
        //copy the path into the buffer
        iOffset = GetCurrentDirectory(MAX_PATH,m_fileName);

        //add the extra backslash
        strcpy(&m_fileName[iOffset++],"\\");
    }

    //copy the file name to the path if it didn't exist
    strcpy(&m_fileName[iOffset],lpfileName);

    //initialize the file handle to NULL
    m_handle = NULL;
}
```

The first thing we do in this version of our class's constructor is create a local variable that holds the offset into our m_filename member variable.

(I explain how to do this later in this chapter.) After that, we verify that our argument, lpfileName, is indeed a valid pointer. We check this with the line:

```
if (!lpfileName)
```

If the logical *not* of lpfileName evaluates to *true* (meaning lpfileName is NULL), then we cease executing our constructor's code by way of the return statement.

> **NOTE:** *It is important to note that even though we* return *from our constructor when an invalid file pointer is found in* lpfileName, *our class is still created and is a legitimate* GenericFile *class. We look at ways to deal with behavior later on in this book.*

Now, if lpfileName is a valid pointer, it is assumed to point to either a file name or a file path and name.

Next, our program uses the strstr function to examine lpfileName for a backslash, as such:

```
if (!strstr(lpfileName,"\\"))
```

The strstr function is a *C++ Standard Library* function that is similar to the InStr function in Visual Basic. It returns the position of the first occurrence of a character in a string. If that string is not found, strstr returns 0. If we find a backslash, we assume the path is a valid path to a file and continue on. But, if we don't find one, we assume that we have been passed a file name only. In this case we will enter our *if* conditional code block and place the name of the current directory m_filename, as shown here:

```
//copy the path into the buffer
iOffset = GetCurrentDirectory(MAX_PATH,m_fileName);

//add the extra backslash
strcpy(&m_fileName[iOffset++],"\\");
```

In case you're not familiar with the WIN32 API, the call to GetCurrentDirectory may not jump out at you as anything special, but it is a commonly used WIN32 API function. As most Visual Basic programmers know, if you want to make this API call from Visual Basic, you have to write a declare statement such as this one:

```
Public Declare Function GetCurrentDirectory Lib "kernel32" _
Alias "GetCurrentDirectory" (ByVal nBufferLength As Long, _
ByVal lpBuffer As String) As Long
```

> **NOTE:** *The reason Visual Basic requires you to write a* Declare *statement is so that Visual Basic can discover enough information about the API function in order to call it. In fact, a Visual Basic* Declare *statement is identical in ideology to a C++ function prototype. The difference is that if your* Declare *statement contains errors, you won't find out until you try to execute the call at run-time. However, if the C++ function prototype contains an error, you won't have to wait until runtime to find out about it because your program won't link.*

Now, based on our existing knowledge of compiling and linking, we know that we have to tell the compiler about GetCurrentDirectory before we can use it in our program, and we do. (This is what I was referring to earlier in the chapter when I said that we had to #include the windows.h file in order to gain access to the WIN32 API.) You see, windows.h #include-es several other header files, one of which is winbase.h. This is the Microsoft-supplied header file that contains the prototype for all of the base WIN32 API functions, structures, and constants. Remember, as far as the C++ compiler is concerned, the call to GetCurrentDirectory is the same as any other function call in our program. Therefore, we must have a prototype for WIN32 API functions as well as any of our own; it just so happens that Microsoft already went to the trouble of putting the API prototypes in a header file for us.

Assuming all goes well with the call to GetCurrentDirectory, our member variable m_filename will point to the name of the current directory. We then use the C runtime function, strcpy, to put a backslash after the path that was just copied into m_fileName by the call to GetCurrentDirectory. An interesting thing to notice here is that we use the variable, iOffSet, to keep track of where we are in the m_filename char array (remember that a char* points to the address of the first member a char array). After the call to GetCurrentDirectory, iOffset contains the length of the name of the current directory. We then use that value as the char array index when copying a backslash into m_filename. A graphical representation of this chain of events is shown in Figure 8-1.

We can see from this diagram that iOffSet always represents our current location in the char array. Notice the use of the *post-fix increment operator* (iOffSet++) in the call to strcpy. It is used to increment iOffSet after copying the backslash to position 7 in the m_filename char array. As you remember from Chapter 4, the post-fix increment operator increments itself after the statement it is a part of is completed. If we mistakenly put the *pre-fix increment operator* (++iOffSet) in the call to strcpy, iOffSet would have been incremented before the

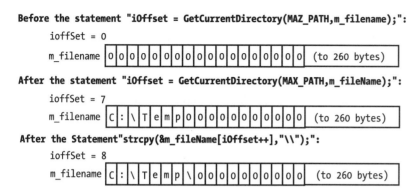

Figure 8-1. Creating the GenericFile class

call to strcpy, and copied the backslash to the wrong position in m_fileName. Be
very careful to avoid these kinds of mistakes, as they lead to bugs that are very
hard to track down!

With these lines of code now executed, our member variable m_fileName will
contain the name of the current directory (or to NULL if lpfileName already has a
backslash in it). We must copy the data at the memory address pointed to by lpfileName into the memory address pointed to by m_fileName[iOffset]. After that
all we do is set our file handle member variable, m_handle, to NULL and we're
done. As a side-note, the nice thing about using iOffSet to keep track of our
pointer position is that we don't need to check where we are in our char array all
of the time. When we reach the line

```
strcpy(&m_fileName[iOffset],lpfileName);
```

we know that &m_fileName[iOffset] is pointing exactly where it should be: either
to the beginning of m_filename or to the position after the last backslash in the
current directory's name. This programming methodology can save many lines of
code, and make a program's logic flow much smoother.

Next comes our class destructor:

```
GenericFile::~GenericFile()  //Destructor
{
    //close the file handle if it's open
    if (m_handle)
    {
        CloseHandle(m_handle);
    }
}
```

Remember that this code will get called when the delete operator terminates an instance of our class. Therefore, it is extremely important to do any per-instance cleanup here, as the object will cease to exist after this code is finished running.

Now, the only thing we do here is check m_handle to see if it contains a file handle. If it does, we close that handle. In a more complex program, we would probably have to free some other types of resources as well.

The GenericFile::Open Functions

We have two versions of the *Open* Function. One that takes a file name as a parameter and another that assumes that the class was created with a parameterized version of the constructor and therefore has already initialized m_filename to the desired file name. Let's first look at the version that does not take a file name parameter:

```
int GenericFile::Open(GF_OPEN_MODE gfo_mode)  //Opens the file
{
    //check that we have a valid file name
    if (!m_fileName[0])
    {
        return 0;
    }

    //Create or Open the file
    m_handle = CreateFile(m_fileName,gfo_mode,
                                    NULL,NULL,OPEN_ALWAYS,NULL,NULL);

    //if the file could not be opened, find out why
    if (m_handle == INVALID_HANDLE_VALUE)
    {
        printf("GetLastError returned %d\n",GetLastError());
    }

    //return true if a file was created
    return ((m_handle != NULL) && (m_handle != INVALID_HANDLE_VALUE));
}
```

This function is pretty straightforward. First, we verify that m_fileName is not NULL. If it is, we return a zero to the caller, which indicates failure. If m_filename is not NULL, we call CreateFile (another WIN32 API function) to open or create the file named in m_filename. I say "open or create" because we pass the OPEN_

ALWAYS flag to the *CreateFile* function. This flag tells CreateFile to try to open the file named in m_filename if such a file exists, or create it if the file does not exist. (I won't go into all of the details of the *CreateFile* function's parameters meanings, but I will give a brief description of each. A detailed description can be found in the Visual Studio help system.)

Following is the prototype for the *CreateFile* function from the Visual Studio help system:

```
HANDLE CreateFile(
  LPCTSTR lpFileName,          // pointer to name of the file
  DWORD dwDesiredAccess,       // access (read-write) mode
  DWORD dwShareMode,           // share mode
  LPSECURITY_ATTRIBUTES lpSecurityAttributes,
                               // pointer to security attributes
  DWORD dwCreationDisposition, // how to create
  DWORD dwFlagsAndAttributes,  // file attributes
  HANDLE hTemplateFile         // handle to file with attributes to
                               // copy
);
```

> **NOTE:** *Remember that most of the types used in the WIN32 API are just* typedef's *of built in types. For example, the WIN32 data type* DWORD *is just a typedef for an* unsigned long. *All of the WIN32 data type mappings are available in the Visual Studio online help system.*

The first parameter, lpFileName (the lp stands for *long pointer*), is a pointer to the name of the file to create or open. dwDesiredAccess (the dw stands for *DWORD*) is one of a set of constants defined in the WIN32 API that describes access to a resource such as a file. The GF_OPEN_MODE enum directly maps these values. We pass NULL as the value for dwShareMode and lpSecurityAttributes. In the first case, dwShareMode, we pass NULL so that CreateFile will use the default share mode. However, in the case of lpSecurityAttributes, we pass NULL to indicate that we don't want to use this feature of the call. (Again, the Visual Studio help file does a good job of detailing all of these meanings.)

The dwCreationDisposition parameter tells create file what to do if the file named in lpFileName already exists. In our case, we tell it to open the existing file. There are other options that enable different reactions to this situation. Just as with dwShareMode and lpSecurityAttributes, we pass NULL to dwFlagsAndAttributes and hTemplateFile to indicate that we want the default value for dwFlagsAndAttributes and to indicate that we won't be using a file template for hTemplateFile.

After our call to `CreateFile`, `m_handle` will contain one of two values: the handle to the file we just opened (or created) if the call was successful, or the value of `INVALID_HANDLE_VALUE` if the call failed. In some cases, it is important to know not only that a function call failed, but also why it failed. This is why we call `GetLastError` when `m_handle` is equal to `INVALID_HANDLE_VALUE` after the call to `CreateFile`. `GetLastError` is an API function that returns the last error code that was encountered during an API call. This way we can find out what the problem is that is preventing the file from being opened and print it to the screen. We can look up this error code to discover the textual representation of the error. In a more robust application we would look up the text of the message using the `FormatMessage` API function, but for our purposes, the error code alone will suffice.

The last thing we do in the function is return the success or failure of the call with the following line of code:

```
return ((m_handle != NULL) && (m_handle != INVALID_HANDLE_VALUE));
```

With this code we tell our code to evaluate our two logical boolean expressions, and then return the logical comparison of them as the return value of our call.

Now let's look at the second version of the call:

```
//Opens the file

int GenericFile::Open(char *lpFileName,GF_OPEN_MODE gfo_mode)
{
    //variable to hold the offset into our buffer
    int iOffset = 0;

    //make sure the file name points to something
    if (!lpFileName)
    {
        return 0;
    }

    //check for a path in the name.
    if (!strstr(lpFileName,"\\"))
    {
        //if no path is found then load the
        // buffer with the current directory
        iOffset = GetCurrentDirectory(MAX_PATH,m_fileName);
```

```
        //add the extra backslash
        strcpy(&m_fileName[iOffset++],"\\");
    }

    //append the file name to the buffer
    strcpy(&m_fileName[iOffset],lpFileName);

    //Check for the existence of a file path and name
    m_handle = CreateFile(lpFileName,gfo_mode,
                                    NULL,NULL,OPEN_ALWAYS,NULL,NULL);

    //if the file could not be opened, find out why
    if (m_handle == INVALID_HANDLE_VALUE)
    {
        printf("GetLastError returned %d\n",GetLastError());
    }

    //return true if a file was created
    return ((m_handle != NULL) && (m_handle != INVALID_HANDLE_VALUE));
}
```

Although slightly longer, this version of the function is virtually identical to the first. In fact, the only difference in this version and the previous version is that in this one we perform a check on the passed in file name to see if it is a path to a file or just a file name as we did in our parameterized constructor. You may be wondering why we didn't write a separate function to do the check for a path in a file name as we require this functionality in more than one place. Well, actually we could have, and *should* have. In fact, as an exercise, you should move this functionality to a protected member function.

You can then replace the code that implements this functionality in each member with a call to your new protected member function. The reason that the member should be protected and not private is because you want to enable access to this functionality from derived classes such as FileChunk. I included a modified version of the *fileBreaker* project on the Web site that accompanies this book (www.apress.com), named *fileBreakerMod*, which does exactly what I described. (But try to do it yourself first…you can do it.)

The GenericFile::SetFileName Function

Our next member implementation is the SetFileName function, which enables a user of our class to explicitly set the name of the file:

```
//Store the path and name of the file

int GenericFile::SetFileName(char *lpfileName)
{
    //variable to hold our position in the m_fileName buffer
    int iOffset = 0;

    //make sure that lpFileName points to something
        if (!lpfileName)
    {
        return 0;
    }

    //check for a path in the string
    if (!strstr(lpfileName,"\\"))
    {
        //copy the path into the buffer
        iOffset = GetCurrentDirectory(MAX_PATH,m_fileName);

        //add the extra backslash
        strcpy(&m_fileName[iOffset++],"\\");
    }

    //return the length of the file name.
    return strlen(strcpy(&m_fileName[iOffset],lpfileName));
```

This code should be starting to look very familiar to you, because this is a portion of the code that is in our parameterized constructor. If it seems like we have created code that enables us to achieve the same result, but in several different ways, it's because we have. Let me explain. You see, although we are creating this class for our own program's use, assume for a moment that we are creating this class to be used by several other developers. Different people will be using our class in different ways; therefore, we must provide a reasonable amount of flexibility in our class. For example, some of the users of our class may want to create an instance of our class without knowing the name of the file that they are creating and then set the name of the file later as shown here:

```
//Create an un-named file
GenericFile gf = new GenericFile();

//Other code here
.. .. .. ..
```

```
//Set the file's name
gf->SetFileName("MyFile.txt");
```

```
//Rest of program here
```

Another user of our class may want to create a file and set its name at the same time as in the following code:

```
//Create a named file
GenericFile gf = new GenericFile("MyFile.txt");
```

Both users executed the same exact lines of C++ code. If you examine the parameterized constructor, you will see that it is made up of the code from the default constructor as well as the code from the SetFileName member function— no more, no less.

The GenericFile::Close Function

The GenericFile::Close function's only job is to close the internal file's handle if it is open, as shown here:

```
int GenericFile::Close()
{
    if (m_handle)
    {
        //close the handle
        CloseHandle(m_handle);
    }

    return !(m_handle = 0);
}
```

As I mentioned previously, the way we check for an open file handle is to see if it contains a NULL value like so:

```
if (m_handle)
```

If it does not, we assume that we have an open file handle. This again is straightforward. The only interesting thing in this function is the way that we send our return value:

```
return !(m_handle = 0);
```

At first glance it looks as if we are checking to see if m_handle is equal to zero, but we aren't. We are actually setting m_handle equal to zero and then sending the logical *not* of that operation as our function's return value. The real trick here is to understand what the return value of an assignment is, so let's take a look. Consider the following code:

```
int x = 0;

printf("x = 10 is equal to %d", x = 10 );
```

This code would cause the number 10 to be written to the screen because the return value of an assignment is always the right-hand value of the assignment. In other words, the value on the right-hand side of the = sign. With this concept now understood, we can see that our *return* statement is actually equivalent to the following:

```
return !(0);
```

after zero is assigned to m_handle. To figure out the return value, we just need to discover the value of !(0) (or !0). Because we know that the *logical not* (!) operator will evaluate to false (0) when applied to a non-zero value and evaluate to true (1) when applied to a zero value, we can say with confidence that this statement will return true. Yes, there is another way to express this concept:

```
m_handle = 0;
if (m_handle == 0)
{
    return 1;
}
return 0;
```

The choice of which syntax to use is up to you. You can see that the first version is much shorter than the second. However, I feel that the second syntax is much easier to read and understand than the first.

The GenericFile::GetFileSize Function

All we do in the GenericFile::GetFileSize function is call the Win32 API function with the same name as our function. The twist here is that we use the *scope resolution* (::) operator in front of the call to *GetFileSize*. The reason that we have to do this is because when the compiler sees a function being called it tries to call it at the most local scope. In our case, if I hadn't prefixed our call to GetFileSize with the scope resolution operator, the compiler would have tried to call the Generic-File version of GetFileSize (which happens to be the function we are calling from). This would have caused the compiler to stop compilation of our program and notify me that GetFileSize doesn't take two parameters.

However, things could be much worse. If our function took the same type and number of parameters as the WIN32 API version, the compiler would happily compile our code and not complain at all. Then when we called GetFileSize we would enter an infinite recursive function call because `GenericFile::GetFileSize` would start recursively calling `GenericFile::GetFileSize`. This would ultimately lead to a stack overflow error.

> **NOTE:** *A recursive function call occurs when a function calls itself. In a very few special situations, this can be a very efficient approach. However, most programmers will never have a legitimate need to call a recursive function.*

By prefixing the call with the scope resolution operator, the compiler knows to look for a global version of GetFileSize and call it if it exists, but more important, it knows not to call the local (class) version of the function, as shown in the following code:

```
int GenericFile::GetFileSize()
{
    if (!m_handle)
    {
        return 0;
    }
    //return the size of the file.
    return (::GetFileSize(m_handle,NULL));

}
```

The GenericFile::GetFileName Function

Now, we use the `GenericFile::GetFileName` function to return the name of our internal file:

```
char *GenericFile::GetFileName()
{
    if (m_fileName)
    {
        //return the name of the file
```

```
        return strdup(m_fileName);
    }
    return 0;
}
```

Traditionally calls like this require that a buffer be passed into the function so that there are no memory allocation issues. What do I mean by *memory allocation issues*? It means that any memory that is allocated must be *freed*. In our function we call strdup, which allocates a block of memory, fills it with a copy of the string we passed to it, and then returns the address of that string to us. The problem is that the memory allocated by strdup in our program never gets freed. This is a classic example of a memory leak, and although this would never cause a problem in our small program, you should never leave a known memory leak.

I challenge you here to re-write the GetFileName function to remove our program's memory leak. (Yes, this will require additional research on your part, but it will be good for your soul.) If you're not able to fix the memory leak at this point in time, don't worry: there is a version of this project on the Web site that accompanies this book (www.apress.com) called fileBreakerFixed, which has incorporated all of the changes I suggested in this chapter.

> **NOTE:** *The subject of allocating, freeing, and using memory is discussed in detail in Chapters 9 and 10.*

The GenericFile::Read Function

The next function we implement is the *Read* function. Its responsibility is to read data from our internal file:

```
int GenericFile::Read(unsigned char *buff,int maxNum)
{
    DWORD numRead = 0;

if (!m_handle)
    {
        return 0;
    }

//read in the specified number of bytes
    if (ReadFile(m_handle,buff,maxNum,&numRead,NULL))
    {
        //return the number read
        return numRead;
```

```
    }

    //return false
    return 0;
}
```

In this function we are simply calling the API function ReadFile in order to read the number of bytes that the user has requested into the buffer that they passed to us, from our class's internal file. If the file cannot be read, we return zero to indicate failure. Otherwise, we return the number of bytes that were read from the file. Following is the prototype of the API function ReadFile:

```
BOOL ReadFile(
    HANDLE hFile,                  // handle of file to read
    LPVOID lpBuffer,               // pointer to buffer that receives data
    DWORD nNumberOfBytesToRead,    // number of bytes to read
    LPDWORD lpNumberOfBytesRead,   // pointer to number of bytes read
    LPOVERLAPPED lpOverlapped      // pointer to structure for data
);
```

I won't go into the details of this API call, as it is fairly self-explanatory. You can ignore the lpOverLapped parameter for now because in most cases you will just pass it NULL. Notice that before the call to ReadFile, we check to see that m_handle is indeed a valid handle. Again, we don't want to operate on an invalid file handle. After the call to ReadFile we simply return the number of bytes read to the caller. Simple, don't you think?

The GenericFile::Write Function

The Genericfile::Write function is exactly like ReadFile, except for the obvious fact that this function writes to a file instead of reading from it, as shown here:

```
int GenericFile::Write(const unsigned char* buff,int maxNum)
{
    DWORD numWritten = 0;

if (!m_handle)
    {
        return 0;
    }

//if all goes well then return the number of bytes written
    if (WriteFile(m_handle,buff,maxNum,&numWritten,NULL))
```

```
    {
        return numWritten;
    }

    //return false
    return 0;
}
```

Here is the WIN32 API declaration of the WriteFile function:

```
BOOL WriteFile(
  HANDLE hFile,                      // handle to file to write to
  LPCVOID lpBuffer,                  // pointer to data to write to file
  DWORD nNumberOfBytesToWrite,       // number of bytes to write
  LPDWORD lpNumberOfBytesWritten,    // pointer to number of bytes written
  LPOVERLAPPED lpOverlapped          // pointer to structure
                                     // for overlapped I/O
);
```

Well, that's it for our GenericFile class. Now we will look at our next class, *FileChunk*, which is a subclass of GenericFile.

The FileChunk Class

Okay, so now we have a class, GenericFile, that represents a complete disk file. But given the requirements for our program, we also need a way to represent a piece (or chunk) of a file. We will use the *FileChunk* class to make this representation.

The FileChunk Header File

Let's take a look at the header file that contains our class's declaration, FileChunk.h:

```
// FileChunk.h: interface for the FileChunk class.
//
//////////////////////////////////////////////////////////////////////

#if !defined(AFX_FILECHUNK_H__837697AC_BC8E_4101_ADA0_5468E024596B__INCLUDED_)
#define AFX_FILECHUNK_H__837697AC_BC8E_4101_ADA0_5468E024596B__INCLUDED_

#if _MSC_VER > 1000
#pragma once
#endif // _MSC_VER > 1000
```

```
#include "genericfile.h"

class FileChunk : public GenericFile
{
public:
    int Read(unsigned char *buff,int maxNum); //Reads data from a file
    //Writes data to a file
    int Write(const unsigned char* buff,int maxNum);
    int GetChunkNumber(); //Gets the FileChunk's chunk number
    //Gets the data size from a FileChunk minus the headers
    int GetRawDataSize();
    FileChunk(char *lpfileName,bool bAlterName = true); //Constructor
    virtual ~FileChunk(); //Destructor

private:
    //Structure to hold FileChunk header information
    typedef struct _chunkId
    {
        int chunkNum;
        char chunkName[MAX_PATH];
    }chunkId;

    char _GetNextChunkNumChar(void);    //Retrieves the next available
//chunk number from the global pool
    int m_chunkNumber;    //Variable to hold the chunk number
    static int m_nextChunkNumber;    //Global chunk counter
};


#endif // !defined(
AFX_FILECHUNK_H__837697AC_BC8E_4101_ADA0_5468E024596B__INCLUDED_)
```

The first thing that we do in this file is #include GenericFile.h. The reason we do this is because the compiler needs the definition of all classes that we will be inheriting from, available at compile time. And because we will be inheriting from GenericFile, we need its declaration (which is in the file GenericFile.h) included in our header file. Notice the use of the *inheritance operator* (:) in our class declaration as follows:

```
class FileChunk : public GenericFile
```

As you will remember from Chapter 6, this notation tells the compiler that we will be inheriting from GenericFile. The public keyword that follows the inheritance operator tells the compiler that we will expose the inherited class publicly. We could also use `private` or `protected` here as well.

You can see that we have declared that we are going to override two of GenericFile's virtual functions, *Read* and *Write* (remember that we also get any non-overridden members from GenericFile as well). We have also declared several functions unique to our class as well as several private members. Let's take a look at these private members now.

struct _chunkId

The `struct_chunkid` structure is designed to hold two pieces of information: the ordinal position of this file chunk in relation to the rest of the chunks and the name of this file chunk on disk. This structure will also serve as the header for each *FileChunk* that is created.

The _GetNextChunkNumChar Function

FileChunk uses the `_GetNextChunkNumChar` function internally. We will look at its details when we discuss the implementation of this class.

m_chunkNumber

This private variable is used to hold the internal chunk number for this *FileChunk*.

m_nextChunkNumber

This private variable is used to hold the next globally available chunk number. How does it do this? Through the use of the keyword `static`, which is also a keyword in Visual Basic. However, the C++ version of the `static` keyword is slightly different than the Visual Basic version, so let me quickly go over it.

In Visual Basic we use the `static` keyword at the procedure (Sub, Function or Property) level in order to preserve a variable's value between procedure calls. This is the case with the C++ version as well. However, the C++ version has some additional capabilities. When it is used in the way that we have used it in our class declaration, the `static` keyword causes the compiler to generate only one copy of the variable for the whole *FileChunk* class, not for each instance of the class. (In fact, this behavior applies to functions as well.) This means that each instance of the *FileChunk* class will share the same variable.

This can be a useful mechanism in certain situations. For instance, if we wanted to be sure that no more than 100 instances of our class were running at any one time we could simply increment the static variable in the class constructor and decrement it in the destructor. This would keep track of how many objects are in existence at any one time. There is one important thing to note here though, and that is that all static variables must be initialized outside of the class.

> **NOTE:** *Although* m_nextChunkNumber *is declared inside of our class, it actually gets initialized outside of our class declaration in the top of the* FileChunk.cpp *file.*

The FileChunk.cpp File

Now that we have examined the declaration of the FileChunk class, let's look at our implementation file, FileChunk.cpp, and then each of its member's implementations:

```cpp
// FileChunk.cpp: implementation of the FileChunk class.
//
//////////////////////////////////////////////////////////////////////

#include "FileChunk.h"

//////////////////////////////////////////////////////////////////////
// Construction/Destruction
//////////////////////////////////////////////////////////////////////

//initialize global counter for the class
int FileChunk::m_nextChunkNumber = 0;

FileChunk::FileChunk(char *lpfileName,bool bAlterName)
{
    int iOffset = 0;     //offset into the variable -- temp

    //get out if there is no filename
    if (!lpfileName)
    {
        return;
    }

    if (bAlterName)
    {
        char temp[255];     //variable to hold the new file name
//copy the filename into the temp variable and capture the length
        iOffset = strlen(strcpy(temp,lpfileName));
```

```
            //append the chunk number to the file name
            temp[iOffset++] = _GetNextChunkNumChar();

            //NULL terminate the filename
            temp[iOffset] = 0;

            //Open the file
            GenericFile::SetFileName(temp);
        }
        else
        {
            GenericFile::SetFileName(lpfileName);

}

FileChunk::~FileChunk()
{

}

int FileChunk::GetChunkNumber()
{
    return m_chunkNumber;
}

int FileChunk::GetRawDataSize()
{
    chunkId cid;
    return (GenericFile::GetFileSize() - sizeof(cid));
}

int FileChunk::Read(unsigned char *buff,int maxNum)
{
    DWORD numRead = 0;
    chunkId cid;

    //allocate a buffer big enough to hold the users data plus the header
    unsigned char *temp = new unsigned char[maxNum + sizeof(cid)];

    //read in the specified number of bytes
    if (numRead = GenericFile::Read(temp,maxNum + sizeof(cid)))
    {
        //strip off the header
```

```
    memcpy(&cid,temp,sizeof(cid));

    //save the chunk number
    m_chunkNumber = cid.chunkNum;

    //get the contents of the file
    memcpy(buff,&temp[sizeof(cid)],maxNum);

    //return the number of bytes read
    return numRead;
}

delete[] temp;

//return false
return 0;
}

int FileChunk::Write(const unsigned char* buff,int maxNum)
{
    //chunk id header
    chunkId cid;

    //allocate a buffer to hold our header and chunk of data
    unsigned char* temp = new unsigned char[maxNum  + sizeof(cid)];

    //var for bytes written
    int iNumWritten = 0;

    //set the chunk number
    cid.chunkNum = m_chunkNumber;

    //copy the name of the chunk into the header
    strcpy(cid.chunkName,m_fileName);

    //copy the chunkID struct to the buffer
    memcpy(temp,&cid,sizeof(cid));

    //copy the chunk to the buffer
    memcpy(&temp[sizeof(cid)],buff,maxNum);

    //call the base class's version of Write
    iNumWritten = GenericFile::Write(temp,maxNum + sizeof(cid));
```

```
    //free our memory
    delete[]temp;

    //return the number of bytes written
    return iNumWritten - sizeof(cid);

}


char FileChunk::_GetNextChunkNumChar()
{
    //assign the chunk number and increment it
    m_chunkNumber = m_nextChunkNumber++;

//return the ASCII version of the number
    return (char)(m_chunkNumber) + 48;
}
```

The FileChunk Constructor

You may notice that there is no default (parameter-less) constructor for this class; there is only our custom constructor, which takes two parameters: lpfileName and bAlterName. The reason we haven't created a default constructor for this class is because there is no practical use for an un-initialized FileChunk (at least not until the developers using our class let us know what it is, at which point we will have to create one). The lpfileName parameter holds the name of the file that the user wants to open or create. bAlterName, is a boolean value that indicates whether we should alter the file name pointed to by lpfileName. The reason we need this variable is because of the fact that we are breaking a file into chunks—we will want to name each chunk as an ordinal increment of the one that came before it, so that a file named *MyProg.exe* could be broken into three chunks named: MyProg.exe0, MyProg.exe1, and MyProg.exe2. But in the case where we are reassembling several file chunks into a complete file, we will want the name to stay intact (because it was already renamed when the chunk was created). Don't worry: this will make sense when we look at the program in action:

```
FileChunk::FileChunk(char *lpfileName,bool bAlterName)
{
    int iOffset = 0;    //offset into the variable -- temp

    //get out if there is no filename
    if (!lpfileName)
    {
        return;
```

```
    }

    if (bAlterName)
    {
        char temp[255];     //variable to hold the new file name
//copy the filename into the temp variable and capture the length
        iOffset = strlen(strcpy(temp,lpfileName));

        //append the chunk number to the file name
        temp[iOffset++] = _GetNextChunkNumChar();

        //NULL terminate the filename
        temp[iOffset] = 0;

        //Open the file
        GenericFile::SetFileName(temp);
    }
    else
    {
        GenericFile::SetFileName(lpfileName);
    }
}
```

You can see that we check to be sure that `lpFileName` contains a valid pointer as our first order of business. You will generally want to be in the habit of checking this first in a function where you have a pointer as one of your critical parameters because if the pointer is invalid, there is no way to continue processing anyway.

After we check the validity of `lpFileName`, we check to see if we should alter the name of the file in `lpFileName`. If so then we enter our *if* condition's code block and append the return value of the `_GetNextChunkNumChar` function (which we will examine next) to our file name and call the `SetFileName` function.

The reason we call `SetFileName` with

```
GenericFile::SetFileName(temp);
```

is because we want to make it clear that this function is contained in our super (inherited from) class's definition. This is a good habit to get into when calling any non-overridden functions from a super class.

The FileChunk Destructor

This is just the standard class destructor, shown here:

```
FileChunk::~FileChunk()
{

}
```

It is worth noting that when a derived class's destructor is called, the compiler automatically calls the base class's destructor. This is a key element of inheritance working properly. It is also important to know so that you don't mistakenly write the same code in both destructors. This is especially important when you free resources in a destructor.

The FileChunk::GetChunkNumber Function

The FileChunk::GetChunkNumber function simply returns the internal m_chunkNumber variable's value to the caller, as shown here:

```
int FileChunk::GetChunkNumber()
{
    return m_chunkNumber;
}
```

The FileChunk::GetRawDataSize Function

The FileChunk::GetRawDataSize function returns the actual data size of a FileChunk, as far as the caller is concerned. The reason I say *as far as the caller is concerned* is because, as you will see when we look at *Read* and *Write* functions, we always have to consider the header that is at the top of every FileChunk when we deal with the size of a FileChunk. This header is simply a *chunkId struct*. When we speak of the RawDataSize, we actually mean the size of the FileChunk on disk, minus the size of the chunkId structure. Therefore, to retrieve the RawDataSize of our chunk, we simply have to call our super class's GetFileSize function (which will retrieve the size of the file chunk on disk) and subtract from it the size of a chunkId struct, which is exactly what we do:

```
int FileChunk::GetRawDataSize()
{
    chunkId cid;
    return (GenericFile::GetFileSize() - sizeof(cid));
}
```

The FileChunk::Read Function

The FileChunk:Read function is used to read a FileChunk object from disk into a memory buffer:

```
int FileChunk::Read(unsigned char *buff,int maxNum)
{
    DWORD numRead = 0;
    chunkId cid;

    //allocate a buffer big enough to hold the users data plus the header
    unsigned char *temp = new unsigned char[maxNum + sizeof(cid)];

    //read in the specified number of bytes
    if (numRead = GenericFile::Read(temp,maxNum + sizeof(cid)))
    {
        //strip off the header
        memcpy(&cid,temp,sizeof(cid));

        //save the chunk number
        m_chunkNumber = cid.chunkNum;

        //get the contents of the file
        memcpy(buff,&temp[sizeof(cid)],maxNum);

        //return the number of bytes read
        return numRead;
    }

    delete[] temp;

    //return false
    return 0;
}
```

Now, you may notice that the first thing that we do in our function is create a local memory buffer that is the size that the user requested, plus the size of a chunkId struct. The reason we add the size of a chunkId struct is, again, because we need to account for the header of the file. Once we retrieve the FileChunk from disk, we use the *Standard C++ Library* function, memcpy, to place the contents of the header of the FileChunk into a chunkId struct. We then put everything following the header into the user passed buffer. This way, we have returned what the user perceives to be the FileChunk. We have also loaded this FileChunk with the values from the header that was in the front of the read operation. (Again, this behavior will make more sense in the context of the main program.)

The FileChunk::Write Function

The FileChunk::Write function is the obvious inverse of the previous one. It writes a FileChunk to disk. Notice that we perform the exact opposite functions as Read and in the reverse order as well:

```
int FileChunk::Write(const unsigned char* buff,int maxNum)
{
    //chunk id header
    chunkId cid;

    //allocate a buffer to hold our header and chunk of data
    unsigned char* temp = new unsigned char[maxNum  + sizeof(cid)];

    //var for bytes written
    int iNumWritten = 0;

    //set the chunk number
    cid.chunkNum = m_chunkNumber;

    //copy the name of the chunk into the header
    strcpy(cid.chunkName,m_fileName);

    //copy the chunkID struct to the buffer
    memcpy(temp,&cid,sizeof(cid));

    //copy the chunk to the buffer
    memcpy(&temp[sizeof(cid)],buff,maxNum);

    //call the base class's version of Write
    iNumWritten = GenericFile::Write(temp,maxNum + sizeof(cid));

    //free our memory
    delete[]temp;

    //return the number of bytes written
    return iNumWritten - sizeof(cid);

}
```

The FileChunk::_GetNextChunkNumChar Function

The `FileChunk::_GetNextChunkNumChar` function is responsible for accessing our class's private static variable, `m_nextChunkNumber`.

```
char FileChunk::_GetNextChunkNumChar()
{
    //assign the chunk number and increment it
    m_chunkNumber = m_nextChunkNumber++;

    //return the ASCII version of the number
    return (char)(m_chunkNumber) + 48;
}
```

Notice that we assign the value of the static variable, `m_nextChunkNumber`, to our instance variable, `m_chunkNumber` and then increment `m_nextChunkNumber` so that it contains the proper value for the next FileChunk class. Now, if you're wondering why we return a char instead of a number, it's because we know that this value is going to be appended to a string that will modify a file name. So, we are saving the caller the step of converting the value to a char.

To help you get a better feel for what is going on here, let's look at an equivalent function in Visual Basic:

```
Public Function GetNextChunkNumChar() As String
    'assign the chunk number and increment it
    m_chunkNumber = m_nextChunkNumber + 1

    'return the ASCII version of the number
    GetNextChunkNumChar = Chr(m_chunkNumber + 48)
End Function
```

As you can see, we are simply returning the ASCII value for the value currently stored in the variable `m_nextChunkNumber`.

Now let's look at the file that puts these two classes to work. We will go through it section by section, as we have done previously.

The `fileBreaker.cpp` File

Any class you create will be utterly useless, unless it is used in some sort of application. Following is the implementation file for our application, `fileBreaker.cpp`:

```
// fileBreaker.cpp : Defines the entry point for the console application.
//

#include "stdafx.h"

int main(int argc, char* argv[])
{
    //check for proper arguments on the command line
    if (!argv[1])
    {
        printf("No parameters passed. Use /? for help.\n");
        return 0;
    }

    //check for help signal
    if (0 == strcmp(argv[1],"/?"))
    {
        //display list of parameters
        printf("Parameters:\n/b | /m FileName [ChunkSize]\n");
        return 0;
    }

    //If we go in here the user wants to break apart the file
    if (0 == strcmp(argv[1],"/b") || 0 == strcmp(argv[1],"/B"))
    {

        //pointer to our file that will be broken apart
        GenericFile *p_gf = new GenericFile(argv[2]);

        if (!p_gf->Open())
        {
            //Print the error to the screen
            printf("Could not open file: %s.",p_gf->GetFileName());

            //Exit the program
            return 0;
        }

        //If no size is specified then default to 1.2 megs
            int iChunkSize = argv[3] != NULL?atoi(argv[3]):1200;

        //Get size in bytes
        iChunkSize *= 1024;
```

```
    if (iChunkSize >= p_gf->GetFileSize() || !p_gf->GetFileSize())
    {
        printf("Last DLL Error: %d.",GetLastError());
}

    //allocate space on the heap
    unsigned char *buff = new unsigned char[iChunkSize];

    int iNumRead = 0;

    do
    {
        //read one chunk
        iNumRead = p_gf->Read(buff,iChunkSize);

        if (!iNumRead)
        {
            printf("could not read from file [%s].",p_gf->GetFileName());
            delete[] buff;
            return 0;
        }

        //store the chunk in the file
        FileChunk *p_fc = new FileChunk(p_gf->GetFileName());

        //open the file
        if (!p_fc->Open())
        {
        printf("Error: could not open the file [%s].\n",
                p_fc->GetFileName());
            p_fc->Close();
            break;
        }

        //write the chunk of data
        if (!p_fc->Write(buff,iNumRead))
        {
            printf("Error: could not write to file [%s].\n",
                    p_fc->GetFileName());
        }

        //Close the file chunk
        p_fc->Close();
```

```
                delete(p_fc);


        }while (iNumRead == iChunkSize);

        //close the file
        if (!p_gf->Close())
        {
            printf("Error: could not close the file [%s].\n",p_gf->GetFileName());
        }

        printf("Operation completed successfully.");

        //clean up our memory allocations
        delete(p_gf);
        delete[](buff);

        return 1;

    }
    //if we enter here, then the user wants to mend the file
    else if (0 == strcmp(argv[1],"/m") || 0 == strcmp(argv[1],"/M"))
    {
        //struct to hold file info
        WIN32_FIND_DATA wfd;

        //Look for the passed in file
        HANDLE hFfile = FindFirstFile(argv[2],&wfd);

        //check to see that the file exists
        if (INVALID_HANDLE_VALUE == hFfile)
        {
            printf("Can't find file [%s].\n",argv[2]);
            exit (0);
        }

        //notify the user of whhat we are doing
        printf("Found first chunk: [%s].\n",wfd.cFileName);

        //allocate stack space for the stripped fle name
        char rawFileName[MAX_PATH];

        //copy the whole name
```

```
strcpy(rawFileName,argv[2]);

//strip off the * from the file name
memcpy(&rawFileName[strlen(argv[2])-1],"\0",1);


//update the user
printf("Rebuilding file %s\n",rawFileName);


//check to make sure we don't try
//to open the file we're rebuilding.
if (!strcmp(wfd.cFileName,strrchr(rawFileName,'\\') + 1))
{
    //if it's the fie we're rebuilding then just skip it
    if (FindNextFile(hFfile,&wfd))
    {
        printf("Recursive file name found!\nSkipping file...\n");
    }
}


GenericFile *p_gf = new GenericFile(rawFileName);

if (!p_gf->Open())
{
    printf("Could not open file: [%s].",p_gf->GetFileName());
}


//keep going until there are no more files
do
{
    //buffer to hold the raw path name
    char ext[MAX_PATH];

    //save the path
    memcpy(ext,rawFileName,strlen(rawFileName));

    //append th current file name
    memcpy(&ext[strlen(rawFileName)],
                &wfd.cFileName[strlen(wfd.cFileName) - 1],2);

    //null terminate it
    ext[strlen(argv[2]) + 2] = 0;

    //create a new FileChunk with renaming turned off
```

```
                    FileChunk *p_fc = new FileChunk(ext,false);

                    //open the file
                    if (!p_fc->Open())
                    {
                        printf("could not open file: [%s].",p_fc->GetFileName());
                        continue;
                    }

                    //buffer to hold the temp data
                    unsigned char *tempBuff =
                                new unsigned char[p_fc->GetRawDataSize()];

                    //read the data from the chunk
                    if (!p_fc->Read(tempBuff,p_fc->GetRawDataSize()))
                    {
                        printf("could not read file: [%s].",p_fc->GetFileName());
                        p_fc->Close();
                        continue;
                    }

                    //write the data to the file opened for restoration
                    if (!p_gf->Write(tempBuff,p_fc->GetRawDataSize()))
                    {
                        printf("could not write to file: [%s].",
                                p_fc->GetFileName());
                        p_fc->Close();
                        continue;
                    }

                    //see if there is another chunk
                    int bFound = FindNextFile(hFfile,&wfd);

                    if (bFound && (strstr(rawFileName,wfd.cFileName)))
                    {
                        bFound = FindNextFile(hFfile,&wfd);
                    }

                    //make sure the chunk isn't the file we are restoring
                    if (!bFound)
                    {
                        //cleanup time
                        p_gf->Close();
```

```
                p_fc->Close();
                delete[](tempBuff);
                break;
            }

            printf("Found next chunk: [%s].\n",wfd.cFileName);

        }while (hFfile);

        printf("File successfully restored!\n");

    }

    return 0;
}
```

As you will notice, our file contains only one function, `main`, which is also our program's entry point (the starting point for our application). You can see that even before our `main` function, we include the file `stdafx.h`. Following is the contents of this file:

```
// stdafx.h : include file for standard system include files,
//  or project specific include files that are used frequently, but
//      are changed infrequently
//

#if !defined(
AFX_STDAFX_H__CE21A7C7_D174_11D3_BC89_B02152C10000__INCLUDED_)
#define AFX_STDAFX_H__CE21A7C7_D174_11D3_BC89_B02152C10000__INCLUDED_

#if _MSC_VER > 1000
#pragma once
#endif // _MSC_VER > 1000

// Exclude rarely-used stuff from Windows headers
#define WIN32_LEAN_AND_MEAN

#include <stdio.h>
#include <stdlib.h>
#include "genericfile.h"
#include "filechunk.h"

// TODO: reference additional headers your program requires here
```

```
//{{AFX_INSERT_LOCATION}}
// Microsoft Visual C++ will insert additional
//declarations immediately before the previous line.

#endif // !defined(AFX_STDAFX_H__CE21A7C7_D174_11D3_BC89_B02152C10000__INCLUDED_)
```

This file's job is to include other files that we will need throughout our program. The first two files that get included, stdio.h and stdlib.h, are the familiar *Standard C++ Library* headers that we have used many times over. And the last two included files are the declarations for our two previously created classes that we will use in our program. Remember that you must always include the declaration of a class before you can use it in a program.

Understanding the Program's Parameters

Our program can do one of two things: break a file into several smaller pieces or reassemble several small pieces into a complete file. It becomes obvious that our program will need to use parameters so that we will know what it is the user is trying to accomplish.

The first parameter we expect is either /b or /m. The /b parameter indicates that we will be *breaking* a file into smaller pieces. If /b is specified as the first parameter, the second parameter is expected to be a path to a file on disk. At this point there may or may not be another parameter, chunksize, which indicates the size we should make each piece of the broken file. If this parameter is not specified then we use 1.2 MB as a default size. However, if our first parameter is /m, we expect that the user wants us to *make* the original whole file from the pieces. When this parameter is passed, we expect the path and file name of the file to be reconstructed, immediately followed by an asterisk. Any parameters passed after this one will be ignored.

You will notice that the first several code blocks of our program simply check the parameters that we were passed. The first and most important test checks to see if argv[1] is NULL. If it is, that means there were no arguments passed (in which case we display an appropriate message for the user).

> **NOTE:** *The reason you always check for command line arguments at array element 1 instead of zero is because the first argument of a C++ program is always the name of the program.*

You can see that I make use of the strcmp in these command line argument checks. strcmp is a case-sensitive *Standard C++ Library* string comparison function. You can also see that I check for the help(/?) switch. If a user passes this as the first parameter, our program displays a list of command line parameters and options.

What we have done to this point is standard practice in a C++ console application, in that we have checked the validity of our command line parameters and displayed helpful information concerning the use of our program. Beyond this point our program boils down to one *if* statement:

```
if (0 == strcmp(argv[1],"/b") || 0 == strcmp(argv[1],"/B"))
```

You can see that with this statement we are checking for a /b or /B parameter.

The /b Command Line Argument

First we will consider the case where /b has been passed to our application. We know that in this case we are going to be breaking apart a file into several smaller pieces. So the first thing we try to do is create a *GenericFile* object using the file passed into our program in argv[2]. If this action fails for any reason, we exit the program. Notice that we use our function calls as the condition in our *if* statements. This technique enables you to handle any negative situation more gracefully. Assuming our GenericFile object as created successfully, we check for the existence of the chunksize parameter, which tells us what size to make our FileChunks, as so:

```
int iChunkSize = argv[3] != NULL?atoi(argv[3]):1200;
```

We use the ternary operator, which is identical to Visual Basic's *IIF* function, to see if the user has specified a chunksize value. The following is what this statement would look like in Visual Basic:

```
Dim iChunkSize As Long
```

```
iChunkSize = IIF(argv3 <> 0,argv3,1200)
```

If the user does not pass a chunksize parameter, we use the default value of 1200KB. We then take that value times 1024 to get the actual number of bytes in chunksize.

Next, we check to see if the file that the user passed us is smaller than the chunksize. If it is then we exit the program because there is no reason to continue. However, if all is well and we have passed all of the aforementioned checks then we enter into our *do-loop*, which does the job of creating the FileChunk objects. Notice our *while* condition at the end of our loop:

```
while (iNumRead == iChunkSize);
```

This statement will fail when our call to

```
iNumRead = p_gf->Read(buff,iChunkSize);
```

returns less than iChunkSize bytes. This will occur when we have reached the end of our file, thus indicating that there is no need to create more chunks. All that our loop does is create FileChunk objects and save them to disk. Once that task is completed we close the GenericFile we used to create our FileChunks from and exit the program. That's all there is to it.

The /m Command Line Argument

Assuming this case, we will need to reassemble several FileChunk objects back into a complete file. The bulk of this algorithm is the use of the *FindFile* API functions that recursively search a directory for files named similarly. I will leave it to you to delve into the details of these API calls but they're pretty straightforward.

Using the FileBreaker Program

To test out the FileBreaker program, open a DOS window and type the following command:

```
filebreaker /b c:\winnt\MyFile.exe 500
```

Be sure to replace c:\winnt\MyFile.exe with the path and name of your file. Assuming MyFile.exe is 2.5MB in size, this command should cause five files to be created, each one 500KB in size. They should be named: MyFile.exe0, My-File.exe1, MyFile.exe2, MyFile.exe3, and MyFile.exe4. To restore the chunks to make the original file, type in the following command at a DOS prompt:

```
filebreaker /m c:\winnt\MyFile.exe*
```

This will cause the *FileChunk*s to be re-assembled into the original file.

Disclaimer

This program is a bit temperamental due to the fact that I have focused on functionality and not usability. For instance the program's parameters need to be entered exactly in the manner described in the above section and you cannot break a file into more than 9 parts. Also, there can be no files with matching names in the folder with the "FileChunks" when using the /m switch. The reason I left out these program features is because in many cases they unnecessarily complicated the code listings. Remember, the focus of this chapter is to teach you how to use your C++ skills to apply the programming knowledge you already have. This does however create an opportunity for you to create a more robust version of this program, and I encourage you to do so.

Conclusion

In this chapter I exposed you to a real-world C++ program. Although primitive in design, the goal here is to get you "battle-ready" for the real development projects later in this book. Please don't try to draw too many good design techniques here, as I tried to load this application with useful techniques more than good design examples. Once you are able to understand the material presented here, you are well on the way to developing your own C++ components for use from VB. Now on to DLLs.

CHAPTER 9

What's the DLL, Man?

I GET A LOT OF TECHNICAL QUESTIONS FROM programmers from all around the world. The subjects of the questions vary broadly, but a lot of them are about the use of Dynamic Link Libraries (DLLs) created in Visual Basic. There seems to be a lack of understanding about the differences between DLLs created in Visual Basic (ActiveX DLLs) and Windows DLLs that are created in languages such as C++ or COBOL. By *Windows DLL*, I am referring to a non-ActiveX DLL such as the WIN32 application programming interface (API) DLLs. In this chapter I discuss the differences between these two types of DLLs, explain the technicalities of Windows DLLs, and provide a tutorial for building a Windows DLL in C++.

When a DLL is Not Really a DLL

Most Visual Basic programmers have used Windows DLLs from within their Visual Basic programs via the Declare statement. (In fact, the entire WIN32 API is housed in a set of Windows DLLs.) So why is it that you can't use the DLLs you create with Visual Basic in the same way? A DLL is a DLL, right? Well, yes and no. Let me explain.

When you create a DLL in Visual Basic you are creating an *ActiveX DLL*, which means you are in essence creating a dwelling place for one or more Component Object Model (COM) Objects. (If you are not familiar with COM objects, don't worry; I cover them in Chapter 11.) This may surprise you, but as a programmer, you should never directly manipulate an ActiveX DLL—you should let COM access it for you. This is what COM is for. Now, I don't want to jump into the subject of COM right now, as I cover it in great depth in Chapters 11, 12, and 13. But, suffice it to say that an ActiveX DLL is not useable in a non-COM environment—you cannot use any functions in an ActiveX DLL through a Declare statement.

> **NOTE:** *There are several products available that enable ActiveX DLLs to act as Windows DLLs. However, I won't discuss these products or the functionality they provide in this book.*

Again, we will cover ActiveX and COM later in this book. For the remainder of this chapter when I refer to a DLL or a Windows DLL, I am referring to the non-ActiveX version. That said, let's get to the business at hand and learn about DLLs!

The Basics of DLLs

A DLL is basically just an .EXE file. A DLL and an .EXE file are both binary files that contain data and executable code. In fact, the only difference in them is that a DLL cannot be "run" on its own; DLLs have to be loaded by a running program before the code contained within them can execute. However, once a DLL is loaded, the program that loaded it can call any functions made publicly available by it (or exported, which I will explain in a moment), as if they were contained in the program's .EXE file. In fact, as far as the program is concerned, a function inside of a loaded DLL is the same as any other in its process space.

How can that be? Well, as a first step in understanding this concept, let's look at what happens when a Visual Basic program that calls a function in a DLL, executes. Consider the following Visual Basic application:

```
Option Explicit

Public Declare Function GetTickCount Lib "Kernel32" () As Long

Public Sub Main()

Call GetTickCount

End Sub
```

This seemingly simple application only Declares and calls one WIN32 API function from within its main function, and then exits. The reason I say *seemingly simple* application is because there is a lot going on behind the scenes that we as Visual Basic programmers never get to see.

To see what exactly happens in this program, I will trace and explain each step. First, when a request is made for the operating system to run this application (by a user double-clicking its icon or typing its name at a command prompt), Windows will try to create a process address space for it and load the program's .EXE file into the newly created process space (at which point all of the code from the .EXE file will be copied into the process' address space). Assuming that Windows is able to successfully do this, the program starts executing Sub Main. Once in Sub Main, our program will attempt to call the WIN32 API function GetTick-Count (which returns the number of milliseconds that the computer has been running since its last boot).

When this call to GetTickCount is made by our application, Visual Basic jumps into action and does the behind the scenes work I spoke of earlier. The first thing it does is attempt to load the DLL named in the Declare statement, which in this case is Kernel32.DLL. It attempts to load this DLL by calling the *LoadLibrary* API function, which is supplied by Windows for the purpose of loading code modules such as DLLs. If LoadLibrary successfully loads the DLL, it returns a module handle (HMODULE), which can be used to manipulate the loaded file. Think of an HMODULE as a file handle for a DLL. Assuming the DLL is found and loaded, Visual Basic then calls GetProcAddress (another WIN32 API function) and passes the handle to the Kernel32.DLL module (which was returned by the call to LoadLibrary) and the name of the function from the Declare statement as its arguments. GetProcAddress looks for a function in a DLL that matches the function name passed as a parameter. GetProcAddress then returns the address of the function inside the DLL if it is found, or NULL if it is not. Assuming the function name from the Declare statement is found in the loaded DLL, Visual Basic will call the function and return its value to our program. It almost makes you start to appreciate all that Visual Basic is doing for us, doesn't it? Almost?

Following is a small C++ program that represents the additional code that Visual Basic has to execute when a Visual Basic program calls a function in a DLL:

```cpp
// DLLCaller.cpp : Defines the entry point for the console application.
//

#include "stdafx.h"
#include <windows.h>

typedef BOOL (__stdcall *pFunc) ();

int main(int argc, char* argv[])
{
    pFunc pf = 0;

    HMODULE hMod = 0;

    hMod = LoadLibrary("kernel32.dll");

    if (!hMod)
    {
        printf("File not found: Kernel32.DLL\n");
        return 0;
    }

    pf = GetProcAddress(hMod,"GetTickCount");

    if (!pf)
    {
        printf(
        "Could not find entry point GetTickCount in Kernel32.DLL\n");
        return 0;
```

```
    }

    printf("GetTickCount returned %d\n",pf());

    return 0;
}
```

> **NOTE:** *Don't worry if parts of the previous code look unfamiliar; I discuss this code in more detail later in this chapter.*

Okay, so now we know how a client calls a function in a DLL, but what we still don't know is how a DLL exposes those functions so that a client can call them. Well, let's find out.

Exporting Functions

In order for a DLL to expose its functions to other programs, it has to *export* them, which simply means that the DLL has to publish the Relative Virtual Address (RVA) at which its exported functions reside.

The reason that the address where the function resides is called the *Relative Virtual Address* is because the address is relative to the address at which the DLL was loaded. Let me explain. When a process loads a DLL, that DLL is loaded at some memory address in the loading process's address space. (This is known as the DLL's *base address*.) Let's assume that a program loads a DLL at address 0x10000000 and that that DLL contains a function, GetData, which resides at RVA 0x00000FFF inside the DLL. In order for the loading application to call the GetData function in the DLL, it has to calculate the address at which the DLL was loaded (0x10000000) and add to it the RVA of the function that it wants to call. In this case, when the DLL is loaded, the function GetData will reside at address 0x10000FFF in the application's address space. By the same token, if the DLL had been loaded at address 0x11000000 in the process's address space, the process would have to call the function GetData at address 0x11000FFF.

This concept is critical in the understanding of dynamic linking. An important point to understand here is that every DLL that loads tries to load at address 0x10000000. If that address is already taken, Windows finds an alternate address at which to load the DLL. (I cover this in more detail in "Rebasing DLLs" in Chapter 10.)

Well, this explains the technicalities of how a DLL exports functions, but we still don't know how to do this in practice. Patience, grasshopper!

The .DEF File

How does a DLL export functions?

    A.   With a .DEF file.
    B.   With a .DUMB file.
    C.   With a .BLIND file.
    D.   With a .MUTE file.

"With a .DEF file."
"Is that your final answer?"
"Yes, Regis, that is my final answer."
"It's a good one! You've just won a million dollars!"
Sorry, I couldn't resist. But the answer is indeed a .DEF (Module DEFinition) file. Now I must warn you that if you that if you look up "exporting functions" in the MSDN online help file, you will find information that will tell you that you can also export functions by using the _declspec(dllexport) modifier. However, this information is incorrect if you are planning on calling your DLL from any language other than C++. (And actually, the C++ programs that could use it would have to be compiled with the same C++ compiler that compiled the DLL.) Why? The answer pertains to something called *name mangling*.

Name Mangling

Name Mangling (also called *Name Decoration*) is a process followed by the compiler to facilitate the handling of overloaded functions. Unfortunately, even if you don't have any overloaded functions in your program, the compiler will still mangle the names. Think of it as "one bad apple can spoil the bunch." Consider the following function in a C++ program:

```
int _stdcall GetData(int x);
```

If you were to build a DLL that contained this function, you would probably expect it to be exported, as GetData, but alas, it would not. It would be exported as _GetData@4.

The reason is because the C++ compiler *mangles* the function name. Now, I won't bore you with the details of name mangling, except to say that there is no standard way of doing it. This means that each C/C++ compiler vendor can and will do it differently. This is where the .DEF file comes into play. You see, a .DEF file tells the linker to export the functions in the DLL exactly as they are listed in the .DEF file.

Let's assume we are going to create a DLL that contains three functions: AddNums, MultiplyNums, and SubtractNums. Here is what a .DEF file would look like for this DLL:

```
;This is the export file for ex01_ch9.DLL
LIBRARY ex01_ch9.DLL

DESCRIPTION    "Test DLL for chapter 9"

EXPORTS
    AddNums          @    1
    SubtractNums     @    2
    MultiplyNums     @    3
```

Notice that the first line in our .DEF file is prefixed with a semi-colon, which denotes a comment (although comments are rare in .DEF files). On the next line we see the LIBRARY keyword. The string following this keyword will become the name of the DLL. (It should match the name given in the project.) Next is the DESCRIPTION keyword. This keyword does just as its name implies; it puts a description string inside of the DLL. The next section we see begins with the keyword EXPORTS. This keyword tells the linker that we are going to be exporting some functions that are named in the list below the EXPORTS keyword. The list is assumed to continue to the end of the file or until another keyword is found; whichever comes first. This section also tells the linker that we want to export the functions *exactly* as they are listed in our EXPORTS section.

Now, take a look at the use of the @ followed by a number. This notation is used to create a specific *ordinal* for each function noted in the .DEF module. An *ordinal* is the physical sequence that a function is placed in memory. A function can be called by its ordinal position instead of its name, but this is strongly discouraged by Microsoft. The reason it is discouraged is because if you add functions to your DLL after its original release, the ordinal position of functions is likely to change, thereby breaking all of your older, ordinal calling clients. You can actually just leave the ordinals out of the .DEF file all together. When you do this, the linker assigns ordinals to the DLL's functions automatically.

Following is the .DEF file with no ordinals:

```
;This is the export file for ex01_ch9.DLL
LIBRARY ex01_ch9.DLL

DESCRIPTION    "Test DLL for chapter 9"
```

```
EXPORTS
    AddNums
    SubtractNums
    MultiplyNums
```

Let's Make a DLL

Now we have enough information to actually create a DLL with C++. Open Visual Studio and select File ➜ New. Select the Projects tab of the New Project dialog box. Once you have done that, select "Win32 Dynamic Link Library" as the project type. When prompted, select "A simple DLL" as the DLL type. At this point you will be presented with an empty DLL project, which only contains one function, DLL-Main. DLLMain is the function that is called by Windows each time a DLL is loaded or unloaded.

Here is what DLLMain looks like:

```
BOOL APIENTRY DllMain( HANDLE hModule,
                       DWORD  ul_reason_for_call,
                       LPVOID lpReserved
                     )
{
    return TRUE;
}
```

We won't dive too deep into this function just yet, but note the two modifiers that precede it: BOOL and APIENTRY. BOOL is a *typedef* for an int and is defined by Windows, in the <windows.h> header file. Now APIENTRY is still just a *typedef* but it is a little more interesting. You see, APIENTRY is a typedef for WINAPI, which is a typedef for _stdcall. But what the heck is _stdcall? Let's find out.

Understanding _stdcall

_stdcall is what is known as a *calling convention*. A calling convention is basically just a fancy way to say the word *rule*. The _stdcall calling convention (or rule) states that the *called* function is responsible for clearing the program's stack when a function returns. Clearing the program's stack entails removing any arguments that were put onto the stack during the current function call. These arguments must be removed when the function returns. Normally, the *calling* function takes on this responsibility by using the _cdecl calling convention. _cdecl is the default calling convention for C++; if you don't specify the calling convention then you get _cedcl. (If you choose not to decide, you still have made a choice.)

_stdcall is the most common cross-language calling convention around, so you will probably never use anything else in your DLLs.

> **NOTE:** *Visual Basic requires* _stdcall *for any DLLs it calls.*

Implementing the DLL's Functions

We now need to implement our functions in actual C++ code, and we will do that in the implementation file, *ex01_ch9.cpp*, which is located on the Web site that accompanies this book (www.apress.com). The code of ex01_ch9.cpp is listed here:

```
// ex01_ch9.cpp : Defines the entry point for the DLL application.
//

#include "stdafx.h"

BOOL APIENTRY DllMain( HANDLE hModule,
                       DWORD  ul_reason_for_call,
                       LPVOID lpReserved
                     )
{
    return TRUE;
}

LONG APIENTRY AddNums(int num1, int num2)
{
    //add the numbers and return the result
    return num1 + num2;
}

LONG APIENTRY SubtractNums(int num1, int num2)
{
    //subtract the numbers and return the result
    return num1 - num2;
}

LONG APIENTRY MultiplyNums(int num1, int num2)
{
    //multiply the numbers and return the result
    return num1 * num2;
}
```

Notice that each of our functions returns a LONG, which is a typedef for a *long*. This data type maps directly to a Visual Basic type, *Long*.

> **NOTE:** *Remember that .DEF files are case sensitive. Be sure that your function names in the .DEF file match the names of the functions in your implementation file exactly.*

For completeness' sake, here are the contents of the #included stdafx.h file, which simply #includes <windows.h>:

```
// stdafx.h : include file for standard system include files,
//  or project specific include files that are used frequently, but
//      are changed infrequently
//

#if !defined
AFX_STDAFX_H__C665B1A3_FEB7_11D3_A7FA_0000C53CCE3D__INCLUDED_)
#define AFX_STDAFX_H__C665B1A3_FEB7_11D3_A7FA_0000C53CCE3D__INCLUDED_

#if _MSC_VER > 1000
#pragma once
#endif // _MSC_VER > 1000


// Insert your headers here
// Exclude rarely-used stuff from Windows headers
#define WIN32_LEAN_AND_MEAN

#include <windows.h>

// TODO: reference additional headers your program requires here

//{{AFX_INSERT_LOCATION}}
// Microsoft Visual C++ will insert
// additional declarations immediately before the previous line.

#endif // !defined(
AFX_STDAFX_H__C665B1A3_FEB7_11D3_A7FA_0000C53CCE3D__INCLUDED_)
```

Believe it or not, all we have to do now is add the .DEF file we saw at the beginning of this chapter to our project (by selecting Project ➔ Add to Project ➔

Files) and we'll be ready to compile our DLL. Once this is done, press F7 to build the DLL.

Verifying the Exports

To be sure our DLL is exporting our functions correctly, we will use DUMPBIN.EXE, a utility that ships with Visual Studio, to examine our DLL's EXPORTS section. The command line for DUMPBIN.EXE is

```
Dumpbin /exports c:\projects\ex01_ch9\debug\ex01_ch9.dll
```

Of course you will want to modify the path after the /exports in your command string so that you will be pointing to the directory containing ex01_ch9.dll on your machine. The output from DUMPBIN.EXE is shown in Figure 9-1.

Notice that our functions are listed exactly as we expect them to be.

Testing the DLL

So we have created a DLL. Now what? We need to try it out and see if it works.

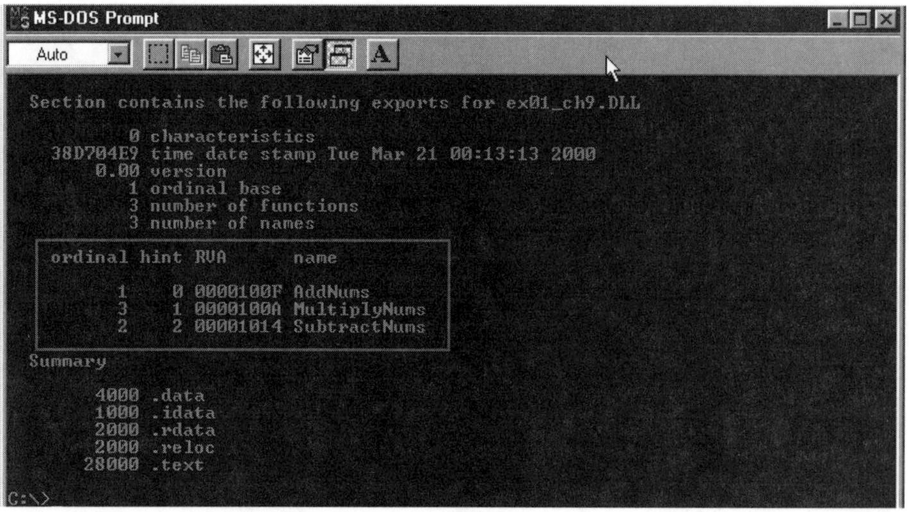

Figure 9-1. The resulting output from DUMPBIN.EXE

To do so we will create a Visual Basic application to do exactly this. Following are the contents of our Visual Basic program:

```
Option Explicit

Public Declare Function AddNums Lib
"c:\apress\chapter9\ex01_ch9\debug\ex01_ch9.dll" _
                              (ByVal num1 As Long, _
                              ByVal num2 As Long) _
                              As Long

Public Declare Function MultiplyNums Lib
"c:\apress\chapter9\ex01_ch9\debug\ex01_ch9.dll" _
                              (ByVal num1 As Long, _
                              ByVal num2 As Long) _
                              As Long

Public Declare Function SubtractNums Lib
"c:\apress\chapter9\ex01_ch9\debug\ex01_ch9.dll" _
                              (ByVal num1 As Long, _
                              ByVal num2 As Long) _
                              As Long

Public Sub main()

Dim lngAddResult As Long
Dim lngMultiplyResult As Long
Dim lngSubtractResult As Long

lngAddResult = AddNums(10, 5)
lngMultiplyResult = MultiplyNums(10, 5)
lngSubtractResult = SubtractNums(10, 5)

MsgBox "AddNums returned " & lngAddResult
MsgBox "MultiplyNums returned " & lngMultiplyResult
MsgBox "SubtractNums returned " & lngSubtractResult

End Sub
```

> **NOTE:** *Notice that in my Declare statements I used the absolute path to*
> ex01_ch9.DLL. *The reason for this is so that I can be sure that I am indeed*
> *testing the right DLL. Be sure to modify this code to point to the actual*
> *path of your DLL.*

When the above program is run, you will see three message boxes, one for
each operation performed.

That's it! We just created our first real Windows DLL. It wasn't too tough, was
it? Now, for the cool part: debugging!

Debugging the DLL

They say, "If you give a man a fish, you feed him for a day. But if you teach a man
to fish, you feed him for a lifetime." In this section you could say that I am going
to teach you how to fish!

The Visual Studio Debugger is the single most amazing tool I have ever used.
It is incredibly intuitive and easy to use. (Okay, so I might be stretching it a bit
here. . . .) It is a truly powerful tool. We already saw how to debug an .EXE from Visual Studio earlier in this book, but debugging a DLL requires a slightly different
approach. However, if you've ever debugged an ActiveX DLL in Visual Basic, you
have already used the technique we are going to use here. The first thing we have
to do is compile our Visual Basic program with "Symbolic Debug Info" by select-

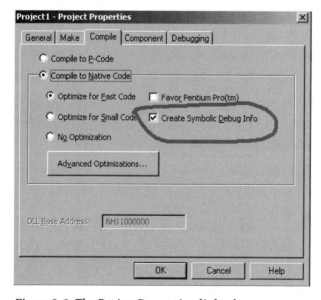

Figure 9-2. The Project Properties dialog box

ing the "Create Symbolic Debug Info" checkbox on the Compile tab of the Project Properties dialog box, as shown in Figure 9-2.

Once our program is compiled, we need to compile our DLL. You should have already done this, but if not, press F7 and build the DLL. Next, open the ex01_ch9.cpp file in Visual Studio (if it isn't already open) and set a break point at the entry point for each function, as shown in Figure 9-3.

You set a breakpoint by putting the cursor on the desired line and pressing F9. Once this is completed, select Project → Settings. This opens the Project Settings dialog box. Select the Debug tab. Next, put the path to the Visual Basic executable file you just compiled in the "Executable for debug session" textbox, as shown in Figure 9-4. Click OK. That's it! We're ready to debug our DLL.

To start the debugging process, press F5. This will cause Visual Studio to load the Visual Basic application that is going to call the DLL. You should almost immediately hit the first breakpoint, which is in the function AddNums. At this point, execution of the Visual Basic application is halted halfway through the call to AddNums. If you want to see something really cool, press ALT+7. This will bring up the Call Stack window, as shown in Figure 9-5.

Notice that your Visual Basic function Module1::Main() is in the call stack. Double-click it and, Voila! You can see exactly where your Visual Basic code halted in order to make the call to ex01_ch9.dll. Is this cool or what? The reason you can see the Visual Basic code here is because you compiled with "Symbolic Debug Info" in your Visual Basic application. If you hadn't selected this option, you

```
// ex01_ch9.cpp : Defines the entry point for the DLL application.
//

#include "stdafx.h"

BOOL APIENTRY DllMain( HANDLE hModule,
                       DWORD  ul_reason_for_call,
                       LPVOID lpReserved
                     )
{
    return TRUE;
}

LONG APIENTRY AddNums(int num1, int num2)
{
    //add the numbers and return the result
    return num1 + num2;
}

LONG APIENTRY SubtractNums(int num1, int num2)
{
    //subtract the numbers and return the result
    return num1 - num2;
}

LONG APIENTRY MultiplyNums(int num1, int num2)
{
    //multiply the numbers and return the result
    return num1 * num2;
}
```

Figure 9-3. The ex01_ch9.cpp file opened in Visual Studio

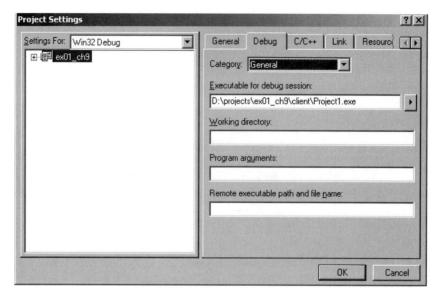

Figure 9-4. The Project Settings dialog box

```
Call Stack                                    ×
⇨ AddNums(int 10, int 5) line 15
   Module1::Main() line 25 + 30 bytes
   MSVBVM60! 6acc4308()
   MSVBVM60! 6acc1bdf()
   MSVBVM60! 6acbe195()
   MSVBVM60! 6acbdef7()
   MSVBVM60! 6acbddfd()
   PROJECT1! __vbaS + 10 bytes
```

Figure 9-5. The Call Stack window

would only see assembly code, which is practically useless for most debugging tasks. From here you can press F10 to step through the rest of the program. Notice how the debugger steps through your Visual Basic code as well as the C++ code. I love this stuff!

Conclusion

In this chapter, I discussed the basic differences between ActiveX DLLs and Windows DLLs. I also covered all of the basic elements of creating, using, and debugging DLLs, and even though our example DLL was very simple in the functions it exported, it gave us the foundation we will need for the next chapter, where we will build a much more robust and useful Windows DLL.

CHAPTER 10

Your First Real DLL

IN CHAPTER 9, WE LEARNED HOW TO CREATE A DLL that we could use in Visual Basic. And although it was a simple DLL in the functionality it provided, it detailed the structure of a DLL and the process involved in creating one. In this chapter we are going to build on the knowledge gained in the previous chapter to create a more useful and realistic DLL.

TrayMan.DLL

The DLL we are going to create is called TrayMan.DLL. This DLL will enable us to put an icon in the system tray, control that icon while it's in the system tray, and remove it from the system tray when we're done with it. However, there are three things I need to discuss before we can continue with this chapter. The first is the way the system tray works and interacts with applications. The second is callback functions, and finally, function pointers. Let's first talk about the way the system tray works.

The System Tray

The system tray is the area at the right hand side of the Windows Start menu. The system tray is designed to enable applications to run and stay available to a user without taking up screen space. The system tray is usually used by applications that run in the "background," such as virus scanners or multimedia applications.

There are many different uses for this particular functionality. So how does the tray actually work? Good question. Following is a typical scenario of how an application and the system tray interact with one another (remember that this is a logical flow; we'll cover the technical flow when we discuss the implementation of our library):

1. An application makes a request for its icon to be added to the system tray. It then passes an icon handle, a unique application identifier, and the address of a callback function (I'll cover this in a moment) to the system tray.

2.   The system tray records the address of the callback function, stores it with the unique application identifier, and loads the icon passed by the application.

3.   The system tray monitors mouse activity for the application's icon, which is now displayed in the system tray.

4.   The system tray calls the application's callback function when a mouse event occurs on that application's icon, passing the message as the callback function's parameter.

5.   The application reacts to the mouse event via the code in its callback function.

6.   Steps 4 and 5 are repeated until the application requests that its icon be removed from the system tray.

7.   Once the application requests to be removed from the system tray, the system tray removes the icon and releases all association with the application.

Now, this process is fairly simple from a conceptual point of view and even the details of implementing it aren't that bad once you've done it a couple of times. Let's now discuss function pointers and then we can start building our DLL.

Callback Functions

I hate it when I try to call someone and the phone line is busy. In fact, a busy signal is probably one of the most annoying sounds I can think of (next to the sound of a cheese grater on a chalkboard). Fortunately, my local phone company just installed a very cool feature in our service area. It's called the "auto-callback" feature, and it works like this: When I call someone and get a busy signal, I can choose to have the phone system monitor that line and call me back when the line is available. Now I no longer have to sit by the phone and press redial, and I can get other things done while I am waiting for the phone to call back when the phone line is free.

A callback function works in pretty much the same way: An application notifies a library or other application that it wants to be alerted when something specific happens. That other application then stores the address of a function for the application that requested notifications, and calls it when the specified event occurs. This continues until the client application notifies the library or other application that it no longer wants to be notified of the specified event.

Now, what I'm about to say may surprise you, but you've been using callback functions extensively in Visual Basic and probably didn't even know it. No way? Let's look at an example of a callback function in Visual Basic and see.

Assume we have a form with a command button on it named *Command1*:

```
Public Sub Command1_Click()
'Do something when Command1 is clicked
End Sub
```

Surprised? Think about what happens when the Visual Basic application that contains the Command1_Click subroutine runs. First, the form is displayed. Then, when the user clicks the Command1 command button, Windows executes the code in the Command1_Click subroutine. Why is the Command1_Click subroutine executed when the user clicks the Command1 button? After all, we never told Windows that the Command1_Click subroutine had anything to do with the control on our form named Command1. Could this be magic? No. You see, although we didn't tell Windows about the relationship between our Command1_Click subroutine and the control on our form named Command1, Visual Basic did. When you draw a control on a form, Visual Basic looks at the name of the control and then assumes that all code routines associated with that control will begin with the string *Command1*. Such that a control named *Command1* will be associated with code routines such as Command1_Click, Command1_MouseDown, and so on. Visual Basic then takes all of the function associated with the control and registers them as callback functions for that control with Windows. In essence, this means that Windows will monitor activity on a control and then look for a callback function associated with that action for that control. If one is found Windows calls it. (Purists may note that this description is not exactly correct and dramatically oversimplifies the actual process, but it is close enough for the purposes of this section.)

Function Pointers

So what exactly is a function pointer? Well, without sounding too sarcastic, it's a pointer to a function. In other words, a function pointer holds the memory address of a function, just as an int pointer holds the address of an int variable.

The following Visual Basic program demonstrates how to retrieve the address of a function (a function pointer) in Visual Basic:

```
Option Explicit

Public Sub Main()
GetFunctionAddress AddressOf MyFunc
End Sub
```

```
Public Function MyFunc() As Long
Dim i As Long
i = i + 1
MyFunc = i
End Function


Public Function GetFunctionAddress(ByVal lngAddress As Long) As Long
MsgBox "The function's address is: 0x" & Hex(lngAddress)
End Function
```

In the previous example, the lngAddress parameter of the GetFunctionAddress function is a function pointer, although you can't do anything with it except pass it to some other function or display it. Why the limitation? Because as with many other cases, Visual Basic tries to protect Visual programmers from themselves. This is somewhat unfortunate because AddressOf would be more useful if you could actually call the function that you had previously obtained the address for. Fortunately, function pointers in C++ do not suffer from this limitation. I must warn you, however, that at first glance function pointer declarations in C++ can look rather scary, but don't be intimidated, we'll go through and examine them piece-by-piece. Following is an example of a function pointer declaration in C++:

```
int (*pFunc)(void);
```

This code declares a function pointer, pFunc, which points to a function that does not take any arguments and returns a value of type int. Do you see why? Just in case it's not clear, take a look at Figure 10-1, which breaks down each section of the function pointer declaration.

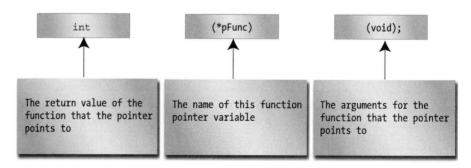

Figure 10-1. A function pointer declaration broken down

As you can see in the following two statements, a function pointer declaration looks almost identical to a function declaration:

```
int (*pFunc)(void); //function pointer declaration
int Func(void); //function declaration
```

Now let's look at an example of how we would use a function pointer in a program. Take a look at the following small program(it contains a function that takes a pointer to a function as an argument:

```
//function that takes an int parameter
int func1(int x)
{
    return 1;
}

//a function that takes a parameter of type 'pointer to function
//that takes a parameter of type int and returns int'
int func2(int (*pF)(int))
{
    return pF(2);
}
int main(int argc, char* argv[])
{
    //pass a pointer to func1 as a parameter of func2
    return func2(func1);
}
```

This small program contains three functions: func1, func2, and main. main is the entry point for the application. func1 is a function that takes one parameter of type int. And func2 is a function that takes a parameter of type *pointer to function* that takes a parameter of type int and returns a value of type int. If you look at the parameter list for func2 you'll see it. It's the same function pointer declaration that we saw earlier. The syntax is a little confusing, but not too bad in this case.

Take a look at the following code:

```
#include "stdafx.h"
#define    NULL    0

int func1(int x,int y, void *pVoid)
{
    return x + y;
}
```

```
int func2(int (*pF)(int,int,void*),int num1, int num2, void *pVoid)
{
    return pF(num1,num2,pVoid);
}

int main(int argc, char* argv[])
{
    return func2(func1,5,2,NULL);
}
```

Believe it or not, this is a more realistic example of using a function pointer in a program. Notice how much more difficult func2 is to decipher in this example than in the previous one. Well, fortunately we can use a C++ typedef to help ease this situation. Consider the following:

```
typedef int myint;
```

By using a *typedef* we make myint an alias for int. We can then use myint like so:

```
typedef int myint
..........
myint td = 0; //variable of type myint (really just an int)
int ntd = 0;  //variable of type int
ntd = td;     //assign an int to another int
..........
```

We can apply this same technique to function pointer declarations to make them easier to read and use. Let's look at a typedef for the function pointer declaration in our second example:

```
typedef int (*pF)(int,int,void*);
```

With this statement we have made the variable pF an alias for the statement:

```
int (*)(int,int,void*);
```

which is the declaration for a pointer to a function that takes three arguments and returns a value of type int. This means I can rewrite the previous application (with the hard to read func2 function) like so:

```
#include "stdafx.h"
#define     NULL    0
```

```
typedef int (*pF)(int,int,void*); //
typedef int myint;

int func1(int x,int y, void *pVoid)
{
    return x + y;
}

int func2(pF pFunc1,int num1, int num2, void *pVoid)
{
    return pFunc1(num1,num2,pVoid);
}

int main(int argc, char* argv[])
{
    return func2(func1,5,2,NULL);
}
```

Notice how much easier it is to read the parameters for func2 when written this way. I always use this technique even if the function pointer declared is relatively simple. I find that it makes the code much easier to read.

Now, look at the code inside of func2:

```
return pFunc1(num1,num2,pVoid);
```

We call the function pointer pFunc1 exactly like we would call the function func1 itself. Pretty cool, don't you think? Hopefully by this point you will agree with me that using function pointers in C++ is pretty straightforward. If not, take a few minutes and play around with the above program until you understand them. Now, let's build that DLL!

Creating the TrayMan.DLL Interface

So it is time to create our TrayMan.DLL. The first question is: Where do we start? The answer is: The interface.

Now when I say interface, I don't mean a Component Object Model (COM) interface or a user interface. I simply mean the set of exported functions that make up our DLL. You see, an interface is really just a way for a user to interact with your software. What does that mean? Well, it means that we need to decide what functions we are going to export from our DLL. As a first step toward doing that, let's make a list of the functionality that we want our DLL to provide as well as names for the functions that will provide that functionality:

- Initialize our DLL (InitTray).

- Add an icon to the system tray (AddToTray).

- Change the icon in the tray (UpdateTrayIcon).

- Update the tip text for the icon in the tray (UpdateTrayTip).

- Remove the icon from the tray (RemoveFromTray).

- Free our library when finished (FreeTray).

Now that we have identified the functions that our library is going to provide, we can actually create our DLL's .DEF (module DEFinition) file. The reason we are starting with this file is because this file is not implementation dependent. This means the .DEF file simply tells the linker what names to export from our DLL, and we already have that information from our list just shown.

Here is the TrayMan.DEF file:

```
LIBRARY         trayman.dll

EXPORTS
    AddToTray
    FreeTray
    InitTray
    RemoveFromTray
    UpdateTrayIcon
    UpdateTrayTip
```

Now we need to create our DLL's header file, which will declare the functions listed in our .DEF file as well as their parameters and return values. Our header file will also define several constants and include several Windows header files. These include the standard WIN32 API headers, `winuser.h` and `windows.h`, as well as one that we have not seen yet, `shellapi.h`. This header file contains all of the tray manipulation functions and structures along with some other useful non-tray related functions.

> **NOTE:** *I used the Visual C++ "Project Wizard" to create the shell for this DLL, by choosing File ➜ New ➜ Win32 Dynamic Link Library. This is exactly the same process we followed in Chapter 9 to create our DLL. The complete project is on the Web site that accompanies this book at* www.apress.com.

Let's go ahead and take a look at the header file in its entirety and then discuss various parts within it:

```
//header file for dll_ex_tray01
#if _MSC_VER > 1000
#pragma once
#endif // _MSC_VER > 1000


// Exclude rarely-used stuff from Windows headers
#define WIN32_LEAN_AND_MEAN

//headers for the WIN32 API calls
#include <windows.h>
#include <winuser.h>

//header file for tray specific API calls
#include <shellapi.h>

//if we're in debug mode then include <stdio.h>
#ifdef TRAYMAN_DEBUG
   #include <stdio.h>
#endif

//This is our unique id that will identify
//the message sent to the client window's from the tray
#define    DLL_EX_TRAY01_MESSAGE   0xBFFE

//constants defining possible icon parameters
enum ICON_TYPE
{
   ICON_AS_STRING = 0,
   ICON_AS_HANDLE = 1
};

//typedef for a function pointer to a WindowProc
typedef long (__stdcall *pWndProcFunc)(HWND hwnd,
                         UINT uMsg,
                         WPARAM wParam,
                         LPARAM lParam);

//typedef for a function pointer to a callback
//with one LONG parameter.
```

```
typedef void (__stdcall *pCbFunc)(LPARAM lParam);
```

```
/*----------------------------------------------------------------
BEGIN -- Exported functions
----------------------------------------------------------------*/
```

```
/*----------------------------------------------------------------
Name:          InitTray

Parameters:        HWND hwnd - The handle to the callers main window

Return Value:   TRUE on success FALSE otherwise

Date:           Tuesday, April 04, 2000 @ (1:50:24 PM)

Notes:          This function initializes the library and
                therefore must be called before any other
                functions in the library.
----------------------------------------------------------------*/
BOOL __stdcall InitTray(HWND hwnd);
```

```
/*----------------------------------------------------------------
Function Name:   AddToTray

Parameters:      char *szTip -   The text to display when the mouse
                                 is held over the icon in the tray

                 pCbFunc cb   -   A pointer to a client function
                                  that will be called when a mouse
                                  event occurs over the icon in the
                                  system tray

                 void *pIcon -   A pointer to either a string or an
                                 icon handle. depends on the value
                                 in iIconType

                 ICON_TYPE iIconType   -   int defining the type of
                                           data inside pIcon

                 bool bAnimated   -   bool flag indicating whether
```

```
                    or not to draw an animation when
                    adding the icon to the tray


Return Value:   TRUE if successful, FALSE otherwise


Date:           Tuesday, April 04, 2000 @ (1:51:38 PM)


Notes:          This function adds an icon to the system tray.
------------------------------------------------------------*/
BOOL __stdcall AddToTray(char *szTip,
                  pCbFunc cb,
                  void *pIcon,
                  ICON_TYPE iIconType = ICON_AS_STRING,
                  bool bAnimated = true);




/*---------------------------------------------------------------
Function Name:   RemoveFromTray


Parameters:      bool bAnimate   -   bool flag indicating whether
                                     or not to draw an animation
                                     when removing the icon from
                                     the tray


Return Value:   TRUE if successful, FALSE otherwise


Date:           Tuesday, April 04, 2000 @ (2:04:52 PM)


Notes:          This function removes a previously added icon from
           the system tray.
------------------------------------------------------------*/
BOOL __stdcall RemoveFromTray(bool bAnimate = true);




/*---------------------------------------------------------------
Function Name:   FreeTray


Parameters:      NONE


Return Value:   TRUE on success, FALSE otherwise
```

Date: Tuesday, April 04, 2000 @ (2:06:28 PM)

Notes: This function frees the library such that a
               call to InitTray is necessary to further use
               the library. This should be the last call in a
               session.
---*/
BOOL __stdcall FreeTray(void);

/*--
Function Name: UpdateTrayTip

Parameters: char *szTip -   A pointer the the new tip to
                    display for

Return Value: TRUE on success, FALSE otherwise

Date: Tuesday, April 04, 2000 @ (2:20:45 PM)

Notes: This function causes the tip text to change for
               an icon

---*/
BOOL __stdcall UpdateTrayTip(char *szTip);

/*--
Function Name: UpdateTrayIcon

Parameters: void *pIcon   -   A pointer to either a string or an
                    icon handle. depends on the value
                    in iIconType

          ICON_TYPE iIconType   -   the type of data pointed
                    to by pIcon

Return Value: TRUE on success, FALSE otherwise

Date: Tuesday, April 04, 2000 @ (2:21:06 PM)

Notes: This function causes the icon in the tray to be
            changed

--*/
BOOL __stdcall UpdateTrayIcon(void *pIcon,
                     ICON_TYPE iIconType = ICON_AS_STRING);

/*---
END -- Exported functions
--*/

//internal functions

//causes an animation to be drawn from a window to the tray
void drawDeflateAnimation(void);

//causes an animation to be drawn from the tray to a window
void drawInflateAnimation(void);

//subclassing function
long __stdcall wndProc(HWND hwnd,
                UINT uMsg,
                WPARAM wParam,
                LPARAM lParam);

//retieves the hwnd of the system tray
HWND getSystemTrayHwnd(void);

//private variable declarations
pWndProcFunc g_prevWndProc;   //Old windows proc.
HICON g_hIcon;   //handle to the icon in the tray
HWND g_hwnd = 0;   //the client's window handle
pCbFunc g_cb;   //the client's callback function
NOTIFYICONDATA g_nid;//Global tray data

Let's examine the file more closely. The first few lines in the header file are:

```
#if _MSC_VER > 1000
#pragma once
#endif // _MSC_VER > 1000

// Exclude rarely-used stuff from Windows headers
#define WIN32_LEAN_AND_MEAN
```

Visual Studio adds these lines when you create a new DLL project. They are standard and are usually included in the file, stdafx.h. (I moved them into this header file to save having two header files.) The statement, #pragma once tells the compiler to include this header file only once during any build. The #define WIN32_LEAN_AND_MEAN causes the compiler to strip out many rarely used declarations from the various Windows header files. (You don't need to worry about either of these things; I only point them out so that you won't wonder what they are doing in our header file.) Next we see the includes for the standard Windows header files, winuser.h and windows.h, and the include for the header file shellapi.h. We then see the line

```
#ifdef TRAYMAN_DEBUG
```

As you may remember, this is a conditional compilation statement. It tells the preprocessor to check to see if the symbol, TRAYMAN_DEBUG, has been previously defined in the program. If the preprocessor finds that the symbol has been previously defined, it processes all of the lines inside the #ifdef – #endif code block, which causes the stdio.h header file to be included.

In this version of TrayMan.DLL, we will not define TRAYMAN_DEBUG, which means stdio.h will not be included in our DLL. The point of putting in this section is to show that if we did define TRAYMAN_DEBUG in our DLL, we would have the ability to use stdio to create a log file or some other type of debugging facility. Of course, these calls to stdio would have to be contained in a #ifdef – #endif code block as well. This is a very common technique for debugging DLLs.

Next we see the statement

```
#define   DLL_EX_TRAY01_MESSAGE    0xBFFE
```

DLL_EX_TRAY01_MESSAGE will identify our icon once we put it in the system tray. In other words, each time something happens to our icon in the tray, the system will use this constant to let us know that our icon is being manipulated. Now, you may be wondering why I chose to define DLL_EX_TRAY01_MESSAGE as 0xBFFE. The reason is that Windows defines constants in the range of 0x8000–0xBFFF as "Messages available for use by applications." So I chose 0xBFFE because it was in this range and it happened to look good to me at the time.

The next code block we see in our header file is the ICON_TYPE enumeration:

```
enum ICON_TYPE
{
   ICON_AS_STRING = 0,
   ICON_AS_HANDLE = 1
};
```

Our DLL accepts an icon by its handle or by the path to its .ico file. As such, the previous enumeration is used in conjunction with a void pointer parameter so that an icon may be passed to a function. By using the ICON_TYPE enumeration along with a void pointer, we can allow either type of icon identifier to be passed. In essence, ICON_TYPE tells us whether our void pointer holds an icon handle or a path to a .ico file. Now there are obviously other ways to accomplish this same effect, such as by adding parameters for both a char* and an HICON to the parameter list for the functions that take icons as parameters, but I feel that this technique is cleaner.

After the ICON_TYPE enumeration, we see the following two function pointer declarations:

```
typedef long (__stdcall *pWndProcFunc)(HWND hwnd,
                                       UINT uMsg,
                                       WPARAM wParam,
                                       LPARAM lParam);

typedef void (__stdcall *pCbFunc)(LPARAM lParam);
```

The first declaration, pWndProcFunc, will be used for sub-classing our client window. (I explain sub-classing later in this chapter.) The second function pointer declaration declares a client callback function. In other words, we will assign the address of a function passed to us by the client that takes a parameter of type LPARAM (a typedef for a long) to a variable of this type. This will enable us to notify the client of any activity that occurs on their icon, once it is placed in the system tray. Now, I mentioned earlier that the function pointer type, pWndProcFunc, is used for sub-classing. But what is *sub-classing*? Many of you may already know the answer to this question, but the following is a quick overview for those that don't.

Sub-classing

Everything in the Windows operating system is a window. Every form, command button, listbox, and just about anything else you can think of is a window. Windows sends messages (which are really just integer values) to each window in the system as different events occur with respect to that window. These messages include WM_LBUTTONDBLCLK, which is sent to a window when the user double-clicks a window; and WM_KILLFOCUS, which is sent to a window just before it loses focus.

There are many different windows messages, so how does a window deal with all of them? With a WindowProc function, or message loop function. A WindowProc function is a function that waits for and deals with incoming windows messages. Let's take a look at a simple Visual Basic application so that we can get a feel for how this works:

```
Option Explicit

Private Sub Form_DblClick()

MsgBox "Form double-clicked!"

End Sub
```

From the viewpoint of a Visual Basic programmer, this program simply reacts to the Form_DblClick event. However, there is a lot going on behind the scenes that Visual Basic does that we never see. When this program starts to run, Visual Basic loads the program's only form into memory; at which point the form officially becomes a window. Visual Basic then attaches a WindowProc function to the form (window), which starts looping, waiting for messages regarding the newly created window to be sent to it by the operating system. When messages are received by the WindowProc function, it checks to see whether it should notify any of the sub routines contained in the application. (In other words, it checks to see whether you have written code for a specific event such as Form_Click()). If the WindowProc function were written in Visual Basic, it might look something like this:

```
Public Function WindowProc(lngMessage As Long) as Long
    Select Case lngMessage
        Case WM_LBUTTONDBLCLK
            Call Form_DblClick()
        Case WM_LBUTTONDOWN
            Call Form_Click()
        Case Else
```

```
            'Do Something Else
       End Select
       WindowProc = 0
End Function
```

As you can see, the `WindowProc` function just maps the messages it receives to the subroutine or function that will deal with that message. The term *sub-classing* refers to the process of replacing the default `WindowProc` that Visual Basic creates for a window, with one that we create ourselves. Why would we ever do this? Well, let's suppose you want to prevent a form from going to the start menu when its minimize button is clicked. If you had to use Visual Basic alone to implement this functionality, you'd be pretty much out of luck. The reason is because Visual Basic doesn't expose a `Form_MinButton_Clicked()` event for you like it does with the `Form_DblClick()` event. In this case you would have to sub-class the form (window) whose minimize event you are trying to trap. In fact, anytime you want to react to an event that Visual Basic doesn't expose to you, you will have to utilize sub-classing.

> **NOTE:** *If you are wondering why Visual Basic doesn't expose all of the possible messages a window could receive, I honestly don't know, either. But it is possibly because Microsoft wanted to keep Visual Basic programmers from trashing their systems too quickly and easily. However, there are third-party tools that allow you to expose all messages for a window.*

The Exported Functions

The next element we see in the header file is the Trayman.DLL interface (declarations of the exported functions). Notice how the comment blocks preceding each function declarations detail all information about the function. The reason this information is so detailed (and always should be) is because in most cases, these comments will be the end user's documentation. In fact, because the end user of your library will most likely be a Visual Basic programmer, you should include a .bas file along with your DLL that contains all of the declares and constants for your library in Visual Basic format so that the developer doesn't have to spend a lot of time doing C++/VB translation. (I will reserve comment on each of the exported functions until we discuss their implementations later in this chapter.)

After the last exported function's declaration we see the declarations of four private (non-exported) functions:

```
//causes an animation to be drawn from a window to the tray
void drawDeflateAnimation(void);

//causes an animation to be drawn from the tray to a window
void drawInflateAnimation(void);

//subclassing function
long __stdcall wndProc(HWND hwnd,UINT uMsg,WPARAM wParam,
                       LPARAM lParam);

//retieves the hwnd of the system tray
HWND getSystemTrayHwnd(void);
```

The last element we see in the header file is the declarations of several private variables:

```
pWndProcFunc g_prevWndProc;    //Old windows proc.
HICON g_hIcon;        //handle to the icon in the tray
HWND g_hwnd = 0;    //the client's window handle
pCbFunc g_cb;        //the client's callback function
NOTIFYICONDATA g_nid;//Global tray data
```

The first variable, g_prevWndProc, is used to save the address of the WindowProc that we are going to replace when we subclass our client's window. The reason we need to save this address is because when we are finished sub-classing we have to replace our replacement WindowProc's address with the original one. This is an important part of sub-classing. The next private variable in our header file is g_hIcon, which is used to store the handle to the icon that the client passes us. After that we see the g_hwnd variable, which is used to hold the handle to our client's main window. Next, we see the variable that will hold our client callback function's address, g_cb. The last of our private variables is g_nid, which is a structure that is used to hold information regarding the icon in the system tray. This structure is defined as follows:

```
struct _NOTIFYICONDATA {
        DWORD cbSize;
        HWND hWnd;
        UINT uID;
        UINT uFlags;
        UINT uCallbackMessage;
        HICON hIcon;
        CHAR    szTip[64];
} NOTIFYICONDATA
```

Let's briefly look at the elements that make up this structure. The first element, cbSize, is an int value that holds the total size of the structure in bytes. This value should always be equal to sizeof(NOTIFYICONDATA). The next element is hWnd, which is the handle to the window that will receive messages, via its WindowProc function, from the icon in the system tray. In our library, this will always be a client supplied window handle. The next element in the structure is uID. This value is used to identify the icon in the system tray, but if your application only puts one icon in the tray, this element is not useful, as TrayMan does not use this element. The element uFlags is a set of flags that denote which elements of the NOTIFYICONDATA structure contain valid data. The possible flags are: NIF_MESSAGE, NIF_ICON, and NIF_TIP. Following the uFlags element is the uCallbackMessage element. This is the value that identifies a message as being sent from the system tray. In our library, this element will hold the constant value DLL_EX_TRAY01_MESSAGE, which we saw defined earlier in our header file. The last element in the structure is szTip, which holds the "tip" that will be displayed when the mouse is held over the icon in the tray. We will explore this structure further once we look at the implementation of our library in the following section.

Implementing TrayMan.DLL

Now it is time to take the interface that we defined in our header file and implement it. We will do this in the file, dll_ex_tray01.cpp, which is listed here:

```
// dll_ex_tray01.cpp : Defines the entry point for the DLL application.
//
#include "dll_ex_tray01.h"

BOOL APIENTRY DllMain(HANDLE hModule,
                      DWORD  ul_reason_for_call,
                      LPVOID lpReserved)
{
    switch (ul_reason_for_call)
    {
        case DLL_PROCESS_ATTACH:
            break;
    }

    return TRUE;
}


/*-------------------------------------------------------------------
```

```
                    BEGIN -- Exported Function Implementations
                    ---------------------------------------------------------------*/


BOOL __stdcall InitTray(HWND hwnd)
{
    //Save the client window handle
    if (!hwnd)
    {
        return FALSE;
    }

    //save the client's hWnd
    g_hwnd = hwnd;
    //initialize the global data elements
    g_hIcon = 0;
    g_prevWndProc = 0;
    g_cb = 0;
    memset(&g_nid,0,sizeof(g_nid));

    //initialize the NOTIFY_ICON_DATA struct
    g_nid.cbSize = sizeof(g_nid);

    return TRUE;
}

BOOL __stdcall AddToTray(char *szTip,pCbFunc cb,void *pIcon,
                        ICON_TYPE iIconType,bool bAnimated)
{
    //flags variable for the NOTIFYICONDATA structure
    int iFlags;

    //be sure that we have a valid hwnd
    if (!g_hwnd)
    {
        return FALSE;
    }

    //be sure that we have a valid callback function address
    if (!cb)
    {
        return FALSE;
    }
    else
    {
```

```
    //save the client callback function address
    g_cb = cb;

    //update the NOTIFYICONDATA flags
    iFlags = iFlags | NIF_MESSAGE;
}


if (ICON_AS_HANDLE == iIconType)
{
    //Load the handle of the passed in Icon
    g_hIcon = (HICON)pIcon;

    //update the NOTIFYICONDATA flags
    iFlags = iFlags | NIF_ICON;
}
else
{
    //Load the handle of the passed in Icon
    g_hIcon = ExtractIcon((HINSTANCE)GetModuleHandle(NULL),
                          (char*)pIcon,0);

    //check for a valid icon handle
    if ((int)g_hIcon == 1 || (int)g_hIcon == NULL)
    {
        return FALSE;
    }
    else
    {
        //add the icon flag to the NOTIFYICONDATA structure
        iFlags = iFlags | NIF_ICON;
    }
}

//load the address of the passed tip string
if (szTip)
{
    //copy the tip string to the NOTIFYICONDATA struct
    strcpy(g_nid.szTip,szTip);

    //add the TIP flag to the NOTIFYICONDATA struct
    iFlags = iFlags | NIF_TIP;
}

//Load the NOTIFYICONDATA structure with the appropriate values.
```

```
            g_nid.hIcon = g_hIcon;
            g_nid.hWnd = (HWND)g_hwnd;

            //add flags to the NOTIFYICONDATA struct
            g_nid.uFlags = iFlags;

            //Set our unique identifier message for the icon in the tray.
            g_nid.uCallbackMessage = DLL_EX_TRAY01_MESSAGE;

            //Send the icon to the tray
            Shell_NotifyIcon(NIM_ADD,&g_nid);

            //check the animation flag
            if (bAnimated)
            {
                drawDeflateAnimation();
            }

            //Start subclassing the client.
            g_prevWndProc = (pWndProcFunc)SetWindowLong(
                             (HWND)g_hwnd,GWL_WNDPROC,(long)wndProc);

            return TRUE;
        }

        BOOL __stdcall UpdateTrayTip(char *szTip)
        {
            //check for a valid pointer
            if (!szTip)
            {
                return FALSE;
            }

            //copy the string into the NOTIFYICONDATA structure
            strcpy(g_nid.szTip,szTip);

            //update the NOTIFYICONDATA flags
            g_nid.uFlags = g_nid.uFlags | NIF_TIP;

            //update the icon in the tray
            Shell_NotifyIcon(NIM_MODIFY,&g_nid);

            return TRUE;
```

```
}

BOOL __stdcall UpdateTrayIcon(void *pIcon,ICON_TYPE iIconType)
{
    //check the icon handle
    if (!pIcon)
    {
        return FALSE;
    }

    //check to see if we are loading our icon
      //from a string or a handle
    if (ICON_AS_HANDLE == iIconType)
    {
        //Load the handle of the passed in Icon
        g_hIcon = (HICON)pIcon;
    }
    else
    {
        //check for a valid string
        if (!pIcon)
        {
            return FALSE;
        }

        //get the handle of the passed in Icon from it's .ico file
        g_hIcon = ExtractIcon((HINSTANCE)GetModuleHandle(NULL),
                              (char*)pIcon,0);

        //check for a valid HICON value
        if ((int)g_hIcon == 1 || (int)g_hIcon == NULL)
        {
            return FALSE;
        }
    }

    //update the NOTIFYICONDATA struct
    g_nid.hIcon = g_hIcon;

    //update the NOTIFYICONDATA flags
    g_nid.uFlags = g_nid.uFlags | NIF_ICON;

    //Change the icon in the tray
```

```
                Shell_NotifyIcon(NIM_MODIFY,&g_nid);
                return TRUE;
            }


        BOOL __stdcall RemoveFromTray(bool bAnimate)
        {
            //remove the icon from the tray
            Shell_NotifyIcon(NIM_DELETE,&g_nid);

            //check for animation flag
            if (bAnimate)
            {
                drawInflateAnimation();
            }

            //check for a valid callback function
            if (g_prevWndProc)
            {
                //release the subclass hook on the client
                SetWindowLong((HWND)g_hwnd,
                               GWL_WNDPROC,(long)g_prevWndProc);
            }

            //check for a valid icon handle
            if (g_hIcon)
            {
                //free the icon
                DestroyIcon(g_hIcon);
            }

            return TRUE;
        }


        BOOL __stdcall FreeTray()
        {
            //Reset all global data
            g_hwnd = 0;
            g_hIcon = 0;
            g_prevWndProc = 0;
            g_cb = 0;
            memset(&g_nid,0,sizeof(g_nid));

            return TRUE;
        }
```

```
/*------------------------------------------------------------------
END -- Exported Function Implementations
-------------------------------------------------------------*/



/*------------------------------------------------------------
PRIVATE "Helper" FUNCTION IMPLEMENTATIONS
-----------------------------------------------------------*/
long __stdcall wndProc(HWND hwnd,UINT uMsg,WPARAM wParam,LPARAM lParam)
{

    //Check for our unique message and then get
      //the Real message from lParam
    if (uMsg == DLL_EX_TRAY01_MESSAGE)
    {
        //Be sure that we have a valid function pointer
        if (g_cb)
        {
            //call the client
            g_cb(lParam);
        }
    }

    //call the default window message handler
    return CallWindowProc(g_prevWndProc,hwnd,uMsg,wParam,lParam);
}

void drawInflateAnimation()
{
    RECT rcTo;
    RECT rcFrom;
    HWND hwndTray;

    //get the handle for the system tray
    hwndTray = getSystemTrayHwnd();

    //get the coordinates of the client window
    GetWindowRect((HWND)g_hwnd,&rcTo);

    //get the coordinates of the system tray
    GetWindowRect((HWND)hwndTray,&rcFrom);

    //draw the animation
```

```
                    DrawAnimatedRects((HWND)g_hwnd,IDANI_CAPTION,&rcFrom,&rcTo);

}

void drawDeflateAnimation()
{
    RECT rcTo;
    RECT rcFrom;
    HWND hwndTray;

    //get the handle for the system tray
    hwndTray = getSystemTrayHwnd();

    //get the coordinates of the client window
    GetWindowRect((HWND)g_hwnd,&rcFrom);

    //get the coordinates of the system tray
    GetWindowRect((HWND)hwndTray,&rcTo);

    //draw the animation
    DrawAnimatedRects((HWND)g_hwnd,IDANI_CAPTION,&rcFrom,&rcTo);

}

HWND getSystemTrayHwnd()
{
    HWND hwndTray;
    HWND hwndStartMenu = FindWindow("Shell_TrayWnd", NULL);
    HWND hwndChild = GetWindow(hwndStartMenu, GW_CHILD);
    int  iClassName = 0;
    char szClass[255];

    //Loop through all siblings until we find the
      //'System Tray' (A.K.A. --> TrayNotifyWnd)
    do
    {
        iClassName = GetClassName(hwndChild,
                                    szClass, sizeof(szClass));

        //If it is the tray then store the handle.
        if (strstr(szClass, "TrayNotifyWnd"))
        {
            hwndTray = hwndChild;
```

```
        break;
    }
    else
    {
        //If we didn't find it, go to the next sibling.
            hwndChild = GetWindow(hwndChild, GW_HWNDNEXT);
    }

}while (true);


    return hwndTray;
}
```

The first function in our file is the entry point function, DllMain. As you may remember from Chapter 9, this function will be called when our function is loaded or unloaded. (We will do some cool stuff with this function in Chapter 14.)

Right after the DllMain function we see the first of our exported functions implementation, InitTray. Our library is designed so that InitTray must be called by a client application before any of the other functions in TrayMan.DLL. The first thing it does is check the hwnd parameter that the client passes in. If this parameter is NULL, the function returns FALSE to the caller. This indicates to the client that the library could not be initialized. (This makes sense because without the client's hwnd, we can't do anything.) Assuming that the client's hwnd is non-zero, we save it in the global variable, g_hwnd.

Next, all of the private global variables in the library are set to 0. This is to ensure that all of our global data is starting in a known state. Notice the use of memset to set every byte in g_nid equal to 0. After doing this we set the size of g_nid equal to the size of the NOTIFYICONDATA structure. Once this is completed, we return TRUE to our client, indicating that the library was successfully initialized. After a successful call to InitTray, our library will be in a state where it can accept calls to the other functions contained within our library.

The next function we implement in our library is AddToTray:

```
BOOL __stdcall AddToTray(char *szTip,pCbFunc cb,void *pIcon,
                    ICON_TYPE iIconType,bool bAnimated)
{
```

This is the function in our library that actually adds an icon to the system tray. The parameters to this function are fairly self-explanatory, but here is the quick rundown of them and what they are used for: szTip contains the tip that will be displayed when the mouse is held over the icon in the tray. The next parameter, cb, is the client supplied callback function. Notice that it is of type pCbFunc, which is the typedef we defined in our header file:

```
typedef void (__stdcall *pCbFunc)(LPARAM lParam);
```

It is important to note that the client callback must be in the exact format as the pCbFunc typedef. (We will examine this closer when we look at the client application at the end of the chapter.) Our function's third parameter, pIcon, is a void pointer that can hold either a pointer to the path for an .ico file, or a handle to an icon. iIconType determines which of these two types pIcon will be interpreted. If iIconType is ICON_AS_STRING, pIcon will be interpreted as a string. Otherwise it will be interpreted as a handle to an icon. The default value for iIconType as detailed in the library header file is ICON_AS_STRING. AddToTray's last parameter, bAnimated, tells it whether to draw an animation when it adds the icon to the system tray. (The animation effect is the same one you see when you minimize a window and it "zooms" to the task bar.)

Now, you may notice that there is a pattern in the first section of AddToTray. The pattern is to check each parameter for validity and return false if it is invalid. Conversely, if the parameter is found to be valid, the parameter is processed appropriately. Notice the use of a bit-wise OR to add flags to the iFlags element of the NOTIFYICONDATA structure as in the following code snippet from the function:

```
//update the NOTIFYICONDATA flags
iFlags = iFlags | NIF_MESSAGE;
```

Once all of the parameters have been verified and the flags and data members have been set, the g_nid structure is loaded with all of the values collected from the functions parameters. When that is complete, our library sends the icon to the tray with the following statement:

```
//Send the icon to the tray
Shell_NotifyIcon(NIM_ADD,&g_nid);
```

Shell_NotifyIcon is a WIN32 API function that is used to add, update, and remove icons from the system tray. The first parameter to Shell_NotifyIcon is one of the following values: NIM_ADD, NIM_MODIFY, NIM_DELETE. The value passed in this parameter determines how Shell_NotifyIcon will act upon the NOTIFYICONDATA structure contained in the function's second parameter. Because we passed NIM_ADD as our flag, Shell_NotifyIcon will add an icon to the tray using the information in g_nid. If we had passed NIM_MODIFY as the flag, Shell_NotifyIcon would modify the icon in the tray according to the information in g_nid. Immediately after we add the icon to the system tray with the call to Shell_NotifyIcon, we check to see if we are going to animate from the client window to the system tray, and call drawDeflateAnimation, accordingly. drawDeflateAnimation is the function in our library that draws an animation from the client window to the system tray. (We will look at drawDeflateAnimation later in this chapter.)

The last thing we do in the AddToTray function is arguably the most important: we sub-class the client's window, as shown here:

```
g_prevWndProc = (pWndProcFunc)SetWindowLong(
                 (HWND)g_hwnd,GWL_WNDPROC,(long)wndProc);
```

We accomplish this with a call to SetWindowLong. SetWindowLong is a WIN32 API function that modifies attributes of a window. In our case we are using it to replace the default WindowProc function for our client's window (due to the fact that we passed the GWL_WNDPROC flag as the second parameter to SetWindowLong) with a custom function we have written.

For the sake of completeness I will detail the parameters for SetWindowLong. The first parameter to SetWindowLong is the handle to the window whose attributes you want to modify. The second parameter for SetWindowLong is the flag that tells SetWindowLong, which attributes of the window to modify. And the last parameter for SetWindowLong is dependent on the flag passed in the second parameter. In this case it is the address of the function that will be replacing the default WindowProc function for the window.

> **NOTE:** *It is extremely important to save the return value of the call to* SetWindowLong *when you pass the* GWL_WNDPROC *flag. The reason is because the return value of* SetWindowLong *is the address of the default* WindowProc *function for our client's window, which we are replacing with our custom* WindowProc.

When we are done sub-classing the client's window, we will need to call SetWindowLong again and pass the address of the original WindowProc as the third parameter to SetWindowLong. If you forgot to capture it in your original call to SetWindowLong, you're going to be in trouble. Notice that we cast the return value of SetWindowLong to be of type pWndProcFunc (which is typedefed in the library's header file). The reason we have to cast this value is because SetWindowLong actually returns a void pointer, which can not be set equal to a value of type pWndProcFunc. Therefore, to store the return value in our pWndProcFunc type variable requires a cast. Now, compared to AddToTray the rest of our exported functions are quite straightforward. So relax; the worst is over.

The function that we implement after AddToTray is UpdateTrayTip:

```
BOOL __stdcall UpdateTrayTip(char *szTip)
```

This function changes the text that is displayed when the mouse is held over the icon in the system tray. After checking the validity of the szTip parameter, we simply copy it to the g_nid structure with the strcpy runtime library function. To actually update the icon's tip we call Shell_NotifyIcon, just as we did in AddToTray, except this time we pass the NIM_MODIFY flag instead of NIM_ADD. This causes Shell_NotifyIcon to update the existing icon in the system tray with the information in g_nid instead of creating a new icon in the tray. Again, this function is straightforward.

Next, we implement the UpdateTrayIcon function:

```
BOOL __stdcall UpdateTrayIcon(void *pIcon,ICON_TYPE iIconType)
```

This function is identical to UpdateTrayTip except for the fact that it modifies the icon in the system tray instead of the icon tip. Again, notice how we use the void pointer parameter, pIcon, in conjunction with the ICON_TYPE enumeration to extract the icon just as we did in the AddToTray function.

The inverse function of AddToTray is RemoveFromTray, which is also the next function we implement:

```
BOOL __stdcall RemoveFromTray(bool bAnimate)
```

The first thing we do in this function is call Shell_NotifyIcon with a flag of NIM_DELETE, which causes the icon to be removed from the system tray. After that we check for the animation flag and call drawInflateAnimation, accordingly. drawInflateAnimation is the opposite effect of drawDeflateAnimation; it draws an animation from the system tray to the client window. The reason we check the animation flag immediately after removing the icon from the tray is so that if we do have to animate, it will appear that the animation is a direct result of the icon being removed from the tray. If we waited, there would be a delay in the animation, causing a less than desirable effect.

After we remove the icon from the system tray and animate if necessary, we "un-sub-class" the client's window with the following call:

```
SetWindowLong((HWND)g_hwnd,GWL_WNDPROC,(long)g_prevWndProc);
```

Notice that this call to SetWindowLong is identical to the call we made to subclass the client's window except for the fact that we pass g_prevWndProc as the address of the new WindowProc function for the client's window. This is precisely why we saved the return value of the first call to SetWindowLong (the address of the original WindowProc for the window). There actually is another use for this value, which we will see when we look at our library's private function wndProc. Once this call is made, the client's window will start using the WindowProc it was before we started sub-classing it.

The last thing we do in the RemoveFromTray function is call DestroyIcon. DestroyIcon is a WIN32 API function that frees the resources allocated by ExtractIcon (which we call in the function AddToTray).

The last exported function in our library is `FreeTray`, which resets all of our library's global data. Once a client calls `FreeTray`, our library is, in effect, shut down. In order for a client to use our library again, they would need to make another call to `InitTray`.

The Helper Functions

We've now seen all of the exported functions in our library. However, there are several other functions that we need to examine, including our library's non-exported helper functions. A *helper function* is a function that is not exported from a library, but assists the public functions of a library do their job. Our library's helper functions are: `getSystemTrayHwnd`, `drawDeflateAnimation`, `drawInflateAnimation`, and `wndProc`.

Let's take a look at each one, starting with `wndProc`:

```
long __stdcall wndProc(HWND hwnd,UINT uMsg,
                       WPARAM wParam,LPARAM lParam)
```

This function is the `WindowProc` replacement function that we use to sub-class our client's window. A `WindowProc` function must conform to the above definition with regard to parameters, return value, and calling convention, as mandated by the Windows operating system. The name of the `WindowProc` function is not important, although I tend to give it a descriptive name such as `wndProc`. This helps to identify it among a list of other functions in a module.

The meanings of the parameters for `WindowProc` function vary depending on the message being sent to the window. In all cases, the `hwnd` parameter identifies the handle of the window where the message is being sent. This enables a sub-classing function to forward the message that is sent to the window (as we will see later in this chapter). The `uMsg` parameter is almost always the actual message being sent to the window, but it doesn't have to be. In fact, the system tray passes the `uCallBackMessage` element of the `NOTIFYICONDATA` structure in this parameter to alert an application that it is receiving a message from the system tray. When this occurs, the actual `WM_` message is passed in the `lParam` parameter. This is why we check `uMsg` for the constant `DLL_EX_TRAY01_MESSAGE`, which we put into `g_nid.uCallBackMessage`:

```
if (uMsg == DLL_EX_TRAY01_MESSAGE)
```

If we find it, we call the client callback function and pass `lParam` (which contains the actual `WM_??` message sent from the tray) as its parameter like so:

```
if (g_cb)
{
    //call the client
    g_cb(lParam);
}
```

> **NOTE:** *We call the client callback function and pass lParam as its parameter only after we check the validity of the client callback function pointer. Never call an invalid function pointer or else, KABOOM!*

At this point it is up to the client application to decide how to react to the message. However, our job in this function is not finished yet. We still have to do something with the messages that don't contain the value `DLL_EX_TRAY01_MESSAGE` in their uMsg parameter. This is where The `CallWindowProc` API call comes into play.

`CallWindowProc` is used to do a onetime call to an inactive `WindowProc` function. By *inactive* I mean a `WindowProc` function that has been temporarily replaced, such as in our case. You see, a `WindowProc` function is responsible for handling all messages sent to a window, which our `WindowProc` function doesn't; our `WindowProc` function only check for one specific message, `DLL_EX_TRAY01_MESSAGE`. Our Visual Basic performs numerous operations based on incoming Windows messages, some of which we can't possibly know. So it is essential to call the original `WindowProc` function like so:

```
return CallWindowProc(g_prevWndProc,hwnd,uMsg,wParam,lParam);
```

The first parameter to `CallWindowProc` is the address of the original `WindowProc` function (this is the other reason why we save this address after calling `SetWindowLong` in the `AddToTray` function). The rest of the parameters to `CallWindowProc` are exactly the same as the parameters from our `WindowProc` function. Notice that we pass them to it verbatim.

> **TIP:** *If you feel that you need more help in understanding sub-classing, get a copy of* Dan Appleman's Visual Basic Programmer's Guide to the Win32 API *(1999, Sams). It contains the easiest to understand explanation of Windows messaging and sub-classing I have read so far.*

The next helper function we look at is `getSystemTrayHwnd`. This function is responsible for obtaining the handle to the system tray window. (Remember that everything in Windows was a window(even the system tray.) This function is not as complicated as it may look. All we are really doing is the following: First we obtain the handle to the system tray itself, Shell_TrayWnd, which is a hidden window (not the box on the right of the task bar). The box on the right side of the task bar is a window named TrayNotifyWnd. This window is a child of the Shell_TrayWnd window. Once we obtained its hwnd, we loop through all of its child windows until we find TrayNotifyWnd like so:

```
do
{
    iClassName = GetClassName(hwndChild,
                                szClass, sizeof(szClass));

    //If it is the tray then store the handle.
    if (strstr(szClass, "TrayNotifyWnd"))
    {
        hwndTray = hwndChild;
        break;
    }
    else
    {
        //If we didn't find it, go to the next sibling.
            hwndChild = GetWindow(hwndChild, GW_HWNDNEXT);
    }

}while (true);
```

Once we obtain the handle of the TrayNotifyWnd window, the function returns it to the caller, which will always be either drawDeflateAnimation or drawInflateAnimation. Both of these functions do exactly the same thing, but in different directions. They both obtain the RECT for both the client's window and the system tray and then call the Win32 API function DrawAnimatedRects, which actually draws the animation on the screen.

> **NOTE:** RECT *is a Win32 API structure that holds the locations of the four corners of a window.*

The Client Application

Our client application consists of one form and one standard module. It is straightforward in its functionality, but it does show some of the capabilities of our DLL when coupled with a Visual Basic client application.

Let's look at the code for the form:

```
Option Explicit

Private Sub cmdIcon_Click()

'Get the path to the new icon
With cdlgMain
    .DialogTitle = "Choose an Icon File..."
    .Filter = "Icon Files (*.ico)|*.ico"
    .ShowOpen

    'If user pressed 'Cancel' then get out
    If .CancelError Then
        Exit Sub
    End If

    'update the label with the path to the icon
    lblIcon.Caption = .FileName

    'Load the picture into the picture box
    picIcon.Picture = LoadPicture(.FileName)

    'Call TrayMan.DLL to update the icon in the system tray
    UpdateTrayIcon .FileName, 0
End With

End Sub
Private Sub cmdAddToTray_Click()

'Hide this form
Me.Hide


'Yuck! but necessary for proper animation effect
DoEvents

'Call TrayMan.DLL to add an icon to the system tray
AddToTray "Double click or press the right mouse button.", _
                    AddressOf CallBack, lblIcon.Caption, 0, True

'Disable the command button
cmdAddToTray.Enabled = False
```

```
End Sub

Private Sub cmdAnimate_Click()

'Check the state of the command button
If cmdAnimate.Caption <> "Stop!" Then
    'Call TrayMan.DLL to initialize the system tray
    InitTray Me.hWnd

    'Add the icon to the system tray
    AddToTray "Now drawing animated icon.", _
                    AddressOf CallBack, "ball1.ico", 0, False

    cmdAnimate.Caption = "Stop!"

    'Disable the command button
    cmdAddToTray.Enabled = False

    'Start the animation timer
    tmrIcon.Enabled = True
Else
    cmdAnimate.Caption = "Animate Tray"

    'Disable the command button
    cmdAddToTray.Enabled = True

    'Stop the animation timer
    tmrIcon.Enabled = False

    'Remove the icon from the tray
    RemoveFromTray False
End If

End Sub

Private Sub Form_Load()

'Call TrayMan.DLL to initialize the system tray
InitTray Me.hWnd

'Set and load the initial icon
lblIcon.Caption = App.Path & "\smile.ico"
picIcon.Picture = LoadPicture(lblIcon.Caption)
```

```
                    End Sub

                    Private Sub Form_QueryUnload(Cancel As Integer, UnloadMode As Integer)

                    'Call TrayMan.DLL to free the system tray before our form unloads
                    FreeTray

                    End Sub

                    Private Sub lblIcon_Change()

                    lblIcon.ToolTipText = lblIcon.Caption

                    End Sub

                    Private Sub mnuChangeIcon_Click()

                    'Stop the timer
                    If tmrIcon.Enabled = True Then
                        tmrIcon.Enabled = False
                    End If

                    Call cmdIcon_Click

                    End Sub

                    Private Sub mnuChangeTip_Click()

                    Dim strInput As String

                    'Get an input string
                    strInput = InputBox("Please enter the tip text.", _
                                        App.EXEName & " -- Change Tray Tip")

                    'Call TrayMan.DLL to update the tip for the icon
                    UpdateTrayTip strInput

                    End Sub

                    Private Sub mnuExit_Click()

                    'Call TrayMan.DLL to remove the icon from the system tray
                    RemoveFromTray False
```

```vb
'Unload the form - don't call FreeTray here because it is already
'going to be called in Form_QueryUnload()
Unload Me

End Sub

Private Sub mnuMessage_Click()

MsgBox "Hello from the tray!"

End Sub

Private Sub mnuShow_Click()

'Call TrayMan.DLL to remove the icon
RemoveFromTray True

'Enable the command button
cmdAddToTray.Enabled = True
frmMain.Visible = True

End Sub

Private Sub tmrIcon_Timer()

'Variable to keep track of the current icon animation frame
Static intNum As Integer
Dim strIconName As String

If intNum = 0 Then
    intNum = 1
End If

'Get the next icon in the animation
strIconName = App.Path & "\ball" & intNum & ".ico"

'Call TrayMan.DLL to update the icon in the system tray
UpdateTrayIcon strIconName, 0

'Set next animation frame icon
If intNum >= 9 Then
    intNum = 1
Else
    intNum = intNum + 1
```

```
End If
End Sub
```

As you can see from the previous code listing, there is nothing special about the client application's code. It is a very simple Visual Basic application. And, in fact, it should be simple because I wrapped all of the difficult code into the Tray-Man.DLL. I will, however, point out some of the important parts of the application.

First, notice that we call InitTray as soon as frmMain is loaded. This is done so that the DLL will be initialized by the time the user sees the form.

```
'Call TrayMan.DLL to initialize the system tray
InitTray Me.hWnd
```

Next, look at our client's hidden menu. This menu will be the popup menu displayed when the user right-clicks the system tray icon. Next, notice that I used a timer to create an animation effect in the system tray by repeated calling UpdateTrayIcon inside of the tmrIcon_Timer event, as shown here:

```
'Get the next icon in the animation
strIconName = App.Path & "\ball" & intNum & ".ico"

'Call TrayMan.DLL to update the icon in the system tray
UpdateTrayIcon strIconName, 0

'Set next animation frame icon
If intNum >= 9 Then
    intNum = 1
Else
    intNum = intNum + 1
End If
```

Lastly, notice that I put the call to FreeTray inside of the Form_QueryUnload event. This is to ensure that the library is freed before our application exits. The rest of the code in the form should be self-explanatory so I won't take time to cover it here, but we do need to look quickly at the basTrayMan module:

```
Option Explicit

'Common Windows Messages
Public Const WM_LBUTTONDOWN = &H201
Public Const WM_LBUTTONDBLCLK = &H203
Public Const WM_RBUTTONDBLCLK = &H206
```

```
Public Const WM_RBUTTONDOWN = &H204


'Enum to tell if you are sending a path to an .ico
'file or a handle to an icon
Public Enum ICON_TYPE
    ICON_AS_STRING = 0
    ICON_AS_HANDLE = 1
End Enum


'Declares for TrayMan.DLL
'Function to initialize the TrayMan library
Public Declare Function InitTray Lib "trayman.dll" _
                                (ByVal lngVal As Long) As Long


'Function to Free the TrayMan library
Public Declare Function FreeTray Lib "trayman.dll" () As Long


'Function to remove the icon from the tray
Public Declare Function RemoveFromTray Lib "trayman.dll" _
                            (ByVal bAnimate As Boolean) As Long


'Function to add the icon to the tray
Public Declare Function AddToTray Lib "trayman.dll" _
                (ByVal szTip As String, _
                 ByVal cbFunc As Long, _
                 ByVal pIcon As Any, _
                 ByVal iIconType As Long, _
                 ByVal bAnimate As Boolean) As Long


'Function to update the tip in the tray
Public Declare Function UpdateTrayTip Lib "trayman.dll" _
                                (ByVal szTip As String) As Long


'Function to update the icon in the tray
Public Declare Function UpdateTrayIcon Lib "trayman.dll" _
                                (ByVal pIcon As Any, _
                                 ByVal iIconType As Long) _
                                As Long


'This is a sample callback function
Public Sub CallBack(ByVal lngParam As Long)

Select Case lngParam
```

```
                    'React when the tray icon is double clicked
                    Case WM_LBUTTONDBLCLK
                            RemoveFromTray True
                            frmMain.cmdAddToTray.Enabled = True
                            frmMain.Visible = True

                    'React when the right mouse button is pressed over the tray icon
                    Case WM_RBUTTONDOWN
                        frmMain.PopupMenu frmMain.mnuMain

            End Select

            End Sub
```

As you can see, this module contains only three elements: the client callback function (CallBack), several WIN32 API WM_ constants, and the Declare statements for TrayMan.DLL. I created the Declare statements by mapping the functions from TrayMan.DLL's header file. The WM_ constants came straight from the Visual Basic API Viewer tool, so I won't spend any time explaining them; however, I do want to examine the one function in our module: CallBack. As I stated earlier, this is our client callback function, which means that this is the function that is called from TrayMan.DLL's wndProc function.

The wndProc function is listed again here for reference:

```c
long __stdcall wndProc(HWND hwnd,UINT uMsg,
                        WPARAM wParam,LPARAM lParam)
{

    //Check for our unique message and then get
      //the Real message from lParam
    if (uMsg == DLL_EX_TRAY01_MESSAGE)
    {
        //Be sure that we have a valid function pointer
        if (g_cb)
        {
            //call the client
            g_cb(lParam);
        }
    }

    //call the default window message handler
    return CallWindowProc(g_prevWndProc,hwnd,uMsg,wParam,lParam);
}
```

In the context of the previous code, our Visual Basic function, `CallBack`, is g_cb. This means that each time a message is sent to the `wndProc` function inside our DLL, it will in turn call our client function, `CallBack` and pass it the `WM_` message it received from the system tray. From the Select-Case block you can see that if `CallBack` receives a `WM_LBUTTONDBLCLK` message, it removes the icon from the tray and "un-hides" the application window. However, if the `WM_RBUTTONDOWN` message is sent, our application displays its hidden menu as a popup menu. From the popup menu the user can do several things, including changing the tip for the icon or actually changing the icon itself. The menu also enables the user to display a message box while the icon is still in the tray.

It is important to remember that I have chosen to only write code to react to the `WM_RBUTTONDOWN` and `WM_LBUTTONDBLCLK` messages, but I could easily add code to handle any message that could be initiated from our icon in the system tray. For example, if I wanted to react to the right mouse button being double-clicked, I could modify the Select-Case block inside of `CallBack` as so:

```
Select Case lngParam
'React when the tray icon is double clicked
Case WM_LBUTTONDBLCLK
        RemoveFromTray True
        frmMain.cmdAddToTray.Enabled = True
        frmMain.Visible = True
Case WM_RBUTTONDBLCLK
        'Do something when the right mouse button
    'is double clicked.
'React when the right mouse button is pressed over the tray icon
Case WM_RBUTTONDOWN
    frmMain.PopupMenu frmMain.mnuMain

End Select
```

Remember that *all* messages from the system tray are sent to our function, but they are simply ignored unless we write code to specifically handle those messages.

Conclusion

By now you should feel pretty confident about writing DLLs in C++. You should also have a better understanding of the interaction between Visual Basic and DLLs than when you started reading this book. I encourage you to experiment with this new-found knowledge and see what kind of creations you can come up with on your own. And now that you understand C++ code, you should start digging around in MSDN documentation. There are new APIs added to Windows daily. Try them out but most important, have fun!

CHAPTER 11

An ATL Primer

IN PREVIOUS CHAPTERS OF THIS BOOK we saw how to create Windows DLLs with C++. We also saw a sample application of how to integrate DLLs written in C++ with applications written in Visual Basic. This ability to encapsulate functions into DLLs and use them from Visual Basic is very powerful indeed, and in many cases, the best solution to a programming problem. However, the current state (and foreseeable future) of the Microsoft world, and therefore the Visual Basic world, is the Component Object Model (COM). As evidence of this, the Windows 2000 operating system has started to transition some of its application program interface (API) from a set of functions exported from DLLs to a set of COM objects exposing the same functionality. In this chapter and the next, we learn how to use the Active Template Library (ATL) to create COM objects in C++, which can be used from Visual Basic. I will also cover the basic concepts of COM ideology and implementation.

> **NOTE:** *COM is extremely complex. There have been many books written about COM, and even some of these books just scratch the surface of it. COM is big! Fortunately you only need to understand the basic ideology of COM and not the underlying technology that drives it in order to work with COM effectively. In this book I will not delve into the underlying details of COM; I will simply stick to the task of creating COM components using the ATL framework, which handles all of the messy details of COM programming for us.*

COM and Interfaces

The Component Object Model is an infrastructure that enables software components to communicate with one another regardless of the programming language in which they were written (and regardless of the machine on which the components reside). To achieve this interoperability, the technology that drives COM must be able to separate a component's interface (the signatures of the methods and properties the component exposes), from its underlying implementation (the source code that executes the methods and properties the component exposes).

To help understand this concept, think back to our DLL example in Chapter 10. We defined a .DEF (module DEFinition) file that had the names of the functions that our DLL (Component) contained, while the actual implementation of those functions was contained in our .cpp file. In a sense, we separated our DLL's interface from its implementation.

Note that a .DEF file has nothing to do with COM—I just want to illustrate the concept of an interface. An *interface*, in the context of COM, is a set of rules describing how a software component can be interacted with by other software components. In other words, an interface describes the properties and methods, as well as their parameters and return value types, an object exposes. And these properties and methods are what other software components use to communicate with and manipulate the object.

Now the wonderful part of interfaces is that they are described in something called Interface Definition Language (IDL), which is programming language-independent. That means that an interface is described in total isolation from any language that may implement it. This enables a programmer to express the true design of an interface without thinking of any restrictions or benefits offered by a specific programming language. This also enables a programmer to implement the interface in any language he or she chooses. The benefits of this are obvious.

So what exactly does it mean to *implement an interface?* Remember that an interface doesn't contain source code to actually execute any of the properties or methods it describes, so some other piece of code must provide its implementation. In fact, the whole point of COM is that you don't know or care how or where an interface is implemented. All you care about is the fact that you are able to use the services promised by a particular interface. A good analogy of this separation of an interface from its implementation is a Web server on the Internet. When you type in a uniform resource locator (URL) in your Web browser, you are using an interface to a Web server somewhere out on the Internet. You don't care about the implementation of that Web server. All you care about is that the Web server returns the file you requested. The fact that a Web server is supposed to return a file to a client based on the URL supplied by the client is essentially the interface that every Web server implements. (The interface is again the set of rules that dictate how one piece of software can be interacted with.) In the case of the Web server, the interface states that a client must request a file in the form of:

```
http://<URL>/<FILENAME>
```

As long as you make your request in this format (conform to the interface) you are guaranteed to receive the file you requested, or a notification that the file could not be found. You don't know (or care) what brand of Web server you are connected to (the Web server implementation) or what platform on which the Web server is running. You also don't know about the actual code that processes your file request. You don't know the language that was used to write the source code for the Web server either. The reason is that all of these things are the Web server's implementation details and from a client's perspective they are inconsequential details.

But wait a minute. Who cares if we know the implementation details of an interface? What's the big deal? Well, once a client knows about the implementation of a specific interface and relies on that implementation, that client becomes intrinsically tied to that implementation. This causes a client to have to be rebuilt each time the interface implementation is changed. This also destroys the whole idea of creating components that can freely talk to each other without regard to the other's implementation.

So now, what about the Web server's interface, where does it fit into all of this? The Web server interface is really just the hypertext transfer protocol (HTTP) specification (which is a set of rules about how documents are transferred around the Internet using HTTP). There is a group in charge of overseeing Internet standards that publishes these rules in a freely available, public document. Each company that wants to create a Web server must use this set of rules (interface) to do so. Now don't get me wrong, there are no Interface Police. If a company decides that their Web server will stray from the interface and only accept requests in the form:

```
http://<FILENAME>/<URL>
```

instead of the format specified in the Web server interface, no one can really stop them. But, it won't take long for clients to get frustrated at the Web servers' noncompliance of the expected Web server interface and quit visiting sites that use that particular Web server. You see, when a software component changes any element of an expected interface it "breaks" the interface. This is strictly prohibited in COM. Once an interface is published (which means that it has been distributed for use by other developers) it can never change, ever!

The nicest part of this separation is that the implementation for an interface can be replaced without the user of the interface ever knowing it. Again referring to the analogy of the Web server, if a company switches from brand "X" of Web server to brand "Z," the clients will not need to be recompiled or even notified of the change. They may notice a change in performance when they connect to the server the next time, but again this is an implementation detail and therefore not a concern of the client. Assuming that brand "Z" Web server is faster than brand "X", the client will have benefited from the improved implementation of the Web server interface without doing anything. As long as the expected Web server interface is intact, the client does not otherwise care about the implementation change.

Remember that the Web server analogy has nothing to do with COM; it only illustrates the separation of an interface from its implementation. However, because COM is what we're after in this chapter, let's look at some real COM interfaces.

The IUnknown Interface

The IUnknown interface is the root of every COM object, which means every COM object has to support the IUnknown interface. (When I say that an object supports an interface, I simply mean that the object provides an implementation of that interface's properties and methods.) IUnknown is a simple interface that contains only three methods: AddRef, Release, and QueryInterface. QueryInterface enables a client to discover what other interfaces an object supports. This is the main job of IUnknown. The other job given to IUnknown is that of *Reference Counting*. Reference counting is a process by which a COM object keeps track of the number of clients currently using it. This is what AddRef and Release are for. Each time a client connects to a specific COM object, AddRef is called. This causes the reference count for that object to be incremented by one. When that client is done using the COM object the client calls Release and thereby decrements the reference count for that COM object. When the reference count for an object reaches 0, the object destroys itself.

Now, I already said that each object has to support IUnknown, but through what mechanism is this made possible? You guessed it: inheritance. You see, just as C++ classes use inheritance to inherit the implementation of another class's methods and properties, interfaces use inheritance as a means of incorporating the properties and methods described in another interface in their own. To say that all COM interfaces are based on IUnknown, means that every interface inherits from either IUnknown directly or from another interface that has already inherited IUnknown. Implementing these interfaces can be very tedious indeed because you have to write code to implement each interface that you want to use as well as the interfaces that it inherits from. You have to write implementations for AddRef, Release, and QueryInterface by hand, from scratch each time you want to write a COM component. It is for this reason COM programming is revered as one of the most difficult tasks in the Windows world.

ATL

As you can start to appreciate, writing a COM object from scratch is a very tedious process, which is where the Active Template Library (ATL) comes into play. ATL is the Visual Basic for COM objects written in C++. You see, just as Visual Basic has made creating COM objects absolutely simple, ATL makes creating COM objects in C++ almost as easy.

ATL is a framework that writes a lot of the mundane, boilerplate code that COM programming requires. One problem a lot of programmers (myself included) have with this is that they like to hand code every byte of data in their programs, but the truth is that this just isn't possible now. In order to be productive in today's environment, you must let your tools do some of the work for you.

I do not propose that you shouldn't know what your tools are doing for you (at least at a reasonable level of knowledge), but once you understand the basic concepts of the code generated by a framework such as ATL, let it do its job and speed the development process along.

ATL uses C++ templates extensively to achieve the type of neutrality required by COM. It's amazing how much COM interfaces and C++ templates resemble each other in an ideological sort of way. Remember from Chapter 7 that a template takes a parameter of a type data type and then uses that type internally to create other data elements and class members. Now, I must tell you that the template usages we saw in Chapter 7 are magnitudes simpler than the usages you will see in ATL, but with some perseverance, you will be able to understand the beauty of ATL's structure.

Functionally, ATL is almost identical to the "Class Builder" utility in Visual Basic in that it enables you to speed the COM object development process by creating all of the necessary "plumbing" of your COM objects for you so that you can concentrate on implementing the object's functionality. You will use the ATL Object Wizard almost exclusively during the process of creating your COM objects.

Testing the Waters

In order to get a better feel for what the ATL is all about, let's build a simple COM object project with it and see what is involved. Open Visual Studio and select File → New. Then select ATL COM AppWizard as the project type and type in the project name **atl_ex01** in the Project Name field, as shown in Figure 11-1.

Press OK. You will then see the screen shown in Figure 11-2.

Press Finish and then OK. At this point you will have an empty ATL COM project. Now it important to note that there are no COM objects in the project at this point in time. We have only created the container to hold COM objects. But this container alone doesn't really do us any good, so let's go ahead and add a COM object to our project. Select New ATL Object from the Insert menu. You will see the screen shown in Figure 11-3.

Notice that you have quite a few choices of types of objects that we can create. For now we will create a "Simple Object." To do this, select Simple Object from the objects list box and press OK. You will see the ATL Object Wizard Properties dialog box as shown in Figure 11-4.

Type **Radio** into the Short Name field. This will be the name of our COM object. Notice that all of the other fields on the dialog box are filled in automatically when you type in the "Short Name" field. Also notice that the interface for our object is named IRadio by default. This is because by standards, interface names are prefixed with an I. Press OK. At this point we have a real live COM object. If you look at the Class View of the project (by selecting Class View tab in the project

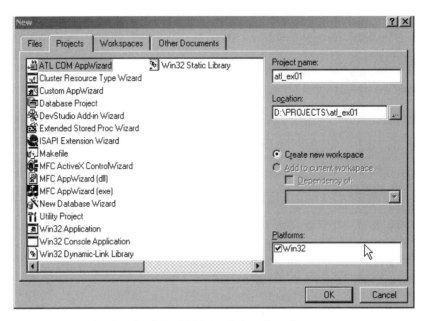

Figure 11-1. Selecting the ATL COM AppWizard project

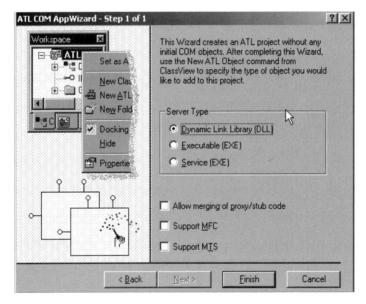

Figure 11-2. The ATL COM AppWizard at work

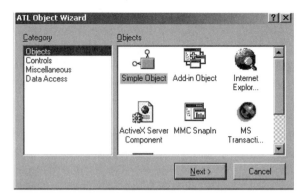

Figure 11-3. The ATL Object Wizard dialog box

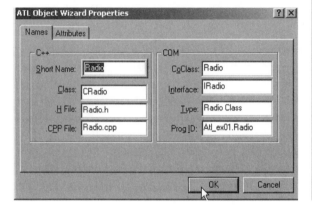

Figure 11-4. The ATL Object Wizard Properties dialog box

Figure 11-5. Viewing the ATL objects from Class View

explorer) you will see our C++ class, CRadio, and our interface IRadio, as shown in Figure 11-5.

Notice the symbol that looks like a lollipop next to our interface. This symbol is the standard notation to indicate a COM interface. Double-click it. This will cause our IDL file, atl_ex01.idl, to open and display the following code (the actual values of the uuid identifiers will differ from what is shown here):

```
// atl_ex01.idl : IDL source for atl_ex01.dll
//

// This file will be processed by the MIDL tool to
// produce the type library (atl_ex01.tlb) and marshalling code.

import "oaidl.idl";
```

```
import "ocidl.idl";
    [
        object,
        uuid(75AE1A60-0A83-4D31-8CE4-39E9417ADABE),
        dual,
        helpstring("IRadio Interface"),
        pointer_default(unique)
    ]
    interface IRadio : IDispatch
    {
    };


[
    uuid(B5B75133-B6E5-4D3A-A96D-1DFD1D8E7A56),
    version(1.0),
    helpstring("atl_ex01 1.0 Type Library")
]
library ATL_EX01Lib
{
    importlib("stdole32.tlb");
    importlib("stdole2.tlb");

    [
        uuid(A92C5BA0-0310-4BA9-B62F-93A07D28FC88),
        helpstring("Radio Class")
    ]
    coclass Radio
    {
        [default] interface IRadio;
    };
};
```

> **NOTE:** *I am going to stay very light on the details of the contents of IDL files. In fact, I only cover the parts absolutely necessary to create components in ATL. However, if you do want to learn more about IDL files and their contents there are some good resources on the MSDN Web site, but the best reference on IDL that I have found to date is* COM IDL and Interface Design *by Dr. Al Major (WROX Press Inc., 1999). He has done a good job of explaining all that goes into designing good COM interfaces with IDL.*

This file contains the interface, IRadio, for our COM object. The Microsoft Interface Definition Language (MIDL) compiler compiles this file when we build our project.

At this point our interface doesn't contain any methods or properties, which means that our component isn't going to be too useful. To remedy this, let's add a method. Right-click the IRadio interface icon in the Class View tab, and select Add Method. You will be presented with the dialog box shown in Figure 11-6.

In the Method Name field, enter **TurnOn**. In the Parameters field enter the following:

```
[in] long InitialVolume, [out,retval] long *retVal
```

Whoa, back up the truck! What the heck is that?! Don't worry: it's just an IDL method (function) declaration. You see, because IDL is not associated with any particular programming language, the way that it describes properties and methods must be programming language-independent. IDL is a language just like any other except for the fact that it doesn't actually generate executable code. Remember, the sole purpose of IDL is to create descriptions of interfaces (and their methods and properties).

Let's examine the TurnOn method declaration a little closer. The first thing we see is the [in] attribute. This is known as a directional attribute because it specifies the direction in which a parameter is passed. Specifically, it denotes that the parameter it prefixes is passed from the client to the COM object. It also implies that the parameter should not be modified by the object it is passed to, and that even if the object modifies it, any changes will be ignored by the client upon return from the method call. It is similar to passing a parameter by value in Visual Basic.

After the [in] attribute, we see the type specifier, long. Note that this is an IDL long, not a C++ long or Visual Basic long. You see, IDL defines it own data

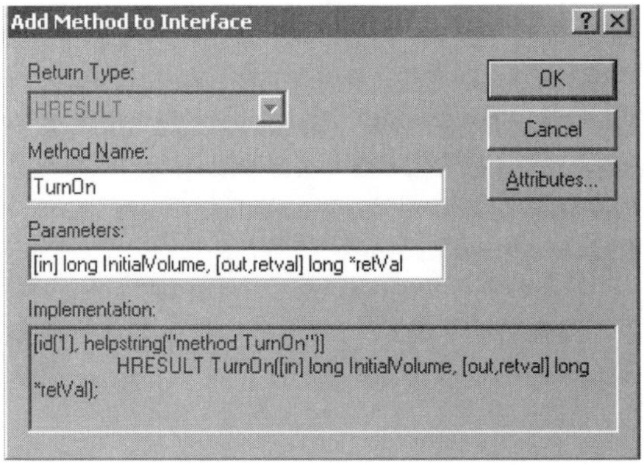

Figure 11-6. The Add Method to Interface dialog box

types, again to promote language independence. Now, following the type specifier long, we have the actual name of our method's first parameter, InitialVolume. Our function's next parameter, retVal, is again prefixed with a directional attribute, out, which indicates that the parameter will be sent from the COM object to the client, but this time it is also prefixed with another attribute, retval. The retval attribute indicates that a parameter is going to be the logical return value for the method. By *logical return value*, I mean the return value as far as the client is concerned. To see what I am talking about, go ahead and press OK on the ATL Object Wizard dialog box (if you haven't already done so). When you do this, the following line is added to our IDL file:

```
[id(1), helpstring("method TurnOn")]
HRESULT TurnOn([in] long InitialVolume, [out,retval] long *retVal);
```

This is the full IDL declaration of the TurnOn method. Don't worry about the first part of the declaration, as we are only concerned with this section of it:

```
HRESULT TurnOn([in] long InitialVolume, [out,retval] long *retVal);
```

By simple deduction it looks like the return value of the function should be of type HRESULT, and it is. But, you may be thinking that retVal was the return value of the method. Let me explain. In COM, every method that returns a value actually has two return values. One is retuned to the client (in this case it is our second parameter, retVal) and the other (the HRESULT) is returned to the COM environment. Why does COM need a return value? Well, you have to remember that there is a lot that can go wrong in a COM method call, mainly due to the fact that there is a good chance that the components are physically on different machines. Think of the HRESULT value as an indicator of the physical success of a method call, and the parameter with the retval attribute as the programmatic (or logical) return value of a method call. It is important to note that the client of the object never sees the HRESULT value. As far as the client is concerned, the logical return value is the only return value.

After all of that we now have a COM interface, IRadio, which contains one method, TurnOn. But we still don't have any implementation for that interface. We need to do that in good old C++. How, you ask? Well, this is the beauty of ATL. Simply open the CRadio node in Class View to reveal the IRadio interface, and double-click the TurnOn method, which is shown in Figure 11-7.

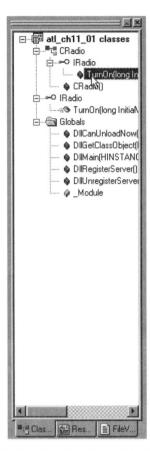

Figure 11-7. The TurnOn Method in Class View

This will open the C++ file, Radio.cpp, which is the file that we will use to implement the IRadio interface. The ATL generated C++ function skeleton looks like this:

```
STDMETHODIMP CRadio::TurnOn(long InitialVolume, long *retVal)
{
    // TODO: Add your implementation code here

    return S_OK;
}
```

Notice that the function returns S_OK. This is a constant of type HRESULT defined by COM to indicate that everything went fine physically with the method call. As you can see, we need to add some C++ code to actually implement our method though. Let's modify the function to look like this:

```
STDMETHODIMP CRadio::TurnOn(long InitialVolume, long *retVal)
{
    MessageBox(NULL,"The radio is now on.","IRadio Implementation",MB_OK);

    if (InitialVolume > 10)
    {
        *retVal = 10;
    }
    else if (InitialVolume < 0)
    {
        *retVal = 1;
    }
    else
    {
        *retVal = InitialVolume;
    }

    return S_OK;
}
```

In our method implementation we added code so that a message box will alert us that the radio is on. We also added code that will make the logical return value of the call the same as the value we passed into the parameter InitialValue. Let's test out this code with a simple Visual Basic application. But before we do that, we need to compile our ATL project. Press F7 (or select Build ... DLL from the Build menu) and create our COM object's container. During the build process you will notice that the IDL file is compiled and that our component is registered in the system registry. Once the library is built, open Visual Basic and create a Standard EXE project. Still in Visual Basic, select Project ➜ References and then check the component we just created, as shown in Figure 11-8.

Next, add a command button (named Command1) to Form1 and add the following code to its click event:

```
Private Sub Command1_Click()

Dim atlObj As New ATL_EX01Lib.Radio

MsgBox "The radio's initial volume is " & atlObj.TurnOn(7)

End Sub
```

When you run the program and click on the command button, you will see the message box from the COM object indicating that the radio is now on, followed by the message box in the Visual Basic application verifying that we re-

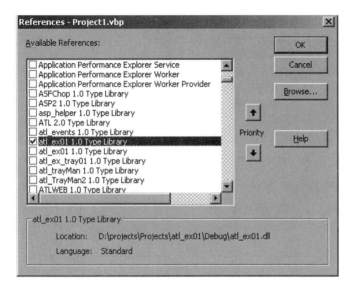

Figure 11-8. Adding a reference to the Radio object from Visual Basic

ceived the proper return value from our method call. Easy, right? Well, maybe *easy* is a little exaggerated, but it's not that difficult either.

Now the question is: How did our implementation get wired to our interface? The answer is simple; ATL did it for us in our C++ class's header file, radio.h. The actual code from that file that wires it is:

```
class ATL_NO_VTABLE CRadio :
    public CComObjectRootEx<CComSingleThreadModel>,
    public CComCoClass<CRadio, &CLSID_Radio>,
    public IDispatchImpl<IRadio, &IID_IRadio, &LIBID_ATL_EX01Lib>
```

Don't even attempt to digest this code, but just look at the structure of it. It is a regular class declaration for CRadio, which indicates that it inherits from three other classes, which happen to be template classes. The reason that you don't necessarily need to worry about this generated code is because it is boilerplate code. This means it is code that does all of the plumbing so that your object can live in a COM environment. It wouldn't be any fun to write this code even if you had to.

Now, this is where our class gets its implementation of IUnknown and all of that other good COM stuff.

Adding More Methods

At this point we could go back and repeat the same process we just finished and add another method to our interface. The reason we can do this is because our interface isn't published yet. However, if we had distributed this interface to other developers, we absolutely could not change any part of it. We would have to create the IRadio2 interface (or some other name) and make the necessary changes to it. This is why it is so important to carefully design your COM interfaces before publishing them.

Adding Properties to the Interface

Just as we added a method to our IRadio interface, we can add properties as well. However, properties in COM aren't really properties, they are actually implemented as a pair of get-set functions, just like properties in a Visual Basic class module.

To see how this works let's add a property to our IRadio interface. Right-click on the IRadio interface in Class View and select Add Property. Select long as the property type and "Volume" as its name. Leave the Parameters field empty. At this point, the Add Property To Interface dialog box should look like the dialog box shown in Figure 11-9.

Press OK. This will add the following lines to the IDL file:

```
[propget, id(2), helpstring("property Volume")]
 HRESULT Volume([out, retval] long *pVal);

[propput, id(2), helpstring("property Volume")]
 HRESULT Volume([in] long newVal);
```

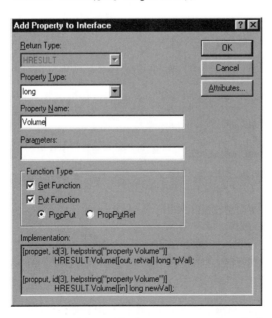

Figure 11-9. The Add Property to Interface dialog box

Notice that these are the two property statements that correlate to the Volume property. You add the implementation in the same way that we added it for the TurnOn method by double-clicking the appropriate node in Class View. Our implementation for these properties looks like this at first:

```
STDMETHODIMP CRadio::get_Volume(long *pVal)
{
    // TODO: Add your implementation code here

    return S_OK;
}


STDMETHODIMP CRadio::put_Volume(long newVal)
{
    // TODO: Add your implementation code here

    return S_OK;
}
```

And then like this after we add the code necessary to properly implement them:

```
STDMETHODIMP CRadio::get_Volume(long *pVal)
{
    *pVal = m_volume;

    return S_OK;
}


STDMETHODIMP CRadio::put_Volume(long newVal)
{
    m_volume = newVal;

    return S_OK;
}
```

> **NOTE:** *The variable* m_volume *that I use in these two property procedures is a private member variable of the* Cradio *class, which I declared in the Radio.h header file.*

Again, if you've ever created a class in Visual Basic that had properties, then this process should look familiar. Notice how our return value still goes to COM.

Now let's modify the Visual Basic application so that we can test the newly added property:

```
Private Sub Command1_Click()

Dim atlObj As New ATL_EX01Lib.Radio

MsgBox "The radio's initial volume is " & atlObj.TurnOn(7)

atlObj.Volume = 5

MsgBox "The volume is " & atlObj.Volume

End Sub
```

After running the modified Visual Basic application, you will see the following series of message boxes shown in Figure 11-10:

Figure 11-10. The test program's output (shown chronologically)

These message boxes prove that our object's property procedures are working properly. We could continue to add properties and methods to our interface in this same manner.

Conclusion

I have probably created as many mysteries as I have solved in this chapter, but don't get overwhelmed. Remember that our job as programmers is to implement our application's logic, not to deal with the mundane details of a Microsoft infrastructure like COM or ATL. Worry about using ATL to help you create fast, lightweight COM objects in C++, and let the details of the underlying technology seep into your brain slowly (as they most assuredly will) as you get more accustomed to the ATL/COM implementation. Otherwise you could spend months just learning what the code generated by ATL does, and still not be any better off as a component developer.

In Chapter 12 we create a COM object that has the same functionality as our TrayMan.DLL from the previous chapter. Come on, this is going to be fun.

CHAPTER 12

The COM Project

IN CHAPTER 11 YOU LEARNED HOW TO CREATE a simple Component Object Model (COM) component with the Active Template Library (ATL). This in turn taught you how to use the ATL framework to create COM components in C++. You will now expand this knowledge to create a more sophisticated COM component that mimics the functionality of the TrayMan.dll we created in Chapter 10. You will also learn some tips and tricks about how to create ATL/COM components so that they can be used more readily from Visual Basic.

> **NOTE:** *As I said before, ATL is a powerful tool for creating COM components in C++. It greatly reduces the amount of code that must be typed by hand, and makes available many helper classes and macros that ease dealing with COM. However, the code generated by ATL can be hard to read and follow. Try not to become distracted (or overwhelmed) by the code you will see as you look through the ATL-generated files.*

Creating the Project

To create a COM version of the TrayMan.DLL project, open Visual Studio. Select File ➔ New and choose the ATL COM AppWizard as the project type. Name it **atl_TrayMan2** and then click OK. Select DLL as the server type and check the "Allow merging of proxy/stub code" checkbox, as shown in Figure 12-1.

> **NOTE:** *Without going into the detail, merging "proxy and stub code" saves you from having to distribute a support DLL for your COM component. It increases the size of the DLL your component is housed in a little bit, but the size increase is usually worth the trade off of shipping an additional DLL.*

At this point you should see an empty project in Visual Studio. Unfortunately, this empty project isn't going to do us much good without any COM classes in it. Therefore, we need to insert an ATL Simple Object into our project by selecting New ATL Object from the Visual Studio Insert menu. This will be our TrayMan class.

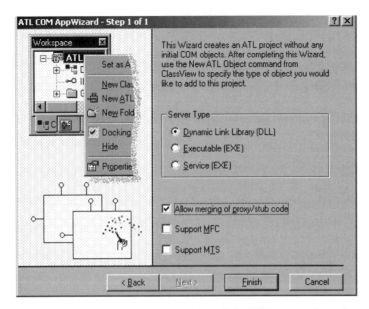

Figure 12-1. The COM App Wizard and the "Allow merging of proxy/stub code" checkbox

> **NOTE:** *Although you may see the words* class *and* object *used interchangeably throughout this book as well as in the COM world in general, they really aren't interchangeable at all. A* class *is a set of methods and properties that define a creatable entity. An* object *is a particular created instance of a class. This means that the ATL Insert menu item, "New ATL Object," should actually say "New ATL Class." I am not sure why the ATL team worded it the way they did. Regardless, as long as you look at the context in which these words are used anytime you see them (in this text or any other) it should be pretty clear which definition is meant.*

In the ATL Object Wizard Properties dialog box, enter **TrayMan** in the Short Name field. This will cause the wizard to automatically fill all of the other fields on this dialog. *Don't press OK yet!* We have to set additional properties for this object that we didn't set in the last chapter's project. Select the Attributes tab in the ATL Object Wizard Properties dialog box, and click the Support Connection Points checkbox, as shown in Figure 12-2.

By setting connection points we enable our component to raise events in its clients. Connection points are essentially the COM equivalent of the client callback function we used in our project in Chapter 10.

Click OK. At this point we are ready to start adding methods to our TrayMan class. Now, because we are going to use the TrayMan DLL from Chapter 10 as the

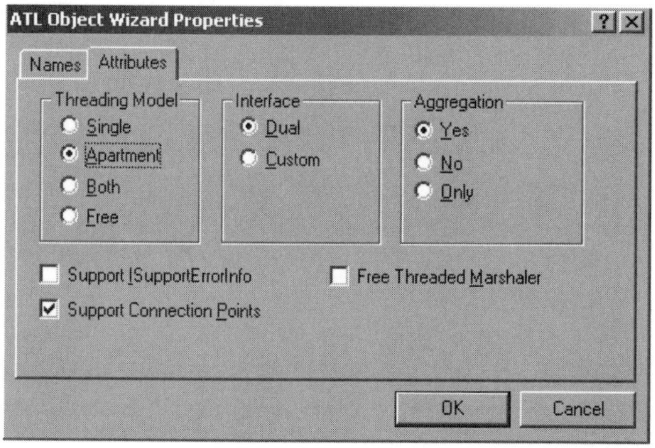

Figure 12-2. The ATL Object Wizard Properties checkbox

blueprint for our class, we will go ahead and use the same method names for our object that it did.

Adding the Methods

In ATL we always start coding with our IDL file. We do this mainly because we are following good object-oriented programming practices and designing our interfaces before we design their implementations. Right? But we also start with it because we want ATL to generate all of the C/C++ stub code for our class's implementation as well as any necessary COM support code for it. Creating our IDL file first will cause this to happen automatically.

Just in case you forgot, to add a method to an ATL object, right-click its icon in the Class View window (in this case ItrayMan), and select Add Method. Let's go ahead and do this for our first method InitTray. Enter **InitTray** in the Method field of the Add Method to Interface dialog box. And then before clicking OK, enter the following into the parameters field:

```
[in] long lngHwnd, [out,retval] long *retVal
```

Click OK. This will cause the wizard to add the InitTray method to the ITrayMan interface in our IDL file, as well as add the stub C++ code for the InitTray function to our implementation file, trayman.cpp. Let's look at the code that was added to the IDL file:

```
[id(1), helpstring("method InitTray")]
HRESULT InitTray([in] long lngHwnd,
    [out,retval] long *retVal);
```

Remember, this is the IDL representation of the InitTray function, not the C++ representation. Any language capable of using COM could use this same IDL definition of the InitTray function and then map it to its native language. Also, keep in mind that the retVal parameter is the actual return value to the client and the HRESULT return value is the return value to COM.

Let's go ahead and look at the IDL file after all of the methods from our TrayMan DLL have been added to it:

```
// atl_TrayMan2.idl : IDL source for atl_TrayMan2.dll
//

// This file will be processed by the MIDL tool to
// produce the type library (atl_TrayMan2.tlb) and marshalling code.

import "oaidl.idl";
import "ocidl.idl";
    [
        object,
        uuid(10FF6CE6-3C50-41D6-8C74-D1BFA66F6DD9),
        dual,
        helpstring("ITrayMan Interface"),
        pointer_default(unique)
    ]
    interface ITrayMan : IDispatch
    {
        typedef [v1_enum] enum
        {
            ICON_AS_STRING = 0,
            ICON_AS_HANDLE = 1
        }ICON_TYPE ;


        [id(1), helpstring("method InitTray")]
                HRESULT InitTray([in] long lngHwnd,
                [out,retval] long *retVal);

        [id(2), helpstring("method AddToTray")]
                HRESULT AddToTray([in] BSTR strTip,
                        [in] VARIANT lngIcon,
                        [in] ICON_TYPE iIconType,
                        [in] long bAnimated,
                        [out,retval] long *retVal);
```

```
        [id(3), helpstring("method Callback")]
            HRESULT Callback([in] long hwnd,
                                      [in] long uMsg,
                            [in] long lParam,
                                      [in] long wParam);


        [id(4), helpstring("method UpdateTrayTip")]
            HRESULT UpdateTrayTip([in] BSTR strTip,
                                      [out,retval] long *retVal);


        [id(5), helpstring("method UpdateTrayIcon")]
            HRESULT UpdateTrayIcon([in] VARIANT pIcon,
                                      [in] ICON_TYPE iIconType,
                                      [out,retval] long *retVal);


        [id(6), helpstring("method RemoveFromTray")]
            HRESULT RemoveFromTray([in] long bAnimate,
                                      [out,retval] long *retVal);


        [id(7), helpstring("method FreeTray")]
            HRESULT FreeTray([out,retval] long *retVal);
    }


[

    uuid(C4C5DD4F-BF0E-4444-9FF4-87E2F598B78B),
    version(1.0),
    helpstring("atl_TrayMan2 1.0 Type Library")
]
library ATL_TRAYMAN2Lib
{

    importlib("stdole32.tlb");
    importlib("stdole2.tlb");


    [

        uuid(5385838A-2069-4EC1-B35C-277F659917F4),
        helpstring("_ITrayManEvents Interface")
    ]
    dispinterface _ITrayManEvents
    {

        properties:
        methods:
        [id(1), helpstring("method MessageArrived")]
                HRESULT MessageArrived([in] long lngMessage);
```

```
    };

    [
        uuid(14F1797C-DD0B-4EDE-A14A-8B4591D4F49B),
        helpstring("TrayMan Class")
    ]
    coclass TrayMan
    {
        [default] interface ITrayMan;
        [default, source] dispinterface _ITrayManEvents;
    };
};
```

Notice that I put the following line in the IDL file:

```
typedef [v1_enum] enum
{
    ICON_AS_STRING = 0,
    ICON_AS_HANDLE = 1
}ICON_TYPE ;
```

This causes an enum to be written in C++ defining these types that is identical to the ICON_TYPES enum in the original TrayMan.dll. You can see all of the functions from our original DLL are now represented in the IDL file. However, we still need to do a couple more things before we leave our IDL file behind.

First, we need to add a method to our connection point interface. This is the method that we will call in our client when we need to send it a message from the system tray. Go to Class View and right-click the _ITrayManEvents interface (this interface was created by ATL for us when we clicked the Support Connection Points checkbox in our project setup dialog box). Select Add Method. This is the same way that we added methods to the ITrayMan interface. Enter **MessageArrived** in the Method Name field of the Add Method to Interface dialog box. Then add the following to the Parameters field:

```
[in] long lngMessage
```

Notice that there is no [out,retval] parameter for this method. This is because this method doesn't return a value to the caller. However, it does still return the HRESULT value to COM. This method will show up in our Visual Basic client as

```
Private Sub TrayManObjectName_MessageArrived(ByVal lngMessage As Long)
```

Now we need to compile our IDL file and implement the connection point we just added the MessageArrived method to. This will cause ATL to create a C++ class that implements the _ITrayManEvents interface.

Switch from Class View to File View and right-click the file atl_trayman.idl depicted in Figure 12-3.

Select Compile. This will compile the IDL file. Go back to Class View, right-click the icon for CTrayMan and select Implement ConnectionPoint. This will bring up the Implement Connection Point dialog box shown in Figure 12-4.

Click the checkbox for the ITrayManEvents interface and click OK. You can now see the newly added C++ class CPRoxy_ITrayManEvents. This class contains the actual code that will do our client callbacks. Double-click this class's icon from Class View. Upon doing so, you will discover that this class contains a single function, Fire_MessageArrived.

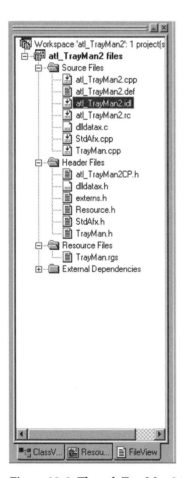

Figure 12-3. The atl_TrayMan2.idl file in Class View

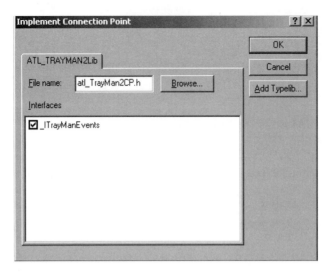

Figure 12-4. The Implement Connection Point dialog box

```
#ifndef _ATL_TRAYMAN2CP_H_
#define _ATL_TRAYMAN2CP_H_



template <class T>
class CProxy_ITrayManEvents :
public IConnectionPointImpl<T,
        &DIID__ITrayManEvents,
        CComDynamicUnkArray>
{
    //Warning this class may be recreated by the wizard.
public:
    HRESULT Fire_MessageArrived(LONG lngMessage)
    {
        CComVariant varResult;
        T* pT = static_cast<T*>(this);
        int nConnectionIndex;
        CComVariant* pvars = new CComVariant[1];
        int nConnections = m_vec.GetSize();

        for (nConnectionIndex = 0; nConnectionIndex < nConnections;
                ConnectionIndex++)
        {
            pT->Lock();
            CComPtr<IUnknown> sp = m_vec.GetAt(nConnectionIndex);
            pT->Unlock();
```

```
        IDispatch* pDispatch = reinterpret_cast<IDispatch*>(sp.p);
        if (pDispatch != NULL)
        {
            VariantClear(&varResult);
            pvars[0] = lngMessage;
            DISPPARAMS disp = { pvars, NULL, 1, 0 };
            pDispatch->Invoke(0x1, IID_NULL, LOCALE_USER_DEFAULT,
                                            DISPATCH_METHOD,
                                            &disp, &varResult,
                                            NULL, NULL);
        }
    }
    delete[] pvars;
    return varResult.scode;


    }
};
#endif
```

Anytime you want to callback to a client, just call this function and pass a long as the parameter. COM and ATL take care of the rest. Unless you have hand coded all of this before, it is hard to appreciate the value in this. But trust me, we have just done a couple hours worth of work with two or three clicks of the mouse!

Implementing the Interface

You can see from the IDL file that in this version of TrayMan the parameter for InitTray is of type long as opposed to type HWND as it was in the original version. The reason for this is that in COM, data type HWND does not exist. You see, COM defines its own set of data types and restricts components to using these COM types. Beyond that, only a subset of COM types are automation compatible (Visual Basic, VBScript, VBA, and so on). Because we are using Visual Basic, we are restricted to this smaller set of types. Included in the automation compatible types are long, which is a 32-bit Visual Basic Long and BSTR, which is a Visual Basic String. If it seems coincidental that automation types match so nicely to Visual Basic, it is not. The automation types were created for, or because of, Visual Basic. Fortunately most non-COM types can be easily cast to COM-compatible types. For instance, an HWND can be cast to a long with a standard cast in the following form:

```
HWND hwnd = FindWindow("MyWindow",NULL);  //Get an HWND value
long lngHwnd = (long)hwnd; //cast the HWND to a long
```

The reason that this can be done so easily is that both an HWND and a COM long are 32-bit signed numbers. They can both hold the same value; it's simply a matter of interpretation, which is what the cast does: it tells the compiler how to interpret the value stored in the variable. We'll see more about this as we continue to look at the C++ code that implements our component's interface later in this chapter.

Converting the TrayMan.DLL Functions

In our COM object's interface definition (IDL file methods), we converted the functions from our TrayMan DLL into COM-friendly versions of the same functions. This involved (with a couple of exceptions) converting all numeric parameters to longs and all char* parameters to BSTRs (we will discuss the BSTR data type more in a moment). The exceptions to this are the AddToTray and UpdateTrayIcon functions. The AddToTray function originally looked like this:

```
BOOL __stdcall AddToTray(char *szTip,pCbFunc cb,void *pIcon,ICON_TYPE
IconType,bool bAnimated)
```

but the COM version was modified to look like this:

```
STDMETHODIMP CTrayMan::AddToTray(BSTR strTip, VARIANT varIcon, ICON_TYPE
iIconType, long bAnimated, long *retVal)
```

You can see that in the new version of AddToTray we removed the parameter, pCbFunc cb, which was our client callback function pointer. We removed this parameter because we can't use function callbacks in COM in the same way that we did in our DLL. COM doesn't assume that an object and its client are going to be in the same process address space or even on the same machine when a function call is made. COM always calls an object's methods without regard of the client's location. This is a very powerful aspect of COM called *Location transparency*. Location transparency frees the programmer from worrying about the physical semantics of calling an object. In other words, the programmer never has to worry about where the object they are calling is located; COM guarantees to take care of finding and calling it. Given this fact it becomes obvious that a function callback will not be guaranteed to work in COM, not to mention the fact that it is strictly against the rules of COM. So then how are we to notify the client of events from our object? We will do it with connection points, which I discuss later in this chapter.

Okay, were almost ready to dig in to the actual function implementations in our TrayMan class. We just need a little detail about the VARIANT and BSTR data types.

The VARIANT Data Type

Notice that we changed the void* pIcon parameter in InitTray to a VARIANT, varIcon. Yes, this is the all too familiar variant that we have grown to love (or hate) in Visual Basic. The reason we changed this parameter is because COM doesn't define a void* data type. COM provides void* -like functionality through the VARIANT data type.

Recall that the reason we needed the void* data type was so that we could pass either a string path to an .ico file or a HICON as the value of pIcon interchangeably. This is why we have to use the VARIANT data type here. A VARIANT in C++ is a large (16-byte) union. Following is the definition of the VARIANT data type in C++:

```
typedef struct tagVARIANT  {
    VARTYPE vt;
    unsigned short wReserved1;
    unsigned short wReserved2;
    unsigned short wReserved3;
    union {
        unsigned char       bVal;       // VT_UI1.
        short               iVal;       // VT_I2    .
        long                lVal;       // VT_I4    .
        float               fltVal;     // VT_R4    .
        double              dblVal;     // VT_R8    .
        VARIANT_BOOL        boolVal;    // VT_BOOL.
        SCODE               scode;      // VT_ERROR.
        CY                  cyVal;      // VT_CY    .
        DATE                date;       // VT_DATE.
        BSTR                bstrVal;    // VT_BSTR.
        IUnknown        FAR* punkVal;   // VT_UNKNOWN.
        IDispatch       FAR* pdispVal;  // VT_DISPATCH.
        SAFEARRAY       FAR* parray;    // VT_ARRAY|*.
        unsigned char   FAR* pbVal;     // VT_BYREF|VT_UI1.
        short           FAR* piVal;     // VT_BYREF|VT_I2.
        long            FAR* plVal;     // VT_BYREF|VT_I4.
        float           FAR* pfltVal;   // VT_BYREF|VT_R4.
        double          FAR* pdblVal;   // VT_BYREF|VT_R8.
        VARIANT_BOOL    FAR* pboolVal;  // VT_BYREF|VT_BOOL.
        SCODE           FAR* pscode;    // VT_BYREF|VT_ERROR.
        CY              FAR* pcyVal;    // VT_BYREF|VT_CY.
        DATE            FAR* pdate;     // VT_BYREF|VT_DATE.
        BSTR            FAR* pbstrVal;  // VT_BYREF|VT_BSTR.
        IUnknown FAR*   FAR* ppunkVal;  // VT_BYREF|VT_UNKNOWN.
```

```
        IDispatch FAR*       FAR* ppdispVal;    // VT_BYREF|VT_DISPATCH.
        SAFEARRAY FAR*       FAR* pparray;    // VT_ARRAY|*.
        VARIANT              FAR* pvarVal;    // VT_BYREF|VT_VARIANT.
        void                 FAR* byref;    // Generic ByRef.
    };
};
```

As you can see, the VARIANT data type contains all other COM automation data types. Therefore, we can safely use it to do what our void pointer did in the previous version of TrayMan. (We will see how to use a VARIANT later in this chapter when we look at the AddToTray function's code listing.) Other than that, the AddToTray method has remained true to the original version with the aforementioned type changes. The UpdateTrayIcon was modified in the same manner as to enable the same type of flexibility.

The BSTR Data Type

As I said before, a BSTR is a Visual Basic string. In fact, the name BSTR is short for *Basic String* (as in Visual *Basic*). A BSTR as used by Visual Basic is essentially an array of Unicode characters. And what exactly is Unicode, you ask?

Unicode is a character set just like the ASCII (American Standard Code for Information Interchange) character set except that instead of only containing 255 characters, Unicode can contain up to 65,536 characters. Using Unicode makes it possible to have a single character set that can contain the characters for any or almost all of the languages in the world. Windows NT uses Unicode internally as does Visual Basic. Now you may be thinking "We used Visual Basic to talk to our TrayMan DLL in Chapter 10 and didn't use Unicode." This is because we declared our String variables "ByVal As String" in our Visual Basic Declare statements. When you do this, you tell Visual Basic that you want an ASCII copy of the variable passed as the parameter declared "ByVal As String." Had we declared our strings in the first version of TrayMan.DLL "As String," which is equivalent to "ByRef As String," we would have passed a pointer to a BSTR. I captured a BSTR in the Memory window in C++, shown in Figure 12-5. The word "Hello" was passed from Visual Basic ByRef.

You can see that each letter is separated by a NULL (or character code 0). This is because you are looking at Unicode; in Unicode each character is two bytes. In ASCII, the letter "H" is represented as 48. In Unicode the letter "H" is represented as 0048—two bytes.

Our Visual Basic clients are going to be passing BSTRs to our functions, so we need to learn to deal with them. Fortunately ATL provides some nifty macros that convert BSTRs to char*s for us. These are very useful in this type of project in which we are calling ASCII application program interface (API) functions exclu-

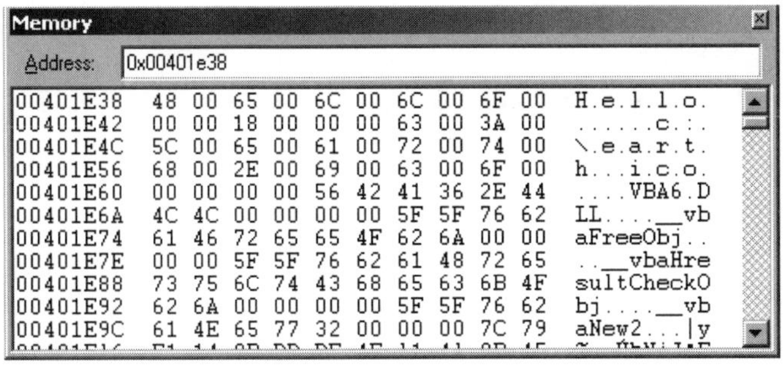

Figure 12-5. The Memory window

sively. We will see these macros in action as we go through the various functions in our class. We won't be using Unicode except to convert it to a `char*` at the beginning of our TrayMan functions that take BSTR parameters. To learn more about Unicode, check out the resources offered by MSDN.

The Full Implementation

Now that the requisite discussions are out of the way, we can start examining the body of each function in the implementation file, trayman.cpp, and their declarations in the header file, trayman.h.

trayman.h

Following is the complete listing from the header file, trayman.h:

```
// TrayMan.h : Declaration of the CTrayMan

#ifndef __TRAYMAN_H_
#define __TRAYMAN_H_

#include "resource.h"       // main symbols
#include "atl_TrayMan2CP.h"

/////////////////////////////////////////////////
// CTrayMan
class ATL_NO_VTABLE CTrayMan :
    public CComObjectRootEx<CComSingleThreadModel>,
    public CComCoClass<CTrayMan, &CLSID_TrayMan>,
    public IConnectionPointContainerImpl<CTrayMan>,
    public IDispatchImpl<ITrayMan,
```

```
                    &IID_ITrayMan, &LIBID_ATL_TRAYMAN2Lib>,
        public CProxy_ITrayManEvents< CTrayMan >,
        public IProvideClassInfo2Impl<&CLSID_TrayMan,&DIID__ITrayManEvents>
{
public:
    CTrayMan()
    {
    }


DECLARE_REGISTRY_RESOURCEID(IDR_TRAYMAN)


DECLARE_PROTECT_FINAL_CONSTRUCT()


BEGIN_COM_MAP(CTrayMan)
    COM_INTERFACE_ENTRY(ITrayMan)
    COM_INTERFACE_ENTRY(IConnectionPointContainer)
    COM_INTERFACE_ENTRY_IMPL(IConnectionPointContainer)
        COM_INTERFACE_ENTRY(IProvideClassInfo)
        COM_INTERFACE_ENTRY(IProvideClassInfo2)
    COM_INTERFACE_ENTRY2(IDispatch, ITrayMan)
END_COM_MAP()


BEGIN_CONNECTION_POINT_MAP(CTrayMan)
CONNECTION_POINT_ENTRY(DIID__ITrayManEvents)
END_CONNECTION_POINT_MAP()



// ITrayMan
public:
    STDMETHOD(FreeTray)(/*[out,retval]*/ long *retVal);
    STDMETHOD(RemoveFromTray)(/*[in]*/ long bAnimate,
                                    /*[out,retval]*/ long *retVal);
    STDMETHOD(UpdateTrayIcon)(/*[in]*/ VARIANT pIcon,
                                    /*[in]*/ ICON_TYPE iIconType,
                                      /*[out,retval]*/ long *retVal);
    STDMETHOD(UpdateTrayTip)(/*[in]*/ BSTR strTip,
                                /*[out,retval]*/ long *retVal);
    STDMETHOD(Callback)(/*[in]*/ long hwnd, /*[in]*/ long uMsg,
            /*[in]*/ long lParam, /*[in]*/ long wParam);
    STDMETHOD(AddToTray)(/*[in]*/ BSTR strTip, /*[in]*/ VARIANT lngIcon,
                            /*[in]*/ ICON_TYPE iIconType,
                            /*[in]*/ long bAnimated,
                            /*[out,retval]*/ long *retVal);
```

```
        STDMETHOD(InitTray)(/*[in]*/ long lngHwnd,
                                    /*[out,retval]*/ long *retVal);
private:
    long m_hWndIndex;
      HWND getSystemTrayHwnd(void);
      void drawInflateAnimation(void);
      void drawDeflateAnimation(void);
    NOTIFYICONDATA m_nid;
    HICON m_hIcon;
    HWND m_hWnd;

    typedef long (__stdcall *pWndProcFunc)(HWND hwnd,
                                           UINT uMsg,
                                           WPARAM wParam,
                              LPARAM lParam);
};


#endif //__TRAYMAN_H_
```

You can see the class declaration of the TrayMan class is much different than the C++ classes that we have seen to date. That is because it uses multiple *inheritance*—which means our class, TrayMan, has more than one class as its base. You can also see that each of the inherited classes is a C++ template class. These template classes are the heart of ATL. They implement IUnknown and other COM interfaces for you. By inheriting from these ATL-provided classes, you save yourself from typing (and debugging) about 250 to 1000 lines of code, depending on your implementation. (Understand that most of the code that you see in the header file was generated by ATL. I have set in bold typeface the additions I made to it.)

Let's quickly review the additions to the header file. First, I added the following line, the inheritance list (the comma separated list of base classes following the class name):

```
public IProvideClassInfo2Impl<&CLSID_TrayMan,&DIID__ITrayManEvents>
```

This is another ATL provided template class. The reason I added it is because Visual Basic requires it in order to receive callbacks. The first parameter is the COM identifier of the ITrayMan interface. This value is generated by ATL and is always in the form CLSID_C++CLASSNAME, such that if your C++ class were named *Radio*, for example, its identifier would be CLSID_Radio. You can do this easily for any object you create in ATL.

The second parameter is the COM identifier for the _ITrayManEvents interface. I took this value from the IDL file. Just look for the name of your connection point, which is _ITrayManEvents in this case, and you will find it.

Next I added

```
COM_INTERFACE_ENTRY(IProvideClassInfo)
COM_INTERFACE_ENTRY(IProvideClassInfo2)
```

These two lines go hand in hand with the first one I added. They finish the routing necessary in order to do callbacks to Visual Basic clients. Other than these lines I added the same global variables that were in the TrayMan.DLL. (I also added one extra variable: m_hwndIndex; we'll see why in a minute.) ATL did all the rest!

> **NOTE:** *Now please don't get frustrated because I have glossed over so much of the code in this file. I encourage you to dig in and learn as much as you can about ATL. However, there just isn't room in this book to even begin to explain it all. To learn more about ATL, I recommend picking up a copy of* ATL Internals *by Brent Rector, Chris Sells, and Jim Springfield (Addison-Wesley, 1999). These guys are the ATL experts (Jim Springfield invented ATL!).*

trayman.cpp

Now for the fun part: writing the C++ code that implements the ITrayMan interface. For each method we added to the ITrayMan interface, a matching C++ function stub was written by ATL in our implementation file, trayman.cpp. Take a look at the InitTray C++ function stub by opening the ITrayMan node in the Class View window and double-clicking the InitTray method:

```
STDMETHODIMP CTrayMan::InitTray(long hWnd, long *retVal)
{
    // TODO: Add your implementation code here
    return S_OK;
}
```

You can see that the function body is empty except for the return of the HRESULT. This is what each of our functions looks like at this point. We must fill in all of the code for each of the methods we declared in the IDL file.

Following is the complete listing from that file. (This listing shows the file after I wrote the appropriate code inside the ATL-generated function stubs.)

```
// TrayMan.cpp : Implementation of CTrayMan
#include "stdafx.h"
#include "Atl_TrayMan2.h"
#include "TrayMan.h"
```

```
#include "externs.h"
#include <shellapi.h>
#include <comdef.h>
/////////////////////////////////////////////
// CTrayMan

#define     DLL_EX_TRAY01_MESSAGE     WM_USER + 0xBffe
#define ICON_AS_STRING              0
#define ICON_AS_HANDLE              1

STDMETHODIMP CTrayMan::InitTray(long hWnd, long *retVal)
{
    //check the passed in parameters
    if ((!hWnd))
    {
        *retVal = FALSE;
    }

    //get the next available hWnd index
    m_hWndIndex = getNextAvailableHWNDIndex();

    //save the client's handle
    m_hWnd = (HWND)hWnd;

    //save the client hwnd
    g_prevWndProc[m_hWndIndex].hWnd = (HWND)m_hWnd;

    //clear the wndProc pointer
    g_prevWndProc[m_hWndIndex].pwndProc = NULL;

    *retVal = TRUE;

    return S_OK;
}

STDMETHODIMP CTrayMan::AddToTray(BSTR strTip, VARIANT varIcon,
                                 ICON_TYPE iIconType,
                                 long bAnimated,
                                 long *retVal)
{
    //declare ATL conversion macros
    USES_CONVERSION;
```

```
char *szTip = W2A(strTip);

//flags variable for the NOTIFYICONDATA structure
int iFlags;

//be sure that we have a valid hwnd
if (!m_hWnd)
{
    return FALSE;
}

//update the NOTIFYICONDATA flags
iFlags = iFlags | NIF_MESSAGE;
//}

if (ICON_AS_HANDLE == iIconType)
{
    //Load the handle of the passed in Icon
    m_hIcon = (HICON)varIcon.intVal;

    //update the NOTIFYICONDATA flags
    iFlags = iFlags | NIF_ICON;
}
else
{
    //ANSI path to icon
    char *szIcon = W2A(varIcon.bstrVal);

    //Load the handle of the passed in Icon using
    m_hIcon = ExtractIcon((HINSTANCE)GetModuleHandle(NULL),szIcon,0);

    int x = GetLastError();

    //check for a vaild icon handle
    if ((int)m_hIcon == 1 || (int)m_hIcon == NULL)
    {
        return FALSE;
    }
    else
    {
        //add the icon flag to the NOTIFYICONDATA structure
        iFlags = iFlags | NIF_ICON;
    }
```

```
}

//load the address of the passed tip string
if (szTip)
{
    //copy the passed in tip string to the NOTIFYICONDATA struct
    strcpy(m_nid.szTip,szTip);

    //add the TIP flag to the NOTIFYICONDATA struct
    iFlags = iFlags | NIF_TIP;
}

//Load the NOTIFYICONDATA structure with the appropriate values.
m_nid.hIcon = m_hIcon;
m_nid.hWnd = (HWND)m_hWnd;

//add flags to the NOTIFYICONDATA struct
m_nid.uFlags = iFlags;

//Set our unique identifier message for the icon in the tray.
m_nid.uCallbackMessage = DLL_EX_TRAY01_MESSAGE;

//set the icon ID
m_nid.uID = 100;

//Start subclassing the client.
g_prevWndProc[m_hWndIndex].pwndProc = (pWndProcFunc)SetWindowLong(
                                      (HWND)m_hWnd,
                                      GWL_WNDPROC,
                    (long)wndProc);

//save the pointer to the object
g_prevWndProc[m_hWndIndex].pObj = this;

//Send the icon to the tray
Shell_NotifyIcon(NIM_ADD,&m_nid);

//check the animation flag
if (bAnimated)
{
    drawDeflateAnimation();
}
```

```
        *retVal = TRUE;

        return S_OK;
}

void CTrayMan::drawDeflateAnimation()
{
    RECT rcTo;
    RECT rcFrom;
    HWND hwndTray;

    //get the handle for the system tray
    hwndTray = getSystemTrayHwnd();

    //get the coordinates of the client window
    GetWindowRect((HWND)m_hWnd,&rcFrom);

    //get the coordinates of the system tray
    GetWindowRect((HWND)hwndTray,&rcTo);

    //draw the animation
    DrawAnimatedRects((HWND)m_hWnd,IDANI_CAPTION,&rcFrom,&rcTo);
}

void CTrayMan::drawInflateAnimation()
{
    RECT rcTo;
    RECT rcFrom;
    HWND hwndTray;

    //get the handle for the system tray
    hwndTray = getSystemTrayHwnd();

    //get the coordinates of the client window
    GetWindowRect((HWND)m_hWnd,&rcTo);

    //get the coordinates of the system tray
    GetWindowRect((HWND)hwndTray,&rcFrom);

    //draw the animation
    //IDANI_CAPTION = 3  -- The definition Is
    //missing from some of the MS header files
    DrawAnimatedRects((HWND)m_hWnd,IDANI_CAPTION,&rcFrom,&rcTo);
```

```
}

HWND CTrayMan::getSystemTrayHwnd()
{
    HWND hwndTray;

    char szShellStr[] = "Shell_TrayWnd";

    char szTrayStr[] = "TrayNotifyWnd";

    HWND hwndStartMenu = FindWindow(szShellStr, NULL);

    HWND hwndChild = GetWindow(hwndStartMenu, GW_CHILD);

    int  iClassName = 0;

    //Loop through all siblings until we find the 'System Tray'
//(A.K.A. --> TrayNotifyWnd)
    do
    {
        char szClass[255];

        iClassName = GetClassName(hwndChild, szClass, 60);

        //If it is the tray then store the handle.
        if (strstr(szClass,szTrayStr))
        {
            hwndTray = hwndChild;
            break;
        }
        else
        {
            //If we didn't find it, go to the next sibling.
            hwndChild = GetWindow(hwndChild, GW_HWNDNEXT);
        }

    }while (true);

    return hwndTray;
}

STDMETHODIMP CTrayMan::UpdateTrayTip(BSTR strTip, long *retVal)
{
```

```
                    //declare ATL conversion macros
                    USES_CONVERSION;

                    //check for a valid pointer
                    if (!strTip)
                    {
                        return FALSE;
                    }

                    //convert tip to ansi
                    char *szTip = W2A(strTip);

                    //copy the tip to the NOTIFYICONDATA structure
                    strcpy(m_nid.szTip,szTip);

                    //update the icon in the tray
                    Shell_NotifyIcon(NIM_MODIFY,&m_nid);

                    *retVal = TRUE;

                    return S_OK;
                }


STDMETHODIMP CTrayMan::UpdateTrayIcon(
                    VARIANT varIcon, ICON_TYPE iIconType,
                    long *retVal)
{
    //declare ATL conversion macros
    USES_CONVERSION;

    //check to see if we are loading our icon from a string or a handle
    if (ICON_AS_HANDLE == iIconType)
    {
        //Load the handle of the passed in Icon
        m_hIcon = (HICON)varIcon.intVal;
    }
    else
    {
        //ANSI path to icon
        char *szIcon = W2A(varIcon.bstrVal);

        //Load the handle of the passed in Icon using UNICODE API call
        m_hIcon = ExtractIcon((HINSTANCE)GetModuleHandle(NULL),szIcon,0);
```

```
        //check for a valid HICON value
        if ((int)m_hIcon == 1 || (int)m_hIcon == NULL)
        {
            return FALSE;
        }
    }

    //update the NOTIFYICONDATA struct
    m_nid.hIcon = m_hIcon;

    //Change the icon in the tray
    Shell_NotifyIcon(NIM_MODIFY,&m_nid);

    *retVal = TRUE;

    return S_OK;
}

STDMETHODIMP CTrayMan::RemoveFromTray(long bAnimate, long *retVal)
{
    //remove the icon from the tray
    Shell_NotifyIcon(NIM_DELETE,&m_nid);

    //check for animation flag
    if (bAnimate)
    {
        drawInflateAnimation();
    }

    SetWindowLong(m_hWnd,GWL_WNDPROC,
                        (long)g_prevWndProc[m_hWndIndex].pwndProc);

    //check for a valid icon handle
    if (m_hIcon)
    {
        //free the icon
        DestroyIcon(m_hIcon);
    }

    *retVal = TRUE;

    return S_OK;
}
```

```
STDMETHODIMP CTrayMan::FreeTray(long *retVal)
{
    //Reset all global data
    m_hWnd = 0;
    m_hIcon = 0;
    memset(&m_nid,0,sizeof(m_nid));

    *retVal = TRUE;
    return S_OK;
}


STDMETHODIMP CTrayMan::Callback(long hwnd,
                                long uMsg, long lParam, long wParam)
{
    Fire_MessageArrived(wParam);
    return TRUE;
}



/*********************************************
Global Function Implementations
*********************************************/
long __stdcall wndProc(HWND hwnd,UINT uMsg,WPARAM wParam,LPARAM lParam)
{
    //Check for our custom tray message
    if (uMsg == DLL_EX_TRAY01_MESSAGE)
    {
        //call the stored pointer to the ITrayMan interface
        g_prevWndProc[findWndProc(hwnd)].pObj->Callback(
                                                (long)hwnd,uMsg,
                                                wParam,lParam);
    }

    //call the default message handler
    return CallWindowProcA(g_prevWndProc[findWndProc(hwnd)].pwndProc,
                                                hwnd,
                                                uMsg,
                                                wParam,
                                                lParam);
}



long __stdcall findWndProc(HWND hWnd)
```

```
{
    //loop through all of the hwnd values in the array
    for (long i = 0; i < sizeof(g_prevWndProc); i++)
    {
        //if a match is found then return its index
        if (g_prevWndProc[i].hWnd == hWnd)
        {
            return i;
        }
    }

    return 0;
}


long getNextAvailableHWNDIndex(void)
{
    return g_hwndIndex++;
}
```

At first glance, this trayman.cpp file looks identical to the one in the original TrayMan.DLL. That's because, pretty much, it is. However, in this version I had to add a few functions due to the fact that we are using COM. Let me explain.

We have a fundamental problem trying to implement TrayMan.DLL functionality in a COM object. The problem is that a COM object is an instance of a COM class. When you create a new instance of a COM class (a COM object), that instance of the object gets its own copy of the class's *instance data*. Instance data is any method or variable that is not declared as static. static data is shared among all instances of a class. Consider the following code:

```
class t1
{
public:
    static int g_num;
    int m_num;
};
```

Each instance of the class t1 will get its own copy of the m_num variable because m_num is instance data (or an instance variable), while every instance of t1 will use the same copy of the variable g_num because g_num is a static variable (or class variable).

The original version of TrayMan called the WIN32 API function SetWindowLong in order to replace the WndProc function for a client window. Windows would then call this replacement WndProc function to notify the window of messages. This was not a problem because the DLL and client were on a one-to-one relationship: each client received its own copy of the DLL's functions.

In our COM version, we don't have this luxury. In the COM version we have to assume that more than one instance of our TrayMan class may be active at one time. The problem, however, is that Windows requires a WndProc function to be a global, non-instance function. This means that the WndProc function we pass to SetWindowLong can't be a member of the TrayMan class. (Actually it could, but this would require a lot of sneaking around behind COM's back, and we just don't want to do that.) So what do we do? Use global data and functions to solve the problem. In addition to static and instance data, there is also *global data*. Global data is data that exists in a process address space, which is accessible by any object (or other entity) in the space. The additional header file, externs.h, contains all of the global data declarations that are going to help us solve our WndProc problem, which is listed here:

```
//function pointer to a WndProc
typedef long (__stdcall *pWndProcFuncCast)
            (struct HWND__ *,unsigned int,unsigned int,long);
//structure to hold instance data
typedef struct tagTRAYMAN_CB
{
    HWND                hWnd;
    pWndProcFuncCast        pwndProc;
    ITrayMan*           pObj;
}TRAYMAN_CB;


//subclassing function
long __stdcall wndProc(HWND hwnd,
                       UINT uMsg,
                       WPARAM wParam,
                       LPARAM lParam);
//helper lookup function
long __stdcall findWndProc(HWND hWnd); //finds the index for a hWnd

//global array of TrayMan instances
TRAYMAN_CB g_prevWndProc[64];    //Old windows proc storage

//helper counter function
long getNextAvailableHWNDIndex(void); //retrieves next available index

//global index counter
long g_hwndIndex = 0;
```

Follow along with me as I explain the theory behind this file's contents (the global data). Take a look at the TRAYMAN_CB struct. It contains three elements: a HWND, a pointer to a WndProc function, and a pointer to an ITrayMan interface. The g_prevWndProc array is an array of TRAYMAN_CBs. The idea behind having an array of TRAYMAN_CB structs is to enable objects to save their HWND, original WndProc, and a pointer to themselves in a global area for later use. When the global WndProc is called by Windows, the HWND parameter will contain the HWND of the client that belongs to a particular object, which is also the object that the WndProc message is destined for. The WndProc can then use the HWND parameter to check each TRAYMAN_CB struct in the g_prevWndProc array. Once it finds a matching HWND in the array, it can then obtain the ITrayMan pointer from that same array element and use it to call the Callback function in the pointed to object, passing along the uMsg, wParam, and lParam values originally passed in by Windows.

All of the functions and variables in the elements.h file are used to accomplish this, as you will see in the body of the TrayMan methods.

InitTray does exactly the same thing as the original version did: it initializes the data elements of the object. It also saves the TRAYMAN_CB data elements in the global g_prevWndProc array. Notice the call to getNextAvailableHWNDIndex. The getNextAvailableHWNDIndex function gets the next global index available. The object saves this index in an instance variable and then uses it in future manipulations of g_prevWndProc. This ensures that the object is altering the right element of the g_prevWndProc array.

The next function we encounter is AddToTray. Again, this version is very close to the original. One difference though is the first few lines of the function:

```
//declare ATL conversion macros
USES_CONVERSION;

char *szTip = W2A(strTip);
```

USES_CONVERSION is an ATL macro that enables the ATL character conversion macros. This is important because the next call we make is to W2A, an ATL macro that converts a Unicode string to an ASCII string. Notice that once we convert the BSTR parameter, strTip, to a char pointer, we use szTip for the remainder of the function. This prevents us from having to work with Unicode strings. Notice how we also use the Unicode conversion function to get a char pointer to the VARIANT, varIcon. AddToTray then continues to do pretty much the same things it did in the original. In fact, the only real difference between the new version and the old one is the following:

```
//Start subclassing the client.
g_prevWndProc[m_hWndIndex].pwndProc =
                           (pWndProcFunc)SetWindowLong(
                                                    (HWND)m_hWnd,
                                                    GWL_WNDPROC,
                                                    (long)wndProc);
//save the pointer to the object
g_prevWndProc[m_hWndIndex].pObj = this;
```

The new version saves the return value of SetWindowLong (which is the pointer to the original WndProc function for the client window) in the g_prevWndProc array. Saving this value will enable the necessary call to CallWndProc once the window is sub-classed. The new version also saves the objects this pointer, which is a pointer to the object's ITrayMan interface functions. Again, this enables the global WndProc function to call the correct instance of the TrayMan class when a message arrives.

The rest of the functions in this file that were carried forward from the original are almost identical to their previous versions (except for the addition of Unicode conversion macros). This is because nothing changed functionally between the DLL version of TrayMan and this version. The changes we are making are necessary due to environment only. We still want the TrayMan component to do the same functions, regardless of the version (COM or DLL) used.

Now, we need to look at the TrayMan::Callback function. The global WndProc function, wndProc, calls this function each time a message arrives for a specific object. It takes the same parameters as a WndProc function. This makes sense because it is simply a surrogate WndProc function for the object in which it resides, which means it is also an instance method (not static or global). This function takes the wParam parameter that is passed to it and passes it to the client via the Fire_MessageArrived Connection Point method.

Looking at the Client Application

The client application we will use to test our COM version of TrayMan is the same client application we used to test the original version, except that I have added the necessary code to call the COM object to it using conditional compilation so that the original source code could be seen for comparison's sake. Following is the client code, which consists of three files: a form, a regular module, and a class module. The class module is used so that we can declare our TrayMan object WithEvents (you can only declare an object WithEvents in a class module). Consequently, all calls to the TrayMan object are routed through the class module.

Form1.frm

Following is the Form1.frm client code:

```vb
Option Explicit

Private Sub cmdIcon_Click()

'Get the name of the icon to load
With cdlgMain
    .DialogTitle = "Choose an Icon File..."
    .Filter = "Icon Files (*.ico)|*.ico"
    .ShowOpen

    'If the user pressed "Cancel" then bail
    If .CancelError Then
        Exit Sub
    End If

    'Load the file name
    lblIcon.Caption = .FileName

    'update the icon in the tray
    If Me.Visible = False Then
        #If COM_TRAYMAN Then
            objTM.comTrayMan.UpdateTrayIcon .FileName, ICON_AS_STRING
        #Else
            UpdateTrayIcon .FileName, 0
        #End If
    End If

    'Load the icon into the image box
    Set Image1.Picture = LoadPicture(.FileName)

End With

End Sub

Private Sub cmdAddToTray_Click()

'Add the icon to the Tray
#If COM_TRAYMAN Then
    objTM.comTrayMan.AddToTray _
```

```
                    "Double click or press the right mouse button.", _
                    lblIcon.Caption, 0, True
#Else
    AddToTray "Double click or press the right mouse button.", _
                AddressOf CallBack, lblIcon.Caption, ByVal 0, True
#End If

'Hide the form
Me.Hide

'Disable the command button
cmdAddToTray.Enabled = False

End Sub

Private Sub cmdAnimate_Click()

If cmdAnimate.Caption <> "Stop!" Then
    'Add the icon to the tray
    #If COM_TRAYMAN Then
        objTM.comTrayMan.AddToTray "Now drawing animated icon.", _
                        App.Path & "\ball1.ico", ByVal 0, False
    #Else
        AddToTray "Now drawing animated icon.", _
                        AddressOf CallBack, _
                        App.Path & "\ball1.ico", ByVal 0, False
    #End If

    cmdAnimate.Caption = "Stop!"

    cmdAddToTray.Enabled = False

    tmrIcon.Enabled = True
Else
    cmdAnimate.Caption = "Animate Tray"

    cmdAddToTray.Enabled = True

    tmrIcon.Enabled = False

    'Remove the icon from the tray
    #If COM_TRAYMAN Then
        objTM.comTrayMan.RemoveFromTray False
    #Else
```

```
        RemoveFromTray False
    #End If

End If

End Sub

Private Sub Form_QueryUnload(Cancel As Integer, UnloadMode As Integer)

'Free the tray
#If COM_TRAYMAN Then
    objTM.comTrayMan.FreeTray
#Else
    FreeTray
#End If

End Sub

Private Sub mnuChangeIcon_Click()

If tmrIcon.Enabled = True Then
    tmrIcon.Enabled = False
End If

Call cmdIcon_Click

End Sub

Private Sub mnuChangeTip_Click()

Dim strInput As String

strInput = InputBox("Please enter the tip text.", _
            App.EXEName & " -- Change Tray Tip")

'Update the tray tip
#If COM_TRAYMAN Then
    objTM.comTrayMan.UpdateTrayTip strInput
#Else
    UpdateTrayTip strInput
#End If

End Sub
```

```vb
            Private Sub mnuExit_Click()

            'Remove the icon from the tray
            #If COM_TRAYMAN Then
                objTM.comTrayMan.RemoveFromTray False
             #Else
                RemoveFromTray False
             #End If

             Unload Me

            End Sub

            Private Sub mnuMessage_Click()

            MsgBox "Hello from the tray!"

            End Sub

            Private Sub mnuShow_Click()

            'Remove the icon from the tray
            #If COM_TRAYMAN Then
                objTM.comTrayMan.RemoveFromTray True
            #Else
                RemoveFromTray True
            #End If

            cmdAddToTray.Enabled = True
            Form1.Visible = True

            End Sub

            Private Sub tmrIcon_Timer()

            'Animate the tray
            Static intNum As Integer

            Dim strIconName As String

            If intNum = 0 Then
                intNum = 1
            End If
```

```
strIconName = App.Path & "\ball" & intNum & ".ico"

#If COM_TRAYMAN Then
    objTM.comTrayMan.UpdateTrayIcon strIconName, ICON_AS_STRING
#Else
    UpdateTrayIcon strIconName, 0
#End If

If intNum >= 9 Then
    intNum = 1
Else
    intNum = intNum + 1
End If

End Sub
```

Module1.bas

Following is the Module1.bas client code:

```
Option Explicit

Public Const WM_LBUTTONDOWN = &H201
Public Const WM_LBUTTONDBLCLK = &H203
Public Const WM_RBUTTONDBLCLK = &H206
Public Const WM_RBUTTONDOWN = &H204

#If COM_TRAYMAN Then
    Public objTM As New clsTrayManWrapper
#Else
    Public Declare Function InitTray Lib "trayman.dll" ( _
                            ByVal lngVal As Long) As Long

    Public Declare Function FreeTray Lib "trayman.dll" () As Long

    Public Declare Function RemoveFromTray Lib "trayman.dll" ( _
                            ByVal bAnimate As Boolean) As Long

    Public Declare Function AddToTray Lib "trayman.dll" ( _
                                        ByVal szTip As String, _
                                        ByVal cbFunc As Long, _
                            ByVal pIcon As String, _
                            ByVal iIconType As Long, _
```

```
                                        ByVal bAnimate As Boolean) _
                                        As Long

            Public Declare Function UpdateTrayTip Lib "trayman.dll" ( _
                            ByVal szTip As String) As Long

            Public Declare Function UpdateTrayIcon Lib "trayman.dll" ( _
                            ByVal pIcon As Any, _
                            ByVal iIconType As Long) _
                            As Long
#End If

Public Sub Main()

'Load the form
Load Form1

'Initialize the tray
#If COM_TRAYMAN Then
    If objTM.comTrayMan.InitTray(Form1.hWnd) = False Then
        MsgBox "Could not initialize the system tray."
    End If
#Else
    If InitTray(Form1.hWnd) = False Then
        MsgBox "Could not initialize the system tray."
    End If
#End If

'Load an initial icon to the image box
Form1.lblIcon.Caption = App.Path & "\smile.ico"

'Show the form
Form1.Show

End Sub


Public Sub CallBack(ByVal lngParam As Long)

'See which message was passed from the tray
Select Case lngParam

    'If the left mouse button was double clicked
```

```
Case WM_LBUTTONDBLCLK
        'Remove the icon from the tray
        #If COM_TRAYMAN Then
            objTM.comTrayMan.RemoveFromTray True
        #Else
            RemoveFromTray True
        #End If

        'Show the form
        Form1.Visible = True

    'If the right mouse button was clicked
    Case WM_RBUTTONDOWN
        'Show the pop-up menu
        Form1.PopupMenu Form1.mnuMain

End Select

End Sub
```

ClsTrayManWrapper.cls

Following is the ClsTrayManWrapper.cls code:

```
Option Explicit

'Declare the object so that it can receive events
Public WithEvents comTrayMan As ATL_TRAYMAN2Lib.TrayMan

Private Sub Class_Initialize()

'Create the object
Set comTrayMan = New ATL_TRAYMAN2Lib.TrayMan

End Sub

Private Sub comTrayMan_MessageArrived(ByVal lngMessage As Long)

'Forward the message
Call Module1.CallBack(lngMessage)

End Sub
```

The only difference in the COM version of the client code and the original (besides the obvious syntactical differences) is the use of a class module. The comTrayMan_MessageArrived subroutine is the subroutine that is called by the Fire_MessageArrived in the TrayMan object.

Conclusion

In this chapter we built a real world COM component with C++ and ATL. Although a lot of the code from this chapter was rather complex, the steps we used to create the component were not. As I said earlier, don't expect to learn ATL overnight or in one chapter of a programming book; it is much too complex of a framework to master it that quickly. The best ways to learn ATL inside and out is to experiment, experiment, experiment!

CHAPTER 13

Advanced Topics

WELL, YOU'VE MADE IT. YOU HAVE TRAVERSED this whole book, and should by now be quite accomplished at writing C++ code. In other words, the work of this book is done. But if the work of the book is done, then what is this chapter about?

This chapter is simply a collection of several advanced topics that didn't really fit neatly elsewhere in the book, but important enough to include. I actually created this chapter for this very reason. I tried to cover topics in this chapter that are advanced, yet still relevant to real world programming. I hope that you will learn something in this chapter that will help you overcome some programming problem, or at a minimum, spark your creativity.

The DLLMain Function

Earlier in this book we learned how to create DLLs in C++. However, there is one aspect about DLLs that we didn't talk about—loading. When a process loads a DLL, the system puts a copy of the DLL's code into the process's address space. But before the loading is complete, the system calls the DLLMain function in that DLL.

Every DLL must have a DLLMain function. If you don't provide one, the compiler will write one for you. If a process tries to load a DLL that doesn't have a DLL main, the load will always fail. When you create a DLL project in Visual C++, the DLL project wizard generates a DLLMain function in your code that looks like this:

```
BOOL APIENTRY DllMain( HANDLE hModule,
                       DWORD  ul_reason_for_call,
                       LPVOID lpReserved
                     )
{
     return TRUE;
}
```

The first parameter, hModule, is the handle to the DLL that can be used to call system functions such as GetModuleFileName. The second parameter, ul_reason_for_call, is a flag that tells the DLL why it is being loaded. The four possible flag values and their meanings are listed in Table 13-1.

Table 13-1. Flags for DLLMain

FLAG	DESCRIPTION
DLL_PROCESS_ATTACH	Passed when a process loads a DLL.
DLL_PROCESS_DETACH	Passed when a process unloads a DLL.
DLL_THREAD_ATTACH	Passed when a new thread in the current process is started.
DLL_THREAD_DETACH	Passed when a new thread in the current process is terminated.

These flags are useful for controlling per-thread values and process data initialization. For instance, the DLL_PROCESS_ATTACH flag is useful for doing any initialization that needs to be done before functions calls are made to the library. Likewise, the DLL_PROCESS_DETACH flag is useful for freeing memory that was allocated during the lifetime of the DLL. The last parameter, lpReserved, is—well, reserved, so don't use it. Following is a simple example of how this function may be implemented:

```
// dll_main.cpp : Defines the entry point for the DLL application.
//

#include "stdafx.h"

#define MsgBox(x) MessageBox(0,x,"DLL_MAIN",MB_OK)

BOOL APIENTRY DllMain( HANDLE hModule,
                       DWORD  ul_reason_for_call,
                       LPVOID lpReserved
                     )
{
    switch (ul_reason_for_call)
    {
        case DLL_PROCESS_ATTACH:
            MsgBox("Process attaching.");
            break;
        case DLL_PROCESS_DETACH:
            MsgBox("Process detaching.");
            break;
        case DLL_THREAD_ATTACH:
            MsgBox("Thread attaching.");
            break;
        case DLL_THREAD_DETACH:
            MsgBox("Thread detaching.");
            break;
```

```
    }

    return TRUE;
}
```

This implementation will show a message box (notice the #define I used to simplify the MessageBox function) when each of the flags is sent to the DLLMain function.

Now, let's create a client to test out the DLL. We will create our client in Visual Basic, by calling the LoadLibrary and FreeLibrary functions. Following is the code for the client:

```
Option Explicit

Private Declare Function LoadLibrary Lib "kernel32" Alias _
                        "LoadLibraryA" (_
                        ByVal lpLibFileName As String) _
                        As Long
Private Declare Function FreeLibrary Lib "kernel32" ( _
                        ByVal hLibModule As Long) _
                        As Long


Private Sub Form_Load()

Dim lngModule As Long

'Load the DLL - causes DLL_PROCESS_ATTACH flag to be passed to DLLMain
lngModule = LoadLibrary("c:\apress\dl_main\debug\dll_main.dll")

'Unload the DLL - causes DLL_PROCESS_DETACH flag to be passed to DLLMain
FreeLibrary lngModule

End Sub
```

This client program causes the message boxes shown in Figure 13-1 and Figure 13-2 to be displayed when it is run. (You will need to change the path in the LoadLibrary call to reflect the proper path to the DLL on your machine.)

Again, it is up to you as to how to effectively use this function, but there will doubtlessly be situations where it will be absolutely necessary. (We will see this applied to a DLL later in this chapter.)

Figure 13-1. The DLL_MAIN message box indicating the DLL_PROCESS_ ATTACH flag was passed

Figure 13-2. The DLL_MAIN message box indicating the DLL_PROCESS_ DETACH flag was passed

Multithreading

Multithreading is one of those topics that causes programmers to either cringe or smile. Cringe if they don't know what multithreading is (or know what it is from a bad experience with it). And smile if they have learned when, how, and why to multithread an application. Most programmers fall into the first group.

Multithreading Basics

So what exactly is multithreading? Multithreading is the ability for an application to create multiple paths of execution for its code. This is not to be confused with *multitasking*, which is the ability of an operating system to appear to run more than one application at a time. The reason I say "appear to" is because the fact of the matter is that a single processor machine can only process one instruction at a time no matter how fast it is. With multitasking, the operating system switches between all of the running applications so fast that it appears that they are running simultaneously. Multitasking is a system-wide mechanism; multithreading is an inter-process mechanism. When an application starts up, the operating system starts running the application's code in a single thread (this is the application's main thread). This thread can then create (or spawn) other threads to help it with its work.

Suppose you have four errands to run in one afternoon. These errands are: buy groceries at the grocery store, buy automotive parts at the auto parts store, buy shoes at the shoe store, and buy a guitar at the music store. You jump into your car and head off to the grocery store. You buy your groceries and then go to the auto parts store, which you go in, and select the appropriate items. Once you finish there you jump back in your car and start driving toward the shoe store. After this you head for your last stop: the music store. And as any true guitar player knows, this stop could take the longest. In this scenario, you have run your errands in a single threaded fashion because only one errand was executed at any one time.

Now, let's look at how these same errands may have been accomplished in a multithreaded scenario. Instead of starting out to do your errands alone, you would get four of your friends to go with you. You would drive to the first stop, the grocery store, and drop off your first friend so that he may start grocery shopping. While he begins to shop, you and your remaining three friends head for the auto parts store. Upon arrival, you drop off another one of your friends. This friend will go into the auto parts store and shop for the items you need. Now at this point, you have one friend shopping for groceries, another shopping for auto parts, and your remaining two friends in the car with you. Now, it's off to the shoe store and one less friend in the car. The last errand is the one to purchase a guitar, so you drop off your last friend, and he goes in to purchase your instrument. At this point you go back and pick up all of your friends from their various tasks and head home. This is an example of multithreading. Each of your friends completed his task in a separate thread.

As you can see, this can be quite efficient. However, sometimes multi-threading can actually prove to be less efficient than a single threaded approach. Imagine if you had only had two errands to do. It is feasible to say that it may have actually taken longer to drop off your friends and pick them up than if you had just run the errands by yourself. The benefits of multithreading are dependent upon the situation in which they are used.

A Multithreaded Example

We now know what a thread is, but still don't know how to create one. There are actually a couple of ways to create threads on the Windows platform. You can either call the WIN32 application program interface (API) function, `CreateThread`, or the C++ Runtime Library function, `beginthread`. It is preferable to use `beginthread` in most cases. `CreateThread` is more useful for Microsoft Foundation Classes (MFC) applications or applications that run in a framework of some type that doesn't rely on C++ Runtime Library functions being available. For our purposes, we will use `beginthread` exclusively.

You may be wondering, if the `CreateThread` API function creates threads, why can't I just call `CreateThread` directly from Visual Basic and create threads that way? I mean `CreateThread` is a WIN32 API just like `SetWindowLong` and `GetTickCount`, and those can be called safely from Visual Basic, right? Well, this has been the basis for many heated discussions among programmers in the Visual Basic community. We, however, won't be getting into this discussion except to say that you should not create threads directly from Visual Basic, ever (except as provided by Visual Basic when creating multithreaded COM components).

> **NOTE:** *If you are interested in learning more about the problems with the usage of threads created in Visual Basic, be sure to read the article by Dan Appleman in Appendix A of this book. Supposedly the next version of Visual Basic will have a facility for creating threads in this manner, but as with many Microsoft promised features, don't believe it until you see it.*

So that we can learn more about how threads work, let's look at a simple C++ console application that uses threads:

```cpp
// basic_threads.cpp : Defines the entry point for the console application.
//
#include "stdafx.h"
#include <process.h>
#include <windows.h>
#include <winbase.h>

void threadProc(void *param)
{
    //print the thread number
printf("Thread %d running...\n",(int*)param);
}

int main(int argc, char* argv[])
{
    for (int i = 0; i < 10 ; i++)
    {
            //create a new thread
            _beginthread(&threadProc,0,(void*)i);
            //take a breath
            Sleep(50);
    }

    return 1;
}
```

This application is actually pretty simple. All it does is enter a for-loop, and call beginthread during each iteration of that loop. Before we go too far though, we need to examine the declaration of beginthread:

```cpp
unsigned long _beginthread( void( __cdecl *start_address )( void * ), unsigned
stack_size, void *arglist );
```

The first parameter for beginthread is a pointer to a cdecl calling convention function that takes one parameter of type void pointer. The next parameter, stack_size, is an unsigned integer that sets the size of the stack for the newly created thread. You will usually pass 0 to this parameter (in which case the new thread will be created with the same size stack as the thread that created it). The last parameter is a void pointer. This is the parameter that will be passed as the argument to the function declared in parameter 1. The reason it is a void pointer is so that you can pass any type of data to the newly created thread.

Okay, I must confess that I haven't been exactly truthful with you on this topic thus far. We aren't going to be using the beginthread function at all in this chapter. We are going to use the improved version of beginthread, beginthreadex. I used beginthread earlier because it is easier to look at than beginthreadex, and I didn't want to scare you with a huge function call right off the bat.

_beginthread versus _beginthreadex

You should always use the improved version of beginthread, beginthreadex. The reason is that beginthreadex is more flexible and safe. Let's look at its declaration:

```
unsigned long _beginthreadex (void *security, unsigned stack_size,
    unsigned ( __stdcall *start_address )( void * ),
    void *arglist, unsigned initflag,
    unsigned *thrdaddr );
```

The first parameter for the beginthreadex function is a pointer to a security descriptor. Don't worry if you don't know what a security descriptor is—this parameter is optional (and usually NULL). In fact, in Windows 95/98, this parameter has to be NULL or the call will fail.

The second parameter for beginthreadex is the same as the second parameter for beginthread, the stack size. Again, this parameter is usually passed as 0 (NULL), indicating to the system that it should create the new thread with the same size stack as the thread that is calling beginthreadex.

The third parameter for beginthreadex is a pointer to the function at which the new thread will begin execution. This starting function parameter is different than the one in the beginthread function in the fact that it is a __stdcall calling convention instead of __cdecl, and it returns an unsigned int instead of a void.

> **NOTE:** *Yes, this means that you could pass a pointer to a function in Visual Basic as the starting address for the thread, but don't even think about try-ing it! It will crash your application. I won't explain why here, but trust me, it will. If you want to know why, search the Internet for "CreateThread and Visual Basic"; this should bring back articles that explain it. You can also check the DevX Web site (www.devx.com), and the Desaware Web site (www.desaware.com). They both have articles that deal with the subject of threads and Visual Basic.*

The next parameter for beginthreadex is the same void pointer parameter from beginthread. It is passed as the parameter to the thread just as in the first example. The next parameter is a start mode flag. Passing a value of 0 in it causes the thread to start running immediately. You can also pass the constant CREATE_SUSPENDED (the Microsoft documentation says to pass CREATE_SUSPEND, but it's just a typo in the Microsoft documentation).

The last parameter is a pointer to an unsigned int that is loaded with the new thread's identifier upon a successful call to beginthreadex. The thread's identifier is useful for several WIN32 API calls, but we will not use it here. The return value of the beginthreadex function is a HANDLE to the newly created thread. This value is also useful for several WIN32 API functions such as ResumeThread. ResumeThread causes a thread created with the CREATE_SUSPENDED flag to start running.

We can now rewrite our previous example application using the beginthreadex function instead of beginthread as so:

```
// basic_threads.cpp : Defines the entry point for the console application.
//
#include "stdafx.h"
#include <process.h>
#include <windows.h>
#include <winbase.h>

unsigned int __stdcall threadProc(void *param)
{
    //print the thread number
    printf("Thread %d running...\n",(int*)param);

    //return the thread number
      return (unsigned int)param;
}

int main(int argc, char* argv[])
{

    for (int i = 0; i <= 10 ; i++)
    {
        //create a new thread
        unsigned int threadID = 0;

        //start a new thread
        HANDLE hThread = (HANDLE)_beginthreadex(NULL,0,
                                        &threadProc,
```

```
                                        (void*)i,
                                        CREATE_SUSPENDED,
                                    &threadID);

        //let the new thread start
        Sleep(10);

        //start the thread
        ResumeThread(hThread);
    }


    return 1;
}
```

You can see that the new version enables our `threadProc` function to return a value whereas the previous version did not. This return value of the thread function is called the thread's "exit code." It can be useful to indicate whether a thread completed its tasks successfully.

Threads and the Sleep Function

You can see that in both versions of the application I call the Win32 API function Sleep immediately after calling `beginthread` or `beginthreadex`. The reason I did this is so that the new thread has a chance to get on its feet, before the thread that created it continues to execute. You see, each thread in the system has a certain amount of the processor's time to execute. This time is referred to as a *time slice*. The processor is constantly switching between all the threads in the system, giving each its own time slice. The WIN32 API's Sleep function enables a thread to allow other threads to execute in its allotted time slice. In our case, calling the Sleep function causes the creating thread to rest and allow the newly created thread to start running. This is important because all created threads exit automatically when the process's main thread exits, and in our case, the main thread would almost definitely exit before the created threads ever started if we had not used Sleep. You can see this effect in action by commenting out the call to Sleep in the source code, recompiling the project, and running the program. There are situations when it is not necessary to use sleep when creating threads. We will see an example of this later in this chapter.

A Multithreaded Visual Basic Application

Did the title get your attention or what? Well, it's not quite true. We are not going to create a multithreaded Visual Basic application; we are going to build a single threaded Visual Basic application that uses a multithreaded DLL. (It is arguable that these are the same thing, but I'm trying to make a point here.)

> **NOTE:** *As I said before, you shouldn't multithread an application just because you can. You should look at your design to determine whether multithreading will be of benefit. Honestly, it's difficult to justify the difficulty and time consumption necessary to create a multithreaded application, but you will have to make those justifications for yourself. They usually become evident with a little pilot-phase benchmarking of the application in question.*

In our application we will assume that we have justified the use of multithreading in the design phase and that we are ready to start coding. Now, our application is pretty straightforward in its functionality. The application consists of a Visual Basic client that calls a single function inside of our DLL, MakeNewThread, which lists all of the files in a specified directory and of a certain file extension. Figure 13-3 depicts the screen from our application after successfully running.

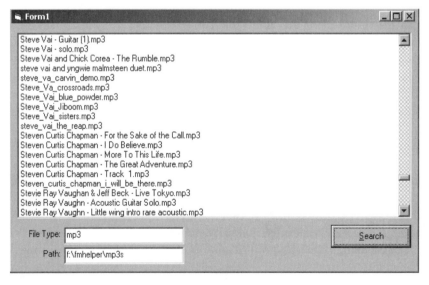

Figure 13-3. multithread_ex_01 at runtime

Now let's take a look at the Visual Basic code for our application:

```
Option Explicit

Private Declare Sub MakeNewThread Lib _
                    "d:\multithread_ex_01.dll" (ByVal strFile As String, _
                    ByVal lngHwnd As Long)

Private Sub cmdSearch_Click()

Dim strData As String

lstFiles.Clear

If txtType.Text = "" Then
    txtType.Text = "*"
End If

strData = txtPath.Text & "\*." & txtType.Text

MakeNewThread strData, lstFiles.hWnd

MsgBox "VB Thread!"

End Sub
```

This code looks pretty simple, doesn't it? That's because it is simple. All we are doing is building a search string from the contents of our two text boxes and passing it to the MakeNewThread function in the DLL, along with the HWND of the lstFiles list box. The reason we pass the HWND of the list box is so that the DLL can update it with the name of each file found via the WIN32 API SendMessage function. To get an idea of how this works, let's look at the code inside the DLL:

```
// multithread_ex_01.cpp : Defines the
// entry point for the DLL application.


#include "stdafx.h"
#include <process.h>
#include <stdio.h>
#include <stdlib.h>
```

```
HWND g_hwndLB = 0;      //HWND of the client listbox
HANDLE hHeap = 0;           //HANDLE to our private heap

BOOL APIENTRY DllMain( HANDLE hModule,
                       DWORD  ul_reason_for_call,
                       LPVOID lpReserved
                     )
{
    switch (ul_reason_for_call)
    {
        //There is a new process loading our DLL
        case DLL_PROCESS_ATTACH:
            //create a private memory chunk for this mapping
            //of the DLL
            hHeap = HeapCreate(NULL,MAX_PATH,MAX_PATH);
            break;

        //We are being unloaded by the process
        case DLL_PROCESS_DETACH:
            //free the private memory chunk
            HeapDestroy(hHeap);
            break;
    }

    return TRUE;
}

unsigned int __stdcall threadProc(void *strData)
{
    int rv = 0;
    WIN32_FIND_DATA w32FD;
    char szMsg[MAX_PATH];

    //open the file search handle
    HANDLE f1 = FindFirstFile((char*)strData,&w32FD);

    //check the results
    if (f1 == INVALID_HANDLE_VALUE)
    {
        //file was not found
        sprintf(szMsg,
                    "No matching files found for search (%s).",
                    strData);
```

```
        MessageBox(0,szMsg,"Background File Search",MB_OK);

        //free the memory from our private heap
        HeapFree(hHeap,NULL,strData);

        return 1;
    }

    //keep listing files till there are no more
    do
    {
        //check to see if we have a directory or not
        if (w32FD.dwFileAttributes & FILE_ATTRIBUTE_DIRECTORY)
        {
            sprintf(szMsg,"%s (Directory)",w32FD.cFileName);
        }
        else
        {
            sprintf(szMsg,"%s",w32FD.cFileName);
        }

        //add the item to the client listbox
        rv = SendMessage(g_hwndLB,LB_ADDSTRING,NULL,(long)szMsg);


        //ceck for another file
        FindNextFile(f1,&w32FD);

    } while (GetLastError() != ERROR_NO_MORE_FILES);

    //free the memory from our private heap
    HeapFree(hHeap,NULL,strData);

    //close the search handle
    FindClose(f1);

    return 1;
}

void __stdcall MakeNewThread(char *strPath, HWND hwndLB)
{
    //check the parameters
    if (!strPath || !hwndLB)
```

```
        {
        }
        else
        {
            //create a block of memory in our private heap
            char *szTemp = (char*)HeapAlloc(hHeap,NULL,MAX_PATH);

            //copy the search path/name into the heap variable
            strcpy(szTemp,strPath);

            //store the client's listbox handle
            g_hwndLB = hwndLB;

            //start a new thread
            HANDLE hThread = (HANDLE)_beginthreadex(NULL,
                                    0,
                                    &threadProc,
                                     szTemp,
                                    CREATE_SUSPENDED,
                                   NULL);

            //start the thread
            ResumeThread(hThread);
        }
}
```

Wow! No wonder the Visual Basic code was so simple; all of the work is being done inside the DLL (as it should be in this case). Let's examine each part of the DLL in detail.

The MakeNewThread Function

The MakeNewThread function is a simple function because all it does is create a new thread for the threadProc function to run in. Actually, it does do one other thing: it creates a private heap for our DLL. A *heap* is a section of memory the system uses to allocate variables and other data in a program. When a process is first started, it gets a default heap. All elements of an application share the default heap, including the actual program executable and any loaded DLLs. However, in our case, we need to create an additional heap for our DLL because Visual Basic has no clue that our DLL is going to be creating a thread. This means that once the call to MakeNewThread returns, Visual Basic assumes that the whole default heap belongs to it again. Therefore, anything we allocate on the heap after that call is susceptible to corruption by Visual Basic, namely the MsgBox function. And because we need the value in the strPath parameter to be guaranteed to be uncorrupted (so that we can pass the correct path to the threadProc function), we have to get it off of the default heap before we return from the MakeNewThread function. (You'll see that we don't actually take strPath off the default heap, we instead create a copy of it on our own heap.)

The heap in the DLLMain function is created with the following call:

```
hHeap = HeapCreate(NULL,MAX_PATH,MAX_PATH);
```

This call causes the system to allocate a new heap. The first parameter of HeapCreate is a flag field that specifies several possible creation options. We pass NULL in our case as to accept the default values. The second parameter to HeapCreate tells the system the initial size to make the heap. The third parameter tells the system the maximum size that the heap can grow to be. We use MAX_PATH for both of these values because that is all the space we are going to need.

Once the heap is created, we can start allocating memory from it, as we do with the following line inside the MakeNewThread function:

```
char *szTemp = (char*)HeapAlloc(hHeap,NULL,MAX_PATH);
```

We then store a copy of the strPath parameter on our new heap thereby ensuring its safety from Visual Basic. Notice that we then pass that copy to the threadProc function. If we had passed strPath directly to threadProc, you can almost guarantee that Visual Basic would have overwritten its value by the time threadProc ever got to use it.

The MakeNewThread Function

Once the call to beginthreadex is made, the MakeNewThread function returns to its caller, Visual Basic. At this point threadProc starts to run in its own newly created thread. The threadProc function then uses the FindFile family of functions to search the specified path for files of the specified extension. Each time it finds one, it calls SendMessage, an API function that sends a message to a particular window with the specified HWND value. In our case, we send messages to the Visual Basic client's list box telling it to add the text in the szMsg parameter value like so:

```
rv = SendMessage(g_hwndLB,LB_ADDSTRING,NULL,(long)szMsg);
```

Once all matching files are found, threadProc calls HeapFree, which releases the memory allocated with the call to HeapAlloc. Once the library is unloaded and receives the call to DLLMain with the DLL_PROCESS_DETACH flag, the DLL calls HeapDestroy, which releases the heap altogether.

Thread Synchronization

Thread *synchronization* is an important part of multithreading. Thread synchronization is the process of ensuring that no two threads are in the same code at the same time. You do this mainly with *CriticalSection objects* and *Mutexes*. There are other synchronization objects available, but these two are the most commonly used for threads.

In the previous version of the "basic_threads" example in this section we actually have a problem with thread synchronization. The problem is that each thread is accessing the threadProc function at potentially the same time. This can, and most likely will, cause unpredictable results to be generated from the program.

Now that we have identified a synchronization problem with our example, let's fix it. We are going to use a Critical Section object to do our thread synchronization. Following is the synchronized version of our example:

```cpp
// basic_threads.cpp : Defines the
// entry point for the console application.
#include "stdafx.h"
#include <process.h>
#include <windows.h>
#include <winbase.h>

#define THREAD_COUNT 10

CRITICAL_SECTION cs;
int g_threadCounter = THREAD_COUNT;

unsigned int __stdcall threadProc(void *param)
{
    //block other threads
    EnterCriticalSection(&cs);

    //print the thread number
    printf("Thread %d running...\n",(int*)param);

    //decrement the counter
    g_threadCounter--;

    //release block on other threads
    LeaveCriticalSection(&cs);
```

```
    //return the thread number
    return (unsigned int)param;
}

int main(int argc, char* argv[])
{
    //initialize the CRITICAL_SECTION object
    InitializeCriticalSection(&cs);

    //loop through all threads
    for (int i = 0; i <= THREAD_COUNT ; i++)
    {
        //create a new thread
        unsigned int threadID = 0;

        //start a new thread
        HANDLE hThread = (HANDLE)_beginthreadex(NULL,0,
                                                &threadProc,
                                                (void*)i,
                                                CREATE_SUSPENDED,
                                            &threadID);

        //start the thread
        ResumeThread(hThread);
    }

    //keep looping until the last thread is finished
    do
    {
    }
    while(g_threadCounter > 0);

    //destroy the CRITICAL_SECTION object
    DeleteCriticalSection(&cs);

    return 1;
}
```

I highlighted the changed sections. You can see that the first thing we
do now is call the InitializeCriticalSection API function passing it our
CRITICAL_SECTION object. This call initializes the object and prepares it for
usage.

Now look at the threadProc function. Notice how we now call EnterCriticalSection at the beginning of the function and LeaveCriticalSection at the end. The first call essentially puts up a roadblock on that section of code to all other threads. The roadblock stays in effect until the LeaveCriticalSection function is called.

> **NOTE:** *If you forget to call* LeaveCriticalSection, *your thread will remain blocked and lockup your application infinitely.*

Now, you will also see that I have implemented a global counter that is decremented by each thread as it finishes running. You will also notice that the main function now has a do-while loop that waits for that global counter to hit zero. The reason we have this counter and loop is to ensure that the main function doesn't exit until all threads are done. Remember that all spawned threads exit when the process that they are part of terminates. Figure 13-4 shows the program at runtime:

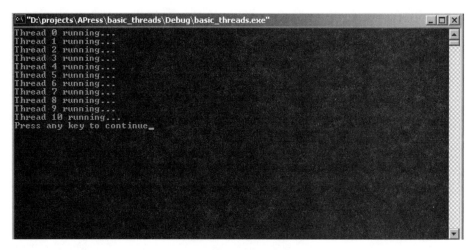

Figure 13-4. The basic_threads application at runtime

Remember that multithreading is a rather complex task to accomplish. It makes debugging an application much more difficult, as well as more coding the application itself. There is much more to writing good, stable multithreaded applications than I have shown here, but this should at least get you on your way. Remember to always think before you code when it comes to multithreading.

Sharing Data in a DLL

As you may already know, each application that loads a DLL gets its own copy of all of the data in the DLL. This means that even if you have a global variable set in the DLL, each process that loads that DLL will get its own copy of the global variable. This is by design. Windows keeps processes separated so that a rogue process cannot interfere with other processes in the system. This is what gives Windows its stability. (Quit laughing!) However, where there's a will, there's a way, and you can indeed share data between applications through a DLL.

Now even more than multithreading, this technique is very difficult to legitimize as a necessity, but you may come across an occasion where it will be the only solution to a problem.

The first thing that we have to do in order to share data in a DLL is to create a "Shared" section in memory. We do this with the #pragma statement. More specifically, we use the data_seg and comment directives of the #pragma statement. The actual syntax is as follows:

```
#pragma data_seg("MY_SHARED_SECTION")
int g_counter = 0;
#pragma data_seg()

#pragma comment(linker,"/Section:MY_SHARED_SECTION,RWS")
```

> **NOTE:** #pragma *directives are compiler- and platform-dependent . The techniques shown here will only work on the Microsoft Visual C++ compiler Version 2.0 or higher running Windows 95/98 or NT/2000.*

The first line tells the compiler to put all of the initialized data that it finds in a section named "MY_SHARED_SECTION" until it hits the line #pragma data_seg(). The #pragma data_seg() line causes the compiler to start putting data back in the place it did before the first #pragma data_seg command was encountered. Following is the code for a DLL that implements shared data:

```
// dll_shared.cpp : Defines the entry point for the DLL application.
//

#include "stdafx.h"
```

```
#pragma data_seg("MY_SHARED_SECTION")
int g_counter = 0;
#pragma data_seg()

#pragma comment(linker,"/Section:MY_SHARED_SECTION,RWS")

BOOL APIENTRY DllMain( HANDLE hModule,
                       DWORD  ul_reason_for_call,
                       LPVOID lpReserved
                     )
{
    return TRUE;
}

int __stdcall GetCount()
{
    return g_counter;
}

int __stdcall IncrementCount()
{
    return g_counter++;
}
```

Notice that this is a very simple DLL. It only contains two exported functions, GetCount and IncrementCount. The GetCount function returns the value of the shared variable, g_counter. And IncrementCount increments it by one. I exported these functions via the following DEF file:

```
LIBRARY "DLL_SHARED.DLL"

EXPORTS
    GetCount
    IncrementCount
```

Now we need a client to test it out. I wrote a simple client that contains a timer, which calls GetCount every 100 milliseconds. It also contains a label, which displays the current value of the global counter as well as a command button that increments the counter by one. Here is the code for the client:

```
Option Explicit

Private Declare Function GetCount Lib _
    "d:\projects\apress\dll_shared\debug\dll_shared.dll" () As Long
Private Declare Function IncrementCount Lib _
    "d:\projects\apress\dll_shared\debug\dll_shared.dll" () As Long

Private Sub cmdCounter_Click()

IncrementCount

End Sub

Private Sub Timer1_Timer()

lblCount.Caption = GetCount

End Sub
```

Figure 13-5 displays the output after starting three instances of the client and pressing the "Increment Count" button three times.

Again, please use this technique judiciously as it does open your application to potential memory violations. You should also synchronize calls to the shared data with a mutex or critical section.

Figure 13-5. DLL data sharing in action

Scripting the IDE

Visual C++ has a lot of nice wizards and macros to help you with some of the more monotonous tasks necessary when writing source code. We have used several of these throughout this book. However, there are times when you will want an automated way of doing something in the Visual C++ Integrated Development Environment (IDE) for which wizard or macro doesn't exist. In this case you can write your own macro to control the Visual C++ IDE. Figures 13-6 and 13-7 depict the effects of running a macro that I wrote—it adds a comment block to a highlighted function declaration.

```
void polyFunc(A *p_objA)
{
    p_objA->func1(100);
}
```

Figure 13-6. Source code before running the "AddCommentBlock" macro

```
/*-------------------------------------------------------------------
Function Name:      void polyFunc(A *p_objA)

Parameters:         **TODO - Add parameter list here**

Return Value:       void

Calling Convention: (default)

Date:               Monday, June 26, 2000 @ (8:30:32 AM)

Notes:

-------------------------------------------------------------------*/
void polyFunc(A *p_objA)
{
    p_objA->func1(100);
}
```

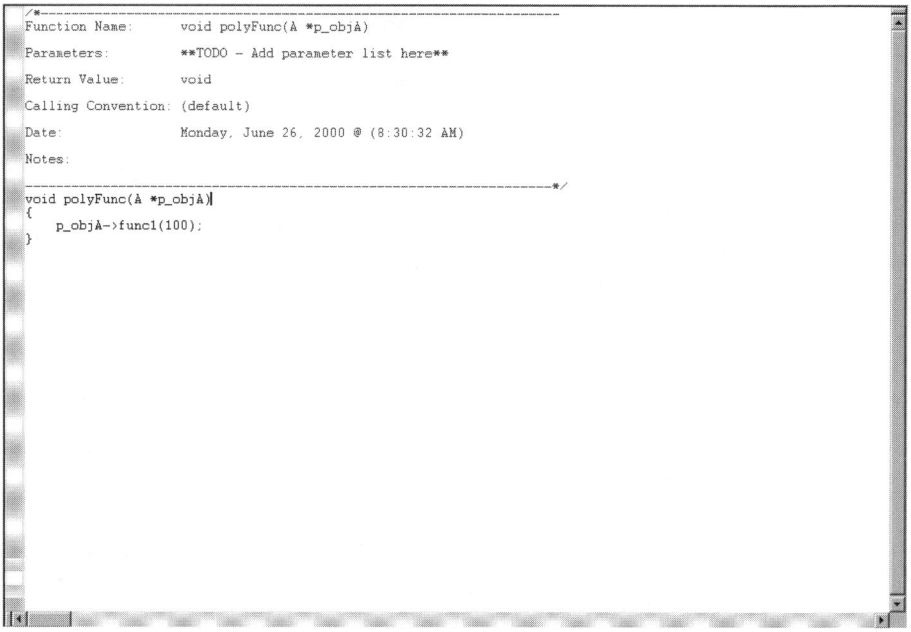

Figure 13-7. Source code after running the "AddCommentBlock" macro

Following is the VBScript code that makes up this macro:

```
'-------------------------------------------------------
'FILE DESCRIPTION: This macro adds a
'comment block header to a function.
'-------------------------------------------------------


Sub AddCommentBlock()

    Dim strFunctionName
    Dim strSelection
    Dim strCallingConv

    strFunctionName = ActiveDocument.Selection

    'Check the calling convention if one exists
    If InStr(1,strFunctionName,"__stdcall") Then
        strCallingConv = "__stdcall"
    ElseIf InStr(1,strFunctionName,"__cdecl") Then
        strCallingConv = "__cdecl"
    ElseIf InStr(1,strFunctionName,"__fastcall") Then
        strCallingConv = "__fastcall"
    Else
        strCallingConv = "(default)"
    End If

    If strFunctionName <> "" And _
                    strFunctionName <> "Enter Function Name" Then
        'Output the comments
        ActiveDocument.Selection = _
                    "/*-----------------------------------" & _
                    vbCrLf & _
        "Function Name:        " & strFunctionName & vbCrLf & _
        vbCrLf & _
            "Parameters:            " & _
                    "**TODO - Add parameter list here**" & vbCrLf & _
        vbCrLf & _
        "Return Value:        " & _
                    Mid(strFunctionName, _
                        1,InStr(1,strFunctionName," ")) & _
                    vbCrLf & _
```

```
            vbCrLf & _
            "Calling Convention:     " & strCallingConv & vbCrLf & _
            vbCrLf & _
            "Date:                   " & _
                    FormatDateTime(Date,vbLongDate) & _
                    " @ (" & time & ")" & vbCrLf & _
            vbCrLf & _
            "Notes:                   " & vbCrLf & _
            vbCrLf & _
            "--------------------------------------------------*/" & _
                    vbCrLf & _
            strFunctionName
    Else
        MsgBox "You must highlight a function declaration " & _
                    "before calling this macro.",vbOkOnly,"Commenter"
    End If

End Sub
```

You can see that the actual VBScript code is pretty straightforward. The main functionality is to string the concatenation piece. Notice the use of the `ActiveDocument.Selection`. This is a member of the Visual Studio object model. The complete Visual Studio object model is documented in the Visual Studio help file and on the MSDN Web site. You can also create add-ins for Visual Studio, which are very much like Visual Basic add-ins.

To create a new macro, select Macro ➜ Tools in Visual Studio. Then select the Edit button. This will cause the New Macro dialog box to be shown. Enter the name of the macro and a short description and click OK. Once this is done, you can write the code of the macro. After creating a macro you can invoke it by again selecting the Macro item from the Tools menu. Select your macro from the list, and click Run. You can also associate toolbars buttons and keystrokes with your macros on the Add-ins and Macros tab of the Customize item on the Visual Studio Tools menu.

Conclusion

I am hopeful you found something of interest in this chapter. (If not, then you probably aren't reading this conclusion anyway!) There are many other cool and useful techniques besides the ones presented in this chapter, so I encourage you to go out and experiment so that you can discover each and every one.

APPENDIX A

A Thread to Visual Basic

WRITTEN BY DANIEL APPLEMAN, THIS article discusses multithreading issues with Visual Basic. You can download the sample code from `ftp.desaware.com/SampleCode/Articles/Thread.zip`.

Just Because You Can, Doesn't Always Mean that You Should

With the appearance of the `AddressOf` operator, an entire industry has developed among authors illustrating how to do previously impossible tasks using Visual Basic. Another industry is rapidly developing among consultants helping users who have gotten into trouble attempting these tasks.

The problem is not in Visual Basic or in the technology. The problem lies in the fact that many authors are applying the same rule to `AddressOf` techniques that many software companies apply to software in general—if you can do something, you should. The idea that the newest and latest technology must, by definition, be the best solution to a problem is prevalent in our industry. This idea is wrong. Deployment of technology should be driven primarily by the problem that you are trying to solve, not by the technology that someone is trying to sell you.

Worse yet, just as companies often neglect to mention the limitations and disadvantages of their tools, authors sometimes fail to stress the consequences of some of the techniques that they describe. And magazines and books sometimes neglect their responsibility to make sure that the programming practices that they describe are sound.

As a programmer, it is important to choose the right tool for the job. It is your responsibility to develop code that not only works now under one particular platform, but that works under all target platforms and system configurations. Your code must be well documented and supportable by those programmers who follow you on the project. Your code must follow the rules dictated by the operating system or standards that you are using. Failure to do so can lead to problems in the future as systems and software are upgraded.

Articles in the *Microsoft Systems Journal* and *Visual Basic Programmer's Journal* introduced to Visual Basic programmers the possibility of using the CreateThread API function to directly support multithreading under Visual Basic. In fact, one reader went so far as to contact me and complain that my book, *Dan Appleman's Visual Basic Programmer's Guide to the Win32 API* (Sams), was fatally flawed because I did not cover this function or demonstrate this technique. This article is in part a response to this reader, and in part a response to other articles written on the subject. This article also serves, in part, as an update to Chapter 14 of my book *Developing ActiveX Components with Visual Basic 5.0: A Guide to the Perplexed* (Sams) with regards to new features supported by Visual Basic 5.0 Service Pack 2.

A Quick Review of Multithreading

If you are already well versed in multithreading technology, you may wish to skip this section and continue from the following sections titled "The Threading Contract" or "New for Service Pack 2."

Everyone who uses Windows knows that it is able to do more than one thing at a time. It can run several programs simultaneously, while at the same time playing a compact disk, sending a fax, and transferring a file. Every programmer knows (or should know) that the computer's CPU can only execute one instruction at a time (we'll ignore the existence of multiprocessing machines for the time being). How can a single CPU do multiple tasks?

It does this by rapidly switching among the different tasks. The operating system holds all of the programs that are running in memory. It allows the CPU to run each program in turn. Every time it switches between programs, it swaps the internal register values including the instruction pointer and stack pointer. Each of these "tasks" is called a thread of execution.

In a simple multitasking system, each program has a single thread of execution. This means that the CPU starts executing instructions at the beginning of the program, and continues following the instructions in the sequence defined by the program until the program terminates.

Let's say the program has five instructions: A, B, C, D, and E that execute in sequence (no jumps in this example). When an application has a single thread, the instructions will always execute in exactly the same order: A, B, C, D and E. True, the CPU may take time off to execute other instructions in other programs, but they will not affect this application unless there is a conflict over shared system resources—another subject entirely.

An advanced multithreading operating system such as Windows allows an application to run more than one thread at a time. Let's say that instruction D in our sample application had the ability to create a new thread that started at instruction B and ran through the sequence C and E. The first thread would still be A, B, C, D, E, but when D executed a new thread would begin that would execute B, C, E (we don't want to execute D again or we'll get another thread).

Exactly what order will the instructions follow in this application?

It could be

Thread 1	A	B	C	D		E
Thread 2			B		C	E

or it could be

Thread 1	A	B	C	D		E
Thread 2			B	C		E

or perhaps

Thread 1	A	B	C	D		E
Thread 2			B	C	E	

In other words, when you start a new thread of execution in an application, you can never know the exact order in which instructions in the two threads will execute relative to each other. The two threads are completely independent.

Why is this a problem?

A Multithreading Simulator

Consider the MTDemo project. (You can download the sample code from `ftp.desaware.com/SampleCode/Articles/Thread.zip`.)

The project contains a single code module that contains two global variables as follows:

```
' MTDemo - Multithreading Demo program
' Copyright © 1997 by Desaware Inc. All Rights Reserved
Option Explicit
Public GenericGlobalCounter As Long
Public TotalIncrements As Long
```

It contains a single form named frmMTDemo1, which contains the following code:

```
' MTDemo - Multithreading Demo program
' Copyright © 1997 by Desaware Inc. All Rights Reserved
Option Explicit
Dim State As Integer
    ' State = 0 - Idle
    ' State = 1 - Loading existing value
    ' State = 2 - Adding 1 to existing value
    ' State = 3 - Storing existing value
    ' State = 4 - Extra delay
Dim Accumulator As Long
Const OtherCodeDelay = 10
Private Sub Command1_Click()
    Dim f As New frmMTDemo1
    f.Show
End Sub
Private Sub Form_Load()
    Timer1.Interval = 750 + Rnd * 500
End Sub
Private Sub Timer1_Timer()
    Static otherdelay&
    Select Case State
        Case 0
            lblOperation = "Idle"
            State = 1
        Case 1
            lblOperation = "Loading Acc"
            Accumulator = GenericGlobalCounter
            State = 2
        Case 2
            lblOperation = "Incrementing"
            Accumulator = Accumulator + 1
            State = 3
        Case 3
            lblOperation = "Storing"
            GenericGlobalCounter = Accumulator
            TotalIncrements = TotalIncrements + 1
            State = 4
        Case 4
            lblOperation = "Generic Code"
            If otherdelay >= OtherCodeDelay Then
```

```
                State = 0
                otherdelay = 0
            Else
                otherdelay = otherdelay + 1
            End If
        End Select
    UpdateDisplay
End Sub
Public Sub UpdateDisplay()
    lblGlobalCounter = Str$(GenericGlobalCounter)
    lblAccumulator = Str$(Accumulator)
    lblVerification = Str$(TotalIncrements)
End Sub
```

This program uses a timer and a simple state machine to simulate multi-threading. The State variable describes the five instructions that this program executes in order. State zero is an idle state. State one loads local variable with the GenericGlobalCounter global variable. State two increments the local variable. State three stores the result into the GenericGlobalCounter variable and increments the TotalIncrements variable (which counts the number of times that the GenericGlobalCounter variable has been incremented). State 4 adds an additional delay representing time spent running other instructions in the program. The UpdateDisplay function updates three labels on the form that show the current value of the GenericGlobalCounter variable, the local accumulator, and the total number of increments.

Each timer tick represents a CPU cycle on the current thread. If you run the program you'll see that the value of the GenericGlobalCounter variable will always be exactly equal to the TotalIncrements variable—which makes sense, because the TotalIncrements variable shows the number of times the thread has incremented the GenericGlobalCounter.

But what happens when you click the Command1 button and start a second instance of the form? This new form simulates a second thread.

Every now and then, the instructions will line up in such a way that both forms load the same GenericGlobalCounter value, increment it, and store it. As a result, the value will only increase by one, even though each thread believed that it had independently incremented the variable. In other words(the variable was incremented twice, but the value only increased by one. If you launch several forms you will quickly see that the number of increments as represented by the TotalIncrements variable grows much more rapidly than the GenericGlobalCounter variable.

What if the variable represents an object lock count—which keeps track of when an object should be freed? What if it represents a signal that indicates that a resource is in use?

This type of problem can lead to resources becoming permanently unavailable to the system, to an object being locked internally in memory, or freed prematurely. It can easily lead to application crashes.

This example was designed to make the problem easy to see—but try experimenting with the value of the OtherCodeDelay variable. When the dangerous code is relatively small compared to the entire program, problems will appear less frequently. While this may sound good, the opposite is true. Multithreading problems can be extremely intermittent and difficult to find. This means that multithreading demands careful design up front.

Avoiding Multithreading Problems

There are two relatively easy ways to avoid multithreading problems:

- Avoid all use of global variables.

- Add synchronization code wherever global variables are used.

The first approach is the one used by Visual Basic. When you turn on multithreading in a Visual Basic application, all global variables become local to a specific thread. This is inherent in the way Visual Basic implements apartment model threading(more on this later.

The original release of Visual Basic 5.0 only allowed multithreading in components that had no user interface elements. This was because they had not figured out at the time a way to make the forms engine thread safe. For example: when you create a form in Visual Basic, VB gives it an implied global variable name (thus if you have a form named Form1, you can directly access its methods using Form1.method instead of declaring a separate form variable). This type of global variable can cause the kinds of multithreading problems you saw earlier. There were undoubtedly other problems within the forms engine as well—making a package that complex safe for multithreading can be quite a challenge.

With service pack 2, Visual Basic's forms engine was made thread safe. One sign of this is that each thread has its own implied global variable for each form defined in the project.

New for Service Pack 2

By making the forms engine thread safe, Service Pack 2 made it possible for you to create multithreading client applications using Visual Basic. This is demonstrated in the MTDemo2 project. (You can download the sample code from ftp.desaware.com/SampleCode/Articles/Thread.zip.)

The application must be defined as an ActiveX EXE program with startup set to Sub Main in a code module as follows:

```
' MTDemo2 - Multithreading demo program
' Copyright © 1997 by Desaware Inc. All Rights Reserved
Option Explicit
Declare Function FindWindow Lib "user32" Alias "FindWindowA"
  (ByVal lpClassName As String, _
  ByVal lpWindowName As String) As Long
Sub Main()
    Dim f As frmMTDemo2
    ' We need this because Main is called on each new thread
    Dim hwnd As Long
    hwnd = FindWindow(vbNullString, "Multithreading Demo2")
    If hwnd = 0 Then
        Set f = New frmMTDemo2
        f.Show
        Set f = Nothing
    End If
End Sub
```

The first time through, the program loads and displays the main form of the application. The Main routine needs some way of finding out whether this is the first thread of the application because it is executed at the start of every thread. You can't use a global variable to find this out because the Visual Basic apartment model keeps global variables specific to a single thread. In this example the FindWindow API function is used to check if the main form of the example has been loaded. There are other ways to find out if this is the main thread, including use of system synchronization objects—but this too is a subject for another time and place. Multithreading is accomplished by creating an object in a new thread.

The object must be defined using a class module. In this case, a simple class module is defined as follows:

```
' MTDemo2 - Multithreading demo program
' Copyright © 1997 by Desaware Inc. All Rights Reserved
Option Explicit
Private Sub Class_Initialize()
    Dim f As New frmMTDemo2
    f.Show
    Set f = Nothing
End Sub
```

We can set the form variable to nothing after it is created because the act of showing the form will keep it loaded:

```
' MTDemo2 - Multithreading demo program
' Copyright © 1997 by Desaware Inc. All Rights Reserved
Option Explicit
Private Sub cmdLaunch1_Click()
    Dim c As New clsMTDemo2
    c.DisplayObjPtr Nothing
End Sub
Private Sub cmdLaunch2_Click()
    Dim c As clsMTDemo2
    Set c = CreateObject("MTDemo2.clsMTDemo2")
End Sub
Private Sub Form_Load()
    lblThread.Caption = Str$(App.ThreadID)
End Sub
```

The form displays its thread identifier in a label on the form. The form contains two launch buttons, one that uses the New operator, the other that uses the CreateObject operator. If you run the program within the Visual Basic environment, you'll see that the forms are always created in the same thread. This is because the Visual Basic environment only supports a single thread. If you compile the program, you'll see that the CreateObject approach creates both the clsMTDemo2 and its form in a new thread.

Why Multithread?

Why all the fuss about multithreading if there is so much potential danger involved? Because, in certain situations, multithreading can dramatically improve performance. In some cases it can improve the efficiency of certain synchronization operations such as waiting for an application to terminate. It allows more flexibility in application architecture.

For example, add a long operation to the form in the MTDemo2 application with code such as this:

```
Private Sub cmdLongOp_Click()
Dim l&
Dim s$
For l = 1 To 1000000
s = Chr$(l And &H7F)
Next l
End Sub
```

Launch several instances of the form using the cmdLaunch1 button. When you click on the cmdLongOp button on any of the forms, you will see that it freezes up operations on all of the other forms. This is because all of the forms are running on a single thread—and that thread is busy running the long loop. If you reproduce this using the cmdLaunch2 button (with a compiled executable) and click the cmdLongOp button on a form, only that form will be frozen—the other forms will continue to be active. They are running in their own execution thread, and the long loop operation only ties up its own thread. Of course, you probably shouldn't be placing these kinds of long operations in your forms in any case. Following is a brief summary of when multithreading has value:

- **ActiveX EXE Server—no shared resources.** When you have an ActiveX EXE server that you expect to share among applications, multithreading prevents the applications from interfering with each other. If one application performs a long operation on an object in a single threaded server, the other applications are frozen out waiting for the server to become available. Multithreading avoids this problem. However, there are cases where you may want to use an ActiveX EXE server to arbitrate access to a shared resource. An example of this is the stock quote server described in my *Developing ActiveX Components with Visual Basic 5.0: A Guide to the Perplexed* book. In this case the single thread runs the stock quote server, which is shared among all of the applications using the server in turn.

- **Multithreading Client—implemented as an ActiveX EXE Server**. A simple form of this approach is demonstrated in the MTDemo2 application. It is used when an application supports multiple windows that must exit within a single application but work completely independently. Internet browsers are a good example of multithreaded clients, where each browser window runs in its own thread. Note that multithreading should not be used as a substitute for good event driven design.

- **Multithreading DLL.** A multithreading DLL does not actually create its own threads. It is simply a DLL that creates objects that run in the same thread that requests the objects. For example: a multithreaded ActiveX control (which is a DLL) creates controls that run in the same thread as the form that contains the control. This can improve efficiency on a multithreaded client such as an Internet browser.

- **Multithreaded Servers DLL or EXE**. In a client server architecture, multithreading can improve performance if you have a mix of long and short client requests. Be careful though—if all of your client requests are of similar length, multithreading can actually slow down the server's average response time! Never assume that the fact that your server is multithreading will necessarily improve performance.

The Threading Contract

Believe it or not, all of this has been in the way of introduction. Some of the material reviews information that is covered in far greater depth in *Developing ActiveX Components with Visual Basic 5.0: A Guide to the Perplexed*; other material describes new information for Service Pack 2.

Now, allow me to ask a question that goes directly to the heart of multithreading using COM (the component object model on which all Visual Basic objects, and those in other windows applications that use OLE are based).

Given: Multithreading is potentially extremely dangerous and specifically—attempting to multithread code that is not designed to support multithreading is likely to cause fatal errors and system crashes.

Question: How is it possible that Visual Basic allows you to create objects and use them under both single and multithreaded environments without any regard to whether they are designed for single or multithreaded use? In other words, how can a multithreaded Visual Basic application use objects that are not designed to be thread safe? How can other multithreaded applications use single threaded Visual Basic objects?

In short: How does COM handle threading issues?

If you know about COM, you know that it defines the structure of a contract. A COM object agrees to follow certain rules so that it can be used successfully from any application or object that supports COM.

Most people think first of the interface part of the contract—the methods and properties that an object exposes. But you may not be aware of the fact that COM also defines threading as part of the contract. And like any part of the COM contract—if you break it, you are in very deep trouble. Visual Basic, naturally, hides most of this from you, but in order to understand what follows, you must learn a little bit about the COM threading models.

The Single Threading Model

A single threaded server is the simplest type of server to implement. It is also the easiest to understand. In the case of an EXE server, the server runs in a single thread. All objects are created in that thread. All method calls to each object supported by the server must arrive in that thread.

But what if the client is running in a different thread? In that case, a proxy object must be created for the server object. This proxy object runs in the client's thread and reflects the methods and properties of the actual object. When a method is called on the proxy object, it performs whatever operations are necessary to switch to the object's thread, then calls the methods on the actual object using the parameters passed to the proxy. Naturally, this is a rather time consuming task—but it does allow the contract to be followed. This process of switching threads and transferring data from the proxy object, to the actual object and back *is called marshalling. It is covered in more depth in chapter 6 in my Developing ActiveX Components with Visual Basic 5.0: A Guide to the Perplexed* book.

In the case of DLL servers, the single threading model demands that all objects in the server be created and called in the same thread as the first object created by the server.

The Apartment Threading Model

Note that apartment model threading as defined by COM does NOT require that each thread have its own set of global variables. That's just how Visual Basic implemented the apartment model. The apartment model states that each object may be created in its own thread; however, once an object is created, its methods and properties may only be called by the same thread that created the object. If another thread wants to access methods of the object, it must go through a proxy.

This is a relatively easy model to implement. If you eliminate global variables (as Visual Basic does), the apartment model grants you thread safety automatically—because each object is effectively running in its own thread, and due to the lack of global variables, the different object threads do not interact with each other.

The Free Threading Model

The free threading model basically says that all bets are off. Any object can be created in any thread. All methods and properties on any object can be called at any time from any thread. The object accepts full responsibility for handling any necessary synchronization.

This is the hardest model to implement successfully, since it demands that the programmer handle all synchronization. In fact, until recently, OLE itself did not support this threading model! However, since marshalling is never required, this is the most efficient threading model.

Which model does your server support? How does an application, or Windows itself, know which threading model a server is using? This information is included in the registry. When Visual Basic creates an object, it checks the registry to determine in which cases a proxy object and marshalling are required.

It is the client's responsibility to adhere strictly to the threading requirements of each object that it creates.

The CreateThread API

Now let's take a look at how the CreateThread API can be used with Visual Basic.

Say you have a class that you want to have running in another thread in order to perform some background operation. A generic class of this type might have the following code (from the MTDemo 3 example):

```
' Class clsBackground
' MTDemo 3 - Multithreading example
' Copyright © 1997 by Desaware Inc. All Rights Reserved
Option Explicit
Event DoneCounting()
Dim l As Long
Public Function DoTheCount(ByVal finalval&) As Boolean
Dim s As String
    If l = 0 Then
        s$ = "In Thread " & App.threadid
        Call MessageBox(0, s$, "", 0)
    End If
    l = l + 1
    If l >= finalval Then
        l = 0
        DoTheCount = True
        Call MessageBox(0, "Done with counting", "", 0)
        RaiseEvent DoneCounting
    End If
End Function
```

The class is designed so that the DoTheCount function can be called repeatedly from a continuous loop in the background thread. We could have placed the loop in the object itself, but you'll see shortly that there are sound reasons for designing the object as shown here. The first time the DoTheCount function is called, a message box appears showing the thread identifier—that way we can verify the thread in which the code is running. The MessageBox API is used instead of the VB MessageBox command because the API function is known to be thread safe. A second message box is shown when the counting is complete, and an event is raised to indicate that the operation is finished.

The background thread is launched using the following code in the frmMTDemo3 form:

```
Private Sub cmdCreateFree_Click()
Set c = New clsBackground
StartBackgroundThreadFree c
```

```
End Sub
The StartBackgroundThreadFree function is defined in modMTBack
module as follows:
Declare Function CreateThread Lib "kernel32" (ByVal _
lpSecurityAttributes As Long, ByVal dwStackSize As Long, _
ByVal lpStartAddress As Long, ByVal lpParameter As Long, _
ByVal dwCreationFlags As Long, _lpThreadId As Long) _
As Long
Declare Function CloseHandle Lib "kernel32" _
(ByVal hObject As Long) As Long
' Start the background thread for this object
' using the invalid free threading approach.
Public Function StartBackgroundThreadFree(ByVal qobj As _
        clsBackground)
    Dim threadid As Long
    Dim hnd&
    Dim threadparam As Long
    ' Free threaded approach
    threadparam = ObjPtr(qobj)
    hnd = CreateThread(0, 2000, AddressOf BackgroundFuncFree, _
            threadparam, 0, threadid)
    If hnd = 0 Then
        ' Return with zero (error)
        Exit Function
    End If
    ' We don't need the thread handle
    CloseHandle hnd
    StartBackgroundThreadFree = threadid
End Function
```

The CreateThread function takes six parameters:

- lpSecurityAttributes is typically set to zero to use the default security attributes.

- dwStackSize is the size of the stack. Each thread has its own stack.

- lpStartAddress is the memory address where the thread starts. This must
  be an address of a function in a standard module obtained using the
  AddressOf operator.

- lpParameter is a long 32-bit parameter that is passed to the function that
  starts the new thread.

- dwCreationFlags is a 32-bit flag variable that lets you control the start of the thread (whether it is active, suspended, and so on). Details on these flags can be found in Microsoft's online 32-bit reference.

- lpThreadId is a variable that is loaded with the unique thread identifier of the new thread.

The function returns a handle to the thread.

In this case we pass a pointer to the clsBackground object that we wish to use in the new thread. ObjPtr retrieves the value of the interface pointer in the qobj variable. After the thread is created, the handle is closed using the CloseHandle function. This does *not* terminate the thread—the thread continues to run until the BackgroundFuncFree function exits. However, if we did not close the handle, the thread object would continue to exist even after the BackgroundFuncFree function exits. All handles to a thread must be closed and the thread terminated in order for the system to free up the resources allocated to the thread.

The BackgroundFuncFree function is as follows:

```
' A free threaded callback.
' This is an invalid approach, though it works
' in this case.
Public Function BackgroundFuncFree(ByVal param As _
    IUnknown) As Long
    Dim qobj As clsBackground
    Dim res&
    ' Free threaded approach
    Set qobj = param
    Do While Not qobj.DoTheCount(100000)
    Loop
    ' qobj.ShowAForm ' Crashes!
    ' Thread ends on return
End Function
```

The parameter to this function is a pointer to an interface (ByVal param as IUnknown). We can get away with this because under COM, every interface is based on IUnknown—so this parameter type is valid regardless of the type of interface originally passed to the function. We must, however, immediately set the param to a specific object type in order to use it. In this case qobj is set to the original `clsBackground` object that was passed to the `StartBackgroundThreadFree` object. The function then enters an infinite loop during which it performs any desired operation, in this case a repetitive count. A similar approach here might be to perform a wait operation that suspends the thread until a system event (such as a process termination) occurs. The thread could then call a method in the class to signal to the application that the event has occurred.

Accessing the `qobj` object is extremely fast because of the free threading nature of this approach(no marshalling is used. You'll notice, however, that if you try to have the `clsBackground` object show a form, the application crashes. You'll also notice that the completion event is never raised in the client form. In fact, even the *Microsoft Systems Journal* that describes this approach includes a great many warnings that there are some things that do not work when you attempt this approach.

Is this a flaw in Visual Basic?

Some people who tried deploying applications using this type of threading have found that their applications fail after upgrading to VB5 service pack 2.

Does this mean that Microsoft has failed to correctly provide backwards compatibility?

The answer to both questions is: No. The problem is not with Microsoft or Visual Basic.

The problem is that the above code is garbage.

The problem is simple—Visual Basic supports objects in both single threaded and apartment models. Let me rephrase this: Visual Basic objects are COM objects that make a statement under the COM contract that they will work correctly as single threaded or apartment model objects. That means that each object expects any method calls to take place on the same thread that created the object.

The example shown above violates this rule. It violates the COM contract.

What does this mean? It means that the behavior of the object is subject to change as Visual Basic is updated. It means that any attempt of that object to access other objects or forms may fail disastrously, and that the failure modes may change as those objects are updated. It means that even code that works now may suddenly fail as other objects are added, deleted, or modified. It means that it is impossible to characterize the behavior of the application, or to predict whether it will work or should work in any given environment. It means that it is impossible to predict whether the code will work on any given system, and that the behavior may vary depending on the operating system in use, the number of processors in use, and other system configuration issues.

You see, once you violate the COM contract, you are no longer protected by those features in COM that allow objects to successfully communicate with each other and with clients.

This approach is programming alchemy. It is irresponsible, and no programmer should ever use it. Period.

The CreateThread API Revisited

Now that I've shown you why the CreateThread API approach that has appeared in some articles is garbage, it's only fair that I make things right and show you how you can, in fact, use this API safely.

The trick is simple—you must simply adhere to the COM threading contract. This takes a bit more work, but the results have proven so far to be reliable.

The MTDemo3 sample shows this in the frmMTDemo3 form with the following code that launches an apartment model background class as follows:

```
Private Sub cmdCreateApt_Click()
    Set c = New clsBackground
    StartBackgroundThreadApt c
End Sub
```

So far this looks very similar to the free threading approach. You create an instance of the class and pass it to a function that starts the background thread. The following code appears in the modMTBack module:

```
' Structure to hold IDispatch GUID
Type GUID
    Data1 As Long
    Data2 As Integer
    Data3 As Integer
    Data4(7) As Byte
End Type
Public IID_IDispatch As GUID
Declare Function CoMarshalInterThreadInterfaceInStream _
Lib "ole32.dll" (riid As GUID, ByVal pUnk As IUnknown, _
ppStm As Long) As Long
Declare Function CoGetInterfaceAndReleaseStream Lib _
"ole32.dll" (ByVal pStm As Long, riid As GUID, _
pUnk As IUnknown) As Long
Declare Function CoInitialize Lib "ole32.dll" _
(ByVal pvReserved As Long) As Long
Declare Sub CoUninitialize Lib "ole32.dll" ()
' Start the background thread for this object
' using the apartment model
```

```
' Returns zero on error
Public Function StartBackgroundThreadApt(ByVal qobj As _
    clsBackground)
    Dim threadid As Long
    Dim hnd&, res&
    Dim threadparam As Long
    Dim tobj As Object
    Set tobj = qobj
    ' Proper marshaled approach
    InitializeIID
    res = CoMarshalInterThreadInterfaceInStream _
            (IID_IDispatch, qobj, threadparam)
    If res <> 0 Then
        StartBackgroundThreadApt = 0
        Exit Function
    End If
    hnd = CreateThread(0, 2000, AddressOf _
            BackgroundFuncApt, threadparam, 0, threadid)
    If hnd = 0 Then
        ' Return with zero (error)
        Exit Function
    End If
    ' We don't need the thread handle
    CloseHandle hnd
    StartBackgroundThreadApt = threadid
End Function
```

The StartBackgroundThreadApt function is a bit more complex than the free threading equivalent. The first new function is called InitializeIID. This function deals with the following code:

```
' Initialize the GUID structure
Private Sub InitializeIID()
    Static Initialized As Boolean
    If Initialized Then Exit Sub
    With IID_IDispatch
        .Data1 = &H20400
        .Data2 = 0
        .Data3 = 0
        .Data4(0) = &HC0
        .Data4(7) = &H46
    End With
    Initialized = True
End Sub
```

You see, we're going to need an interface identifier—a 16-byte structure that uniquely identifies an interface. In particular, we're going to need the interface identifier for the IDispatch interface (more information on IDispatch can be found in *Developing ActiveX Components with Visual Basic 5.0: A Guide to the Perplexed*). The InitializeIID function simply initializes the IID_IDispatch structure to the correct values for the IDispatch interface identifier. This value is obtained originally using a registry viewer utility. Why do we need this identifier?

Because in order to adhere to the COM threading contract, we need to create a proxy object for the clsBackground object. The proxy object needs to be passed to the new thread instead of the original object. Calls by the new thread on the proxy object will be marshaled into the current thread.

The CoMarshalInterThreadInterfaceInStream performs an interesting task. It collects all of the information needed to create a proxy for a specified interface and loads it into a stream object. In this example we use the IDispatch interface because we know that every Visual Basic class supports IDispatch, and we know that IDispatch marshalling support is built into Windows—so this code will always work. We then pass the stream object to the new thread. This object is designed by Windows to be transferable between threads in exactly this manner, so we can pass it safely to the CreateThread function. The rest of the StartBackgroundThreadApt function is identical to the StartBackgroundThreadFree function.

The BackgroundFuncApt function is also more complex than the free threaded equivalent as shown here:

```
' A correctly marshaled apartment model callback.
' This is the correct approach, though slower.
Public Function BackgroundFuncApt(ByVal param As Long) _
    As Long
    Dim qobj As Object
    Dim qobj2 As clsBackground
    Dim res&
    ' This new thread is a new apartment, we must
    ' initialize OLE for this apartment
        ' (VB doesn't seem to do it)
    res = CoInitialize(0)
    ' Proper apartment modeled approach
    res = CoGetInterfaceAndReleaseStream(param,
            IID_IDispatch, qobj)
    Set qobj2 = qobj
    Do While Not qobj2.DoTheCount(10000)
    Loop
    qobj2.ShowAForm
    ' Alternatively, you can put a wait function here,
```

```
' then call the qobj function when the wait is satisfied
' All calls to CoInitialize must be balanced
CoUninitialize
End Function
```

The first step is to initialize the OLE subsystem for the new thread. This is necessary for the marshalling code to work correctly. The `CoGetInterfaceAndReleaseStream` creates the proxy object for the original `clsBackground` object and releases the stream object used to transfer the data from the other thread. The `IDispatch` interface for the new object is loaded into the `qobj` variable. It is now possible to obtain other interfaces—the proxy object will correctly marshal data for every interface that it can support. Now you can see why the loop is placed in this function instead of in the object itself. When you call the `qobj2.DoTheCount` function for the first time, you'll see that the code is running in the original thread! Every time you call a method on the object, you are actually calling the method on the proxy object. Your current thread is suspended, the method request is marshaled to the original thread, and the method called on the original object in the same thread that created the object. If the loop was in the object, you would be freezing up the original thread.

The nice thing about this approach is that everything works. The `clsBackground` object can show forms and raise events safely. Of course it can—it's running in the same thread as the form and its client—as it should be. The disadvantage of this approach is, of course, that it is slow. Thread switches and marshalling are relatively slow operations. You would never actually want to implement a background operation as shown here.

But this approach can work extremely well if you can place the background operation in the `BackgroundFuncApt` function itself! For example: you could have the background thread perform a background calculation or a system wait operation. When it is complete, it can call a method on the object, which will raise an event in the client. By keeping the number of method calls small relative to the amount of work being done in the background function, you can achieve very effective results.

What if you want to perform a background operation that does not need to use an object? Obviously, the problems with the COM threading contract vanish. But other problems appear. How will the background thread signal completion to the foreground thread? How will they exchange data? How will the two threads be synchronized? All of these things are possible with appropriate use of API calls. (Refer to the book, *Visual Basic 5.0 Programmer's Guide to the Win32 API*, for information on synchronization objects such as Events, Mutexes, Semaphores and Waitable Timers.)

It also includes examples of memory-mapped files which can be helpful in exchanging data between processes. You may be able to use global variables to exchange data as well—but be aware that this behavior is not guaranteed by Visual

Basic (in other words, even if it works now, there is no assurance that it will work in the future). I would encourage you to use API based techniques to exchange data in this case. However, the advantage of the object-based approach shown here is that it makes the problem of exchanging data between threads trivial— simply do it through the object.

Conclusion

I once heard from an experienced Windows programmer that OLE is the hardest technology he's ever needed to learn. I agree. It is a vast subject and parts of it are very difficult to understand. Visual Basic, as always, hides much of the complexity from you.

There is a strong temptation to take advantage of advanced techniques such as multithreading using a "tips and techniques" approach. This temptation is encouraged by articles that sometimes present a particular solution, inviting you to cut and paste their techniques into your own applications.

When I wrote my original *Visual Basic Programmer's Guide to the Windows API*, I explicitly disavowed that approach. I felt that it is generally irresponsible to include code in an application that you don't understand, and that real knowledge, while hard to gain, is worth the effort even in the short run.

Thus my API books were designed not to provide quick answers and easy solutions, but to teach API usage to such a degree that programmers can intelligently apply even the most advanced techniques correctly, quickly going beyond what is shown in the book. I applied this same approach to *Developing ActiveX Components with Visual Basic 5.0: A Guide to the Perplexed,* which spends a great deal of time discussing the principles of ActiveX, COM, and object oriented programming before getting into implementation details.

Much of my career in the Visual Basic field, and much of Desaware's business, has been based on teaching Visual Basic programmers advanced techniques. The reader who inspired this article by criticizing me for holding back on threading technology and thus betraying this principle missed the point.

Yes, I teach and demonstrate advanced techniques—but I try never to miss the bigger picture. The advanced techniques that I teach must be consistent with the rules and specifications of Windows. They must be as safe to use as possible. They must be supportable in the long run. They must not break when Windows or Visual Basic changes.

I can claim only partial success—it's a hard line to draw sometimes, and Microsoft is at liberty to change the rules whenever they wish. But I always keep it in mind and try to warn people where I think I may be pushing the limit.

I hope this multithreading discussion shown here demonstrates the dangers of applying "simple techniques" without a good understanding of the underlying technology. I can't promise that the apartment model version of CreateThread usage is absolutely correct—only that it is safe to the best of my understanding and testing.

There may be other factors that I have missed—OLE is indeed complex and both the OLE DLLs and Visual Basic itself keep changing. I can only say that to the best of my knowledge, the code I've shown does obey the COM rules and that empirical evidence shows that Visual Basic 5.0's runtime is sufficiently thread-safe to run background thread code in a standard module.

Visual Basic 6

The following comments were written after the release of VB6.

Sigh. . . . It seems that many readers missed my original point. The idea was not to encourage VB programmers to use `CreateThread` with Visual Basic. It was to explain clearly and accurately why you shouldn't use `CreateThread` with Visual Basic.

So, when Visual Basic 6 turned out to be considerably less thread-safe than VB5, breaking the sample programs referenced by this article, what could I do? I suppose I could go back and revise the samples and try to make them work with VB6. But then the same problem might arise with later versions of Visual Basic as well.

Visual Basic offers good support of multithreading including multithreaded clients in ActiveX servers (this is described quite thoroughly in the latest edition of *Developing COM/ActiveX Components*). I strongly encourage you to stay within the rules defined by the Visual Basic documentation and not use the `CreateThread` API with Visual Basic.

For those who insist on pursuing `CreateThread` further, to start with, you should eliminate all Declare statements and use a type library instead. I don't promise that this will fix the problem, but my initial testing indicates that it is a necessary first step.

SpyWorks 6.2

It seems that telling people not to use `CreateThread` wasn't a satisfactory answer after all. I continued to receive requests for information on how to create threads both for background operations and to use NT synchronization objects from VB DLLs. As you probably know, when enough people ask for something that isn't easy or possible to do with Visual Basic, sooner or later it shows up as a new feature in SpyWorks. With version 6.2, we've included a component called `dwBackThread` that allows you to create objects from your VB DLL in their own thread and then trigger background operations. The component handles all of the necessary marshaling and cleanup for you so that it's as safe as one can be when doing multithreading. Most important—it follows all of the COM threading rules, so you don't have to worry about pieces of VB or components you use suddenly failing to work. See our product pages on SpyWorks for further details.

Visual Basic Strings: The BSTR Data Type

WHEN I STARTED WRITING THIS BOOK, I couldn't decide where to explain Visual Basic's String data type, the BSTR, because it did not integrate easily into any one chapter; yet it is important to understand if you are going to be writing components for Visual Basic. Therefore, I chose to cover the topic in an appendix in which I could explain BSTRs and how to work with them, without clouding the content of a chapter in the book. In this appendix I will explain what BSTRs are, how to allocate, manage and free them, and how to pass them to and from Visual Basic.

What Is a BSTR?

A BSTR is a pointer to an array of null terminated Unicode characters. In fact, a BSTR is to Unicode characters what a char* is to ANSI characters, with one important exception: there is a 4-byte "length" field preceding each BSTR. This 32-bit length field is stored in the four bytes of memory directly in front of the BSTR and contains the length of the BSTR at the current time. This means that a BSTR is technically not a pointer because a pointer by definition points to the beginning address of a variable. In the case of a BSTR, it points to the address of the fifth byte of what is essentially a data structure. Figure B-1 illustrates the layout of the string "ABCDEFG" as a BSTR in memory.

> **NOTE:** *Although BSTRs will usually contain an array of Unicode characters, it is perfectly legal for a BSTR to contain an array of ANSI characters; however, this is usually only done by or for a Visual Basic client, or as a means to transport binary data in a COM scenario. An example of this ANSI usage of a BSTR is seen later in this appendix.*

You can see that each character occupies two bytes. This is because all Unicode characters are 16-bit characters even if only eight bits are non-null. You will also notice that the character string "ABCDEFG" in Figure B-1 is followed by a

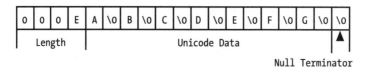

Figure B-1. The layout of the BSTR in memory

null terminator just like a char*. This is the case with all BSTRs. However, unlike a char* the null terminator is not used to determine the length of the string because a BSTR can contain embedded nulls. Also, the terminating null at the end of a BSTR is **not** part of the length of the BSTR. Again referring to Figure B-1, you can see that the string "ABCDEFG" is prefixed in memory by the 32-bit value 0x0E (decimal 14), which is the number of characters (7) times 2 bytes for each character. This sums up to a length of 14 bytes for the BSTR. The null terminator was not included when calculating the length of the BSTR, nor is it a part of the BSTR.

If it's starting to sound like BSTRs are a little more complicated than other types of character strings, it's because they are! In fact, working with BSTRs can be quite a daunting task. The reason is that they have to be very carefully managed by COM. Why? For one thing, each BSTR assumes that the four bytes preceding it contain its length, so it is critical that those four bytes are not corrupted. And because the BSTR can contain embedded nulls its size cannot be determined by searching for a null terminator. Essentially, if it ever loses the four bytes preceding it, or if it is corrupted somehow, the BSTR is sunk! And consequently so is the program or component using it. Fortunately, there is a set of functions that are especially made, and required, to work with BSTRs. These functions are the BSTR System functions.

The BSTR System Functions

The BSTR System functions are COM/Win32 API functions that allocate, manage, and free BSTRs. Rather than elaborate here, I recommend a great article on MSDN by Bruce McKinney called "Strings the OLE Way" that, although slightly dated, contains currently useful information on BSTRs and their associated system functions. (The article is included as "Appendix C" in this book). In *this* appendix I will concentrate on using the BSTR wrapper classes, _bstr_t and CComBSTR, which take care of the messy details of allocations and management of BSTRs. However, the fact that there are wrapper classes doesn't let you off the hook for following the COM rules regarding BSTRs.

The BSTR Management Rules

There are a few rules dictated by COM that you have to follow when working with BSTRs. These rules are in place to allow the clients and servers to pass BSTRs around by reference or by value, without any memory access violations or memory leaks on either side. Follow these simple rules and you should avoid the common pitfalls of using BSTRs.

1. Never free a BSTR passed to you by value or as an [in] parameter.

2. Free and allocate a new, or re-allocate any BSTR passed in by reference or as an [in,out] parameter. Do not free the re-allocated BSTR.

3. Allocate but *do not* free any BSTR returned to a client or passed in as an [out] or [out,retval] parameter.

4. Never modify a BSTR directly: use the BSTR API functions or a BSTR wrapper class.

The BSTR Wrapper Classes

Due to the complexity of working with BSTRs, Microsoft created wrapper classes to address many of the technical semantics of dealing with BSTRs and to make the lives of developers working with BSTRs much easier. There are two main wrapper classes in use today: _bstr_t and CComBSTR. CComBSTR is part of the *Active Template Library* (ATL) while _bstr_t is a compiler COM support class. I prefer to use _bstr_t even when using ATL, but both are easy to use. All of the examples in this appendix will use _bstr_t.

Using _bstr_t

_bstr_t is a class just like any other C++ class, and can therefore be used as such. For instance, to create an empty _bstr_t you simply use the following syntax:

```
_bstr_t s; //create an empty _bstr_t
```

Then to assign a value to the newly created _bstr_t you use the overloaded assignment operator like so:

```
s = "Hello There" ; //create an empty _bstr_t
```

To return a BSTR to a client use the copy method as such:

```
return s.copy(); //return a copy of the contained BSTR
```

Fortunately, the copy function does all of the necessary allocation on the BSTR for you. And the underlying BSTR is freed when the _bstr_t object goes out of scope.

As you can see, using the _bstr_t is very straightforward and intuitive. In fact, the _bstr_t wrapper makes using the notoriously difficult BSTR data type down-right easy! The main thing that becomes simpler is the fact that the BSTR gets au-tomatically allocated and freed for you (by calling the BSTR system functions in-ternally by the _bstr_t object) when the _bstr_t object is declared or when it goes out of scope. However, even though dealing with BSTRs is made easier by the _bstr_t, you are still responsible for following the BSTR rules listed earlier in this text. Here is a sample program that shows the BSTR rules actually being applied. I created this project in the same manner as the COM project in Chapter 11. Follow the steps listed there, except for the obvious name changes where applicable. This project is also available on the Web site for the book at www.apress.com.

First, the IDL file for the COM class BSTRTest, COM_bstr_test.idl:

```
// COM_bstr_test.idl : IDL source for COM_bstr_test.dll
//


// This file will be processed by the MIDL tool to
// produce the type library (COM_bstr_test.tlb) and marshalling code.

import "oaidl.idl";
import "ocidl.idl";
    [
        object,
          uuid(6F1B4D79-4F44-44F5-80B0-E205E63734D1),
        dual,
          helpstring("IBSTRTest Interface"),
          pointer_default(unique)
    ]
    interface IBSTRTest : IDispatch
    {
        [id(1), helpstring("method UseBSTRPassedIn")]
                HRESULT UseBSTRPassedIn([in] BSTR strIn);

        [id(2), helpstring("method UseBSTRPassedInOut")]
                HRESULT UseBSTRPassedInOut([in,out] BSTR *strInOut,
                [out,retval] long *retVal);
        [id(3), helpstring("method UseBSTRPassedOut")]
                HRESULT UseBSTRPassedOut([out] BSTR *strOut,
                [out,retval] long *retVal);
    };
```

```
[
    uuid(DA131245-EF77-4EB4-AD52-CCF28C53F853),
    version(1.0),
    helpstring("COM_bstr_test 1.0 Type Library")
]
library COM_BSTR_TESTLib
{
    importlib("stdole32.tlb");
    importlib("stdole2.tlb");

    [
        uuid(72F7DB36-7B04-402A-86E8-CC114F443D84),
        helpstring("BSTRTest Class")
    ]
    coclass BSTRTest
    {
        [default] interface IBSTRTest;
    };
};
```

Notice the directional parameters like [in], [in,out] and [out] in the IDL file. These parameters dictate the BSTR rule that must be followed by the client and component alike.

Now let's look at the header file for the library COM_BSTR_TESTLib, BSTRTest.h:

```
// BSTRTest.h : Declaration of the CBSTRTest

#ifndef __BSTRTEST_H_
#define __BSTRTEST_H_

#include "resource.h"        // main symbols


/////////////////////////////////////////////////////
// CBSTRTest
class ATL_NO_VTABLE CBSTRTest :
    public CComObjectRootEx<CComSingleThreadModel>,
    public CComCoClass<CBSTRTest, &CLSID_BSTRTest>,
    public IDispatchImpl<IBSTRTest, &IID_IBSTRTest,
                                    &LIBID_COM_BSTR_TESTLib>
{
public:
    CBSTRTest()
```

```
            {
            }

    DECLARE_REGISTRY_RESOURCEID(IDR_BSTRTEST)

    DECLARE_PROTECT_FINAL_CONSTRUCT()

    BEGIN_COM_MAP(CBSTRTest)
        COM_INTERFACE_ENTRY(IBSTRTest)
        COM_INTERFACE_ENTRY(IDispatch)
    END_COM_MAP()

    // IBSTRTest
    public:
        STDMETHOD(UseBSTRPassedOut)(
                            /*[out]*/ BSTR *strOut,
                            /*[out,retval]*/ long *retVal);
        STDMETHOD(UseBSTRPassedInOut)(
                            /*[in,out]*/ BSTR *strInOut,
                            /*[out,retval]*/ long *retVal);
        STDMETHOD(UseBSTRPassedIn)(/*[in]*/ BSTR strIn);
    };


    #endif //__BSTRTEST_H_
```

Notice that each of the "by reference" BSTR parameters for the methods are pointers to BSTRs, while the "by value" BSTR parameter are just BSTRs.

Now let's look at the implementation file for library COM_BSTR_TESTLib, BSTRTest.cpp:

```
// BSTRTest.cpp : Implementation of CBSTRTest
#include "stdafx.h"
#include <comdef.h>
#include "COM_bstr_test.h"
#include "BSTRTest.h"


/////////////////////////////////////////////////
// CBSTRTest

STDMETHODIMP CBSTRTest::UseBSTRPassedIn(BSTR strIn)
{
    //Use the passed in BSTR
    MessageBox(0,(char*)(_bstr_t(strIn)),"COM_bstr_test",MB_OK);
```

```
    return S_OK;
}


STDMETHODIMP CBSTRTest::UseBSTRPassedInOut(BSTR *strInOut, long *retVal)
{
    //make a copy of the bstr
    _bstr_t strTemp(*strInOut,TRUE);

    //create a new string value in the copy
    strTemp = "New Value!";

    //reallocate the BSTR
    SysReAllocString(strInOut,(wchar_t*)strTemp);

    //return the length of the new value
    *retVal = strTemp.length();

    //strTemp's destructor takes care of its cleanup

    return S_OK;
}


STDMETHODIMP CBSTRTest::UseBSTRPassedOut(BSTR *strOut, long *retVal)
{
    //create a BSTR wrapper
    _bstr_t s;

    //put a value in the wrapper
    s = "This is the new value!";

    //return a new BSTR
    *strOut = s.copy();

    return S_OK;
}



BSTR __stdcall PassAndReturnBSTR(/*parameter must be a
                                  "StrPtr(str)" & "ByVal As Long" in VB
                                  */BSTR strIn)
{
    int len = SysStringLen(strIn);

    //create an ANSI string
```

```
        char *lp_s = new char[len + 1];

        //null terminate the string
        lp_s[len] = 0;

        //copy the passed in *ANSI* BSTR to the char*
        wcstombs(lp_s, strIn,len);

        //create a new *ANSI* BSTR to hold the old one
        BSTR s = SysAllocStringByteLen(lp_s,strlen(lp_s));

        //free memory
        bdelete[] lp_s;

        //return the newly created *ANSI* BSTR
        return s;
}

BSTR __stdcall PassAndReturnBSTRByRefAsString(/*parameter must be a
                                            "ByRef As String" in VB
                                            */BSTR *strIn)
{
        int len = SysStringByteLen(*strIn);

        //create an ANSI string
        char *lp_s = new char[len + 1];

        //null terminate the string
        lp_s[len] = 0;

        //copy the passed in *ANSI* BSTR to the char*
        memcpy(lp_s,*strIn,len);

        //create a new *ANSI* BSTR to hold the old one
        BSTR s = SysAllocStringByteLen(lp_s,len);

        //free memory
        delete[] lp_s;

        //return the newly created *ANSI* BSTR
        return s;
}
```

You can see that each function follows the appropriate BSTR rule depending on the direction of the BSTR parameter. You will also notice that the exported non-COM function, `PassAndReturnBSTR`, is defined in this file. You can see that it treats the BSTR differently than the COM functions do. The reason for this is that Visual Basic treats each version differently. Anytime Visual Basic passes a string to or from a Declare function, it passes and expects an ANSI, null terminated string. This is somewhat frustrating, but what are you to do? Just be thankful that there is a way to deal with this behavior. You can see from the function that I wrote, `PassAndReturnBSTR`, that I have returned a BSTR created with the `SysAllocStringByteLen` API function, which is one of the BSTR system functions. This function creates a BSTR with an ANSI string inside of it (which is technically considered binary data). This is what Visual Basic wants to see returned from a function that returns a Visual Basic `String` data type. You will also notice when you look at the Visual Basic client code listed below that the parameter for the `PassAndReturnBSTR` function is `Declared` as `ByVal As Long`. Observe that the actual parameter is passed using the controversial Visual Basic `StrPtr` function. The reason that the parameter is declared and passed this way is so Visual Basic won't convert the BSTR to an ANSI version (as it does with all Strings in a `Declare` statement) before sending it to the component. To prove that Visual Basic converts even `ByRef As String` parameters to ANSI BSTRs before calling remote functions, I have included the `PassAndReturnBSTRByRefAsString` function. You will notice that the client `Declare` statement calls this parameter `ByRef As String`, which would make you think that the value passed to the function would be a Unicode BSTR, but it's not. Visual Basic converts it to an ANSI BSTR before sending it. Notice that in this version of the DLL function I don't have to do any ANSI/Unicode conversion because the BSTR has already been converted.

Here is the Visual Basic client code that demonstrates the functions in the library:

```
Option Explicit

Private Declare Function PassAndReturnBSTR Lib _

"d:\projects\apress\COM_bstr_test\debug\COM_bstr_test.DLL" _
                            (ByVal strIn As Long) As String

Private Declare Function PassAndReturnBSTRByRefAsString Lib _

"d:\projects\apress\COM_bstr_test\debug\COM_bstr_test.DLL" _
                            (ByRef strIn As String) As String

Public s As String
```

```vbnet
                Private Sub cmdDeclareByRef_Click()

                Dim strIn As String
                Dim strReturn As String

                strIn = "Dll call value"

                MsgBox "Passing Value:" & strIn

                strReturn = PassAndReturnBSTRByRefAsString(strIn)

                MsgBox "Returned Value:" & strReturn

                End Sub
                Private Sub cmdDeclare_Click()

                Dim strIn As String
                Dim strReturn As String

                strIn = "Dll call value"

                MsgBox "Passing Value:" & strIn

                strReturn = PassAndReturnBSTR(StrPtr(strIn))

                MsgBox "Returned Value:" & strReturn

                End Sub

                Private Sub cmdIn_Click()

                Dim s As New COM_BSTR_TESTLib.BSTRTest

                'Call the "[in] BSTR" parameter
                s.UseBSTRPassedIn "This is my BSTR"

                End Sub

                Private Sub cmdInOut_Click()

                Dim s As New COM_BSTR_TESTLib.BSTRTest
                Dim strRetVal As String
```

```
strRetVal = "This is my BSTR"

MsgBox "Before call: " & strRetVal

'Call the "[in,out] BSTR" parameter
s.UseBSTRPassedInOut strRetVal

MsgBox "After call: " & strRetVal

End Sub

Private Sub cmdOut_Click()

Dim s As New COM_BSTR_TESTLib.BSTRTest
Dim strRetValWithParen As String
Dim strRetValWithoutParen As String
Dim lngRetVal As Long

'Call the "[out] BSTR*" param without parentheses -
' VB leaves strRetValWithoutParen alone
s.UseBSTRPassedOut strRetValWithoutParen
MsgBox "Called without parentheses: " & strRetValWithoutParen

'Call the "[out] BSTR*" param with parentheses -
'VB makes strRetValWithParen const?
s.UseBSTRPassedOut (strRetValWithParen)
MsgBox "Called with parentheses: " & strRetValWithParen

'Call the "[out] BSTR*" param with parentheses -
' VB makes strRetValWithParen const?
lngRetVal = s.UseBSTRPassedOut(strRetValWithParen)
MsgBox "Called with parentheses using return value: " & strRetValWithParen

End Sub
```

Conclusion

As you can see, using BSTRs in your C++ components requires that you understand exactly what BSTRs are and how to use them properly, although your task is made considerably easier by using the BSTR wrapper classes instead of using BSTRs directly. If you follow the examples for using BSTRs shown in this appendix, you should easily incorporate BSTRs or the BSTR wrapper classes in your components and programs.

Article 3.
Strings the OLE Way

by Bruce McKinney
April 18, 1996

THE DIFFERENCE BETWEEN MICROSOFT VISUAL BASIC strings and Visual C++ strings is the difference between "I'll do it" and "You do it." The C++ way is fine for who it's for, but there aren't many programmers around anymore who get a thrill out of allocating and destroying their own string buffers. In fact, most C++ class libraries (including the Microsoft Foundation Classes, or MFC) provide string classes that work more or less on the Basic model, which is similar to the model of Pascal and FORTRAN.

When you manage an array of bytes (or an array of books or beer bottles or babies), there are two ways of maintaining the lengths. The marker system puts a unique marker at the end of the array. Everything up to the marker is valid. The count system adds a special array slot containing the number of elements. You have to update the count every time you resize the array. Both systems have their advantages and disadvantages. The marker system assumes you can find some unique value that will never appear in the array. The count system requires tedious bookkeeping to keep the count accurate.

The C language and most of its offspring use the marker system for storing strings, with the null character as the marker. All the other languages I know use the count system. You might argue that the majority indicates the better choice, but even if you buy that, C still gets the last laugh. Many of the leading operating systems of the world (all the flavors of Unix, Windows, and OS/2, for example) expect strings passed to the system to be null-terminated. As a result, languages such as Pascal and FORTRAN support a special null-terminated string type for passing strings to the operating system. Basic doesn't have a separate type for null-terminated strings, but it has features that make passing null-terminated strings easy.

As a language-independent standard, OLE can't afford to take sides. It must accommodate languages in which null is not a special character, but it must also be able to output null-terminated strings for its host operating system. More importantly, OLE recognizes that requiring the operating system to manage strings is inherently more stable and reliable in a future computing world where strings may be transferred across process, machine, and eventually Internet boundaries. I've been told that the name *BSTR* is a compression of Basic STRing, but in fact a BSTR looks a lot more like a Pascal string than like the strings Basic old-timers remember.

In any case, C++ programmers have some unlearning to do when it comes to writing strings for OLE. But before you can get into BSTR details, you need to clearly understand the difference between Unicode and ANSI strings.

Unicode Versus ANSI

Stringwise, we are cursed to live in interesting times. The world according to Microsoft (and many other international companies) is moving from ANSI to Unicode characters, but the transition isn't exactly a smooth one.

Most of the Unicode confusion comes from the fact that we are in the midst of a comprehensive change in the way characters are represented. The old way uses the ANSI character set for the first 256 bytes, but reserves some characters as double-byte character prefixes so that non-ANSI character sets can be represented. This is very efficient for the cultural imperialists who got there first with Latin characters, but it's inefficient for those who use larger character sets. Unicode represents all characters in two bytes. This is inefficient for the cultural imperialists (although they still get the honor of claiming most of the first 128 characters with zero in the upper byte), but it's more efficient (and more fair) for the rest of the world.

Different Views of Unicode

Eventually, everybody will use Unicode, but nobody seems to agree on how to deal with the transition.

- **Windows 3.*x***—Doesn't know a Unicode from a dress code, and never will.

- **16-bit OLE**—Ditto.

- **Windows NT**—Was written from the ground up first to do the right thing (Unicode) and secondly to be compatible (ANSI). All strings are Unicode internally, but Windows NT also completely supports ANSI by translating internal Unicode strings to ANSI strings at run time. Windows NT programs that use Unicode strings directly can be more efficient by avoiding frequent string translations, although Unicode strings take about twice as much data space.

- **Windows 95**—Uses ANSI strings internally. Furthermore, it doesn't support Unicode strings even indirectly in most contexts—with one big exception.

- **32-bit OLE**—Was written from the ground up to do the right thing (Unicode) and doesn't do ANSI. The OLE string types—OLESTR and BSTR—are Unicode all the way. Any 32-bit operating system that wants to do OLE must have at least partial support for Unicode. Windows 95 has just enough Unicode support to make OLE work.

- **Visual Basic**—The designers had to make some tough decisions about how they would represent strings internally. They might have chosen ANSI, because it's the common subset of Windows 95 and Windows NT, and converted to Unicode whenever they needed to deal with OLE. But since Visual Basic 4.0 is OLE inside and out, they chose Unicode as the internal format, despite potential incompatibilities with Windows 95. The Unicode choice caused many problems and inefficiencies both for the developers of Visual Basic and for Visual Basic developers—but the alternative would have been worse.

- **The Real World**—Most existing data files use ANSI. The .WKS, .DOC, .BAS, .TXT, and most other standard file formats use ANSI. If a system uses Unicode internally but needs to read from or write to common data formats, it must do Unicode-to-ANSI conversion. Someday there will be Unicode data file formats, but today they're pretty rare.

What does this mean for you? It means you must make choices about any program you write:

- If you write using Unicode internally, your application will run only on Windows NT, but it will run faster. Everything is Unicode, inside and out. There are no string translations—except when you need to write string data to standard file formats that use ANSI. An application written this way won't be out-of-date when some future iteration of Windows 9*x* gets Unicode.

- If you write using ANSI internally, your application will run on either Windows NT or Windows 95, but it will run slower under Windows NT because there are a lot of string translations going on in the background. An application written this way will someday be outdated when the whole world goes Unicode, but it may not happen in your lifetime.

The obvious choice for most developers is to use the ANSI version because it works right now for all 32-bit Windows platforms. But I'd like to urge you to take a little extra time to build *both* versions.

If you choose to write your application using both ANSI and Unicode, Win32 and the C run-time library both provide various types and macros to make it easier to create portable programs from the same source. To use them, define the symbol _UNICODE for your Unicode builds and the symbol _MBCS for your ANSI builds. The samples already have these settings for the Microsoft Developer Studio.

> **NOTE:** *As far as this article is concerned, there is no difference between double-byte character strings—DBCS—and multi-byte character strings—MBCS. Similarly, "wide character" and "Unicode" are synonymous in the context of this article.*

A WCHAR Is a wchar_t Is an OLECHAR

Just in case you're not confused enough about ANSI and Unicode strings, everybody seems to have a different name for them. Furthermore, there's a third type of string called a single-byte character string (SBCS), which we will ignore in this article.

In the Win32 API, ANSI normally means MBCS. The Win32 string functions (lstrlenA, lstrcpyA, and so on) assume multi-byte character strings, as do the ANSI versions of all application programming interface (API) functions. You also get Unicode versions (lstrlenW, lstrcpyW). Unfortunately, these aren't implemented in Windows 95, so you can't use them on BSTRs. Finally, you get generic macro versions (lstrlen, lstrcpy) that depend on whether you define the symbol UNICODE.

The C++ run-time library is even more flexible. For each string function, it supports a single-byte function (strlen); a multi-byte function (_mbslen); a wide character (wcslen), and a generic macro version (_tcslen) that depends on whether you define _UNICODE, _MBCS, or _SBCS. Notice that the C run-time library tests _UNICODE while Win32 tests UNICODE. We get around this by defining these to be equivalent in OLETYPE.H.

Win32 provides the MultiByteToWideChar and WideCharToMultiByte functions for converting between ANSI and Unicode. The C++ run-time library provides the mbstowcs and wcstombs functions for the same purpose. The Win32 functions are more flexible, but not in any way that matters for this article. We'll use the simpler run-time versions.

Types also come in Unicode and ANSI versions, but to add to the confusion, OLE adds its own types to those provided by Win32 and ANSI. Table C-1 lists some of the types and type coercion macros you need to be familiar with.

Table C-1. Types and Type Coercion Macros

TYPE	DESCRIPTION
char	An 8-bit signed character (an ANSI character).
wchar_t	A typedef to a 16-bit unsigned short (a Unicode character).
CHAR	The Win32 version of char.
WCHAR	The Win32 version of wchar_t.
OLECHAR	The OLE version of wchar_t.
_TCHAR	A generic character that maps to char or wchar_t.
LPSTR, LPCSTR	A Win32 character pointer. The version with C is const.
LPWSTR, LPCWSTR	A Win32 wide character pointer.
LPOLESTR, LPCOLESTR	An OLE wide character pointer.
LPTSTR, LPCTSTR	A Win32 generic character pointer.
_T(*str*), _TEXT(*str*)	Identical macros to create generic constant strings.
OLESTR(*str*)	OLE macro to create generic constant strings.

Do you notice a little redundancy here? A little inconsistency? The sample code uses the Win32 versions of these types, except when there isn't any Win32 version or the moon is full.

In normal C++ programming, you should use the generic versions of functions and types as much as possible so that your strings will work in either Unicode or ANSI builds. In this series, the String class hides a lot of the detail of making things generic. Generally it provides overloaded ANSI and Unicode versions of functions rather than using generic types. When you have a choice, you should use Unicode strings rather than ANSI or generic strings. You'll see how and why this nontypical coding style works later.

> **NOTE:** *Versions of Visual C++ before 4.0 had a DLL called OLE2ANSI that automatically translated OLE Unicode strings to ANSI strings behind the scenes. This optimistic DLL made OLE programming simpler than previously possible. It was indeed pleasant to have the bothersome details taken care of, but performance-wise, users were living in a fool's paradise. OLE2ANSI is history now, although conditional symbols for it still exist in the OLE include files. The OLECHAR type, rather than the WCHAR type, was used in OLE prototypes so that it could be transformed into the CHAR type by this DLL. Do not define the symbol OLE2ANSI in the hopes that OLE strings will magically transform themselves into ANSI strings. There is no Santa Claus.*

What Is a BSTR?

The BSTR type is actually a typedef, which in typical Windows include file fashion, is made up of more typedefs and defines. You can follow the twisted path yourself, but here's what it boils down to:

```
typedef wchar_t * BSTR;
```

Hmmm. A BSTR is actually a pointer to Unicode characters. Does that look familiar? In case you don't recognize this, let me point out a couple of similar typedefs:

```
typedef wchar_t * LPWSTR;
typedef char * LPSTR;
```

So if a BSTR is just a pointer to characters, how is it different from the null-terminated strings that C++ programmers know so well? Internally, the difference is that there's something extra at the start and end of the string. The string length is maintained in a long variable just before the start address being pointed to, and the string always has an extra null character after the last character of the string. This null isn't part of the string, and you may have additional nulls embedded in the string.

That's the technical difference. The philosophical difference is that the contents of BSTRs are sacred. You're not allowed to modify the characters except according to very strict rules that we'll get to in a minute. OLE provides functions for allocating, reallocating, and destroying BSTRs. If you own an allocated BSTR, you may modify its contents as long as you don't change its size. Because every BSTR is, among other things, a pointer to a null-terminated string, you may pass one to any string function that expects a read-only (const) C string. The rules are much tighter for passing BSTRs to functions that modify string buffers. Usually, you can only use functions that take a string buffer argument and a maximum length argument.

All the rules work on the honor system. A BSTR is a BSTR by convention. Real types can be designed to permit only legal operations. Later we'll define a C++ type called String that does its best to enforce the rules. The point is that BSTR servers are honor-bound to follow the rules so that BSTR clients can use strings without even knowing that there are rules.

The BSTR System Functions

My descriptions of the OLE BSTR functions are different from and, in my opinion, more complete than the descriptions in OLE documentation. I had to experiment to determine some behavior that was scantily documented, and I checked the include files to get the real definitions, so I am confident that my descriptions are valid and will work for you.

For consistency with the rest of the article, the syntax used for code in this section has been normalized to use Win32 types such as LPWSTR and LPCWSTR. The actual prototypes in OLEAUTO.H use const OLECHAR FAR * (ignoring the equivalent LPCOLESTR types). The original reasons for using OLECHAR pointers rather than LPCWSTRs don't matter for this article.

You need to read this section only if you want to fully understand how the String class (presented later) works. But you don't really need to understand BSTRs in order to use the string class.

BSTR SysAllocString(LPCWSTR wsz);

Given a null-terminated wide character string, allocates a new BSTR of the same length and copies the string to the BSTR. This function works for empty and null strings. If you pass in a null string, you get back a null string. You also get back a null string if there isn't enough memory to allocate the given string, as shown in the following example:

```
// Create BSTR containing "Text"
bs = SysAllocString(L"Text")
```

BSTR SysAllocStringLen(LPCWSTR wsz, unsigned len);

Given a null-terminated wide-character string and a maximum length, allocates a new BSTR of the given length and copies up to that length of characters from the string to the BSTR. If the length of the copied string is less than the given maximum length, a null character is written after the last copied character. The rest of the requested length is allocated, but not initialized (except that there will always be a null character at the end of the BSTR). Thus the string will be doubly null-terminated—once at the end of the copied characters and once at the end of the allocated space. If NULL is passed as the string, the whole length is allocated, but not initialized (except for the terminating null character). Don't count on allocated but uninitialized strings to contain null characters or anything else in particular. It's best to fill uninitialized strings as soon after allocation as possible.

```
// Create BSTR containing "Te"
bs = SysAllocStringLen(L"Text", 2)
// Create BSTR containing "Text" followed by \0 and a junk character
bs = SysAllocStringLen(L"Text", 6)
```

BSTR SysAllocStringByteLen(LPSTR sz, unsigned len);

Given a null-terminated ANSI string, allocates a new BSTR of the given length and copies up to that length of bytes from the string to the BSTR. The result is a BSTR with two ANSI characters crammed into each wide character. There is very little you could do with such a string, and therefore not much reason to use this function. It's there for string conversion operations such as Visual Basic's StrConv function. What you really want is a function that creates a BSTR from an ANSI string, but this isn't it (we'll write one later). The function works like SysAllocStringLen if you pass a null pointer or a length greater than the length of the input string.

BOOL SysReAllocString(BSTR * pbs, LPWSTR wsz);

Allocates a new BSTR of the same length as the given wide-character string, copies the string to the BSTR, frees the BSTR pointed to by the first pointer, and resets the pointer to the new BSTR. Notice that the first parameter is a pointer to a BSTR, not a BSTR. Normally, you'll pass a BSTR pointer with the address-of operator.

```
// Reallocate BSTR bs as "NewText"
f = SysReAllocString(&bs, "NewText");
```

BOOL SysReAllocStringLen(BSTR * pbs, LPWSTR wsz, unsigned len);

Allocates a new BSTR of the given length, and copies as many characters as fit of the given wide-character string to the new BSTR. It then frees the BSTR pointed to by the first pointer and resets the pointer to the new BSTR. Often the new pointer will be the same as the old pointer, but you shouldn't count on this. You can give the same BSTR for both arguments if you want to truncate an existing BSTR. For example, you might allocate a BSTR buffer, call an API function to fill the buffer, and then reallocate the string to its actual length, as illustrated by the following example:

```
// Create uninitialized buffer of length MAX_BUF.
BSTR bsInput = SysAllocStringLen(NULL, MAX_BUF);
// Call API function to fill the buffer and return actual length.
cch = GetTempPathW(MAX_BUF, bsInput);
// Truncate string to actual length.
BOOL f = SysReAllocStringLen(&bsInput, bsInput, cch);
```

unsigned SysStringLen(BSTR bs);

Returns the length of the BSTR in characters. This length does not include the terminating null. This function will return zero as the length of either a null BSTR or an empty BSTR.

```
// Get character length of string.
cch = SysStringLen(bs);
```

unsigned SysStringByteLen(BSTR bs);

Returns the length of the BSTR in bytes, not including the terminating null. This information is rarely of any value. Note that if you look at the length prefix of a BSTR in a debugger, you'll see the byte length (as returned by this function) rather than the character length.

void SysFreeString(BSTR bs);

Frees the memory assigned to the given BSTR. The contents of the string may be completely freed by the operating system, or they may just sit there unchanged. Either way, they no longer belong to you and you had better not read or write to them. Don't confuse a deallocated BSTR with a null BSTR. The null BSTR is valid; the deallocated BSTR is not.

```
// Deallocate a string.
SysFreeString(bs);
```

BSTR SysAllocStringA(LPCSTR sz);

The same as SysAllocString, except that it takes an ANSI string argument. OLE doesn't provide this function; it's declared in BString.H and defined in BString.Cpp. Normally, you should only use this function to create Unicode BSTRs from ANSI character string variables or function return values. It works for ANSI string literals, but it's wasted effort because you could just declare Unicode literals and save yourself some run-time processing.

```
// Create BSTR containing "Text".
bs = SysAllocStringA(sz)
```

```
BSTR SysAllocStringLenA(LPCSTR sz, unsigned len);
```

The same as `SysAllocStringLen`, except that it takes an ANSI string argument. This is my enhancement function, declared in BString.H.

```
// Create BSTR containing six characters, some or all of them from sz.
bs = SysAllocStringLenA(sz, 6)
```

The Eight Rules of BSTR

Knowing what the BSTR functions do doesn't mean you know how to use them. Just as the BSTR type is more than its typedef implies, the BSTR functions require more knowledge than documentation states. Those who obey the rules live in peace and happiness. Those who violate them live in fear—plagued by the ghosts of bugs past and future.

The trouble is, these rules are passed on in the oral tradition; they are not carved in stone. You're just supposed to know. The following list is an educated attempt—based on scraps of ancient manuscripts, and revised through trial and error—to codify the oral tradition. Remember, it is just an attempt.

Rule 1: Allocate, destroy, and measure BSTRs only through the OLE API (the Sys functions)

Those who use their supposed knowledge of BSTR internals are doomed to an unknowable but horrible fate in future versions. (You have to follow the rules if you don't want bugs.)

Rule 2: You may have your way with all the characters of strings you own

The last character you own is the last character reported by **SysStringLen**, not the last non-null character. You may fool functions that believe in null-terminated strings by inserting null characters in BSTRs, but don't fool yourself.

Rule 3: You may change the pointers to strings you own, but only by following the rules

In other words, you can change those pointers with **SysReAllocString** or **SysReAllocStringLen**. The trick with this rule (and rule 2) is determining whether you own the strings.

Rule 4: You do not own any BSTR passed to you by value

The only thing you can do with such a string is copy it or pass it on to other functions that won't modify it. The caller owns the string and will dispose of it according to its whims. A BSTR passed by value looks like this in C++:

```
void DLLAPI TakeThisStringAndCopyIt(BCSTR bsIn);
```

The BCSTR is a typedef that should have been defined by OLE, but wasn't. I define it like this in OleType.H:

```
typedef const wchar_t * const BCSTR;
```

If you declare input parameters for your functions this way, the C++ compiler will enforce the law by failing on most attempts to change either the contents or the pointer.

The Object Description Language (ODL) statement for the same function looks like this:

```
void WINAPI TakeThisStringAndCopyIt([in] BCSTR bsIn);
```

The BCSTR type is simply an alias for BSTR because MKTYPLIB doesn't recognize const. The [in] attribute allows MKTYPLIB to compile type information indicating the unchangeable nature of the BSTR. OLE clients such as Visual Basic will see this type information and assume you aren't going to change the string. If you violate this trust, the results are unpredictable.

Rule 5: You own any BSTR passed to you by reference as an in/out parameter

You can modify the contents of the string, or you can replace the original pointer with a new one (using SysReAlloc functions). A BSTR passed by reference looks like this in C++:

```
void DLLAPI TakeThisStringAndGiveMeAnother(BSTR * pbsInOut);
```

Notice that the parameter doesn't use BCSTR because both the string and the pointer are modifiable. In itself the prototype doesn't turn a reference BSTR into an in/out BSTR. You do that with the following ODL statement:

```
void WINAPI TakeThisStringAndGiveMeAnother([in, out] BSTR * pbsInOut);
```

The [in, out] attribute tells MKTYPLIB to compile type information indicating that the string will have a valid value on input, but that you can modify that value and return something else if you want. For example, your function might do something like this:

```
// Copy input string.
bsNew = SysAllocString(*pbsInOut);
// Replace input with different output.
f = SysReAllocString(pbsInOut, L"Take me home");
// Use the copied string for something else.
UseString(bsNew);
```

Rule 6: You must create any BSTR passed to you by reference as an out string

The string parameter you receive isn't really a string—it's a placeholder. The caller expects you to assign an allocated string to the unallocated pointer, and you'd better do it. Otherwise the caller will probably crash when it tries to perform string operations on the uninitialized pointer. The prototype for an out parameter looks the same as one for an in/out parameter, but the ODL statement is different:

```
void WINAPI TakeNothingAndGiveMeAString([out] BSTR * pbsOut);
```

The [out] attribute tells MKTYPLIB to compile type information indicating that the string has no valid input but expects valid output. A container such as Visual Basic will see this attribute and will free any string assigned to the passed variable before calling your function. After the return the container will assume the variable is valid. For example, you might do something like this:

```
// Allocate an output string.
*pbsOut = SysAllocString(L"As you like it");
```

Rule 7: You must create a BSTR in order to return it

A string returned by a function is different from any other string. You can't just take a string parameter passed to you, modify the contents, and return it. If you did, you'd have two string variables referring to the same memory location, and unpleasant things would happen when different parts of the client code tried to modify them. So if you want to return a modified string, you allocate a copy, modify the copy, and return it. You prototype a returned BSTR like this:

```
BSTR DLLAPI TransformThisString(BCSTR bsIn);
```

The ODL version looks like this:

```
BSTR WINAPI TransformThisString([in] BSTR bsIn);
```

You might code it like this:

```
// Make a new copy.
BSTR bsRet = SysAllocString(bsIn);
// Transform copy (uppercase it).
_wcsupr(bsRet);
// Return copy.
return bsRet;
```

Rule 8: A null pointer is the same as an empty string to a BSTR

Experienced C++ programmers will find this concept startling because it certainly isn't true of normal C++ strings. An empty BSTR is a pointer to a zero-length string. It has a single null character to the right of the address being pointed to, and a long integer containing zero to the left. A null BSTR is a null pointer pointing to nothing. There can't be any characters to the right of nothing, and there can't be any length to the left of nothing. Nevertheless, a null pointer is considered to have a length of zero (that's what SysStringLen returns).

When dealing with BSTRs, you may get unexpected results if you fail to take this into account. When you receive a string parameter, keep in mind that it may be a null pointer. For example, Visual Basic 4.0 makes all uninitialized strings null pointers. Many C++ run-time functions that handle empty strings without any problem fail rudely if you try to pass them a null pointer. You must protect any library function calls:

```
if (bsIn != NULL) {
    wcsncat(bsRet, bsIn, SysStringLen(bsRet));
}
```

When you call Win32 API functions that expect a null pointer, make sure you're not accidentally passing an empty string:

```
cch = SearchPath(wcslen(bsPath) ? bsPath : (BSTR)NULL, bsBuffer,
        wcslen(bsExt) ? bsExt : (BSTR)NULL, cchMax, bsRet, pBase);
```

When you return functions (either in return values or through out parameters), keep in mind that the caller will treat null pointers and empty strings the same. You can return whichever is most convenient. In other words, you have to clearly understand and distinguish between null pointers and empty strings in your C++ functions so that callers can ignore the difference in Basic.

In Visual Basic, a null pointer (represented by the constant vbNullString) is equivalent to an empty string. Therefore, the following statement prints True:

```
Debug.Print vbNullString = ""
```

If you need to compare two strings in a function designed to be called from Visual Basic, make sure you respect this equality.

Those are the rules. What is the penalty for breaking them? If you do something that's clearly wrong, you may just crash. But if you do something that violates the definition of a BSTR (or a VARIANT or SAFEARRAY, as we'll learn later) without causing an immediate failure, results vary.

When you're debugging under Windows NT (but not under Windows 95) you may hit a breakpoint in the system heap code if you fail to properly allocate or deallocate resources. You'll see a message box saying "User breakpoint called from code at 0xXXXXXXXX" and you'll see an *int 3* instruction pop up in the disassembly window with no clue as to where you are or what caused the error. If you continue running (or if you run the same code outside the debugger or under Windows 95), you may or may not encounter a fate too terrible to speak of. This is not my idea of a good debugging system. An exception or an error dialog box would be more helpful, but something is better than nothing, which is what you get under Windows 95.

A BSTR Sample

The Test.Cpp module contains two functions that test BSTR arguments. They're the basis of much of what I just passed on as the eight rules. The TestBStr function exercises each of the BSTR operations. This function doesn't have any output or arguments, but you can run it in the C++ debugger to see exactly what happens when you allocate and reallocate BSTRs. The TestBStrArgs function tests some legal and illegal BSTR operations. The illegal ones are commented out so that the sample will compile and run. This article is about the String class, not raw BSTR operations, so I'll leave you to figure out these functions on your own. It's probably more interesting to study this code than to run it, but the BSTR button in the Cpp4VB sample program does call these functions.

Before you start stepping through this sample with the Microsoft Developer Studio, you'll have to tell the debugger about Unicode. You must decide whether you want arrays of unsigned shorts to be displayed as integer arrays or as Unicode strings. The choice is pretty obvious for this project, but you'll be up a creek if you happen to have both unsigned short arrays and Unicode strings in some other project. The debugger can't tell the difference. You probably won't have this kind of problem if your compiler and debugger interpret wchar_t as an intrinsic type.

To get the Microsoft debugger to display wchar_t arrays as Unicode, you must open the Tools menu and select Options. Click the Debug tab and enable Display Unicode Strings. (Note that this applies to Visual C++ versions 5 and later.)

For Visual C++ version 5, you can use the *su* format specifier on all Unicode variables in your watch window (although this won't help you in the locals window). To get a little ahead of ourselves, you can add the following line to make the String class described in the next section display its internal BSTR member as a Unicode string:

```
; from BString.h
String =<m_bs,su>
```

Comments in AUTOEXP.DAT explain the syntax of format definitions. Comments in AUTOEXP.DAT explain the syntax of format definitions. You don't need to do this for Visual C++ version 6.

The String Class

One reason for writing server DLLs is to hide ugly details from clients. We'll take care of all the Unicode conversions in the server so that clients don't have to, but handling those details in every other line of code would be an ugly way to program. C++ provides classes so that we can hide ugly details even deeper. The String class is designed to make BSTR programming look almost as easy as programming with Basic's String type. Unfortunately, structural problems (or perhaps lack of imagination on my part) make this worthy goal unachievable. Still, I think you'll find the String type useful.

> **NOTE:** *I know that it's presumptuous of me to name my BSTR class wrapper String, my VARIANT class wrapper Variant, and my SAFEARRAY class wrapper SafeArray. Most vendors of classes have the courtesy to use some sort of class naming convention that avoids stealing the most obvious names from the user's namespace. But I've been using the Basic names for other OLE types through typedefs. Why not use them for the types that require classes? After all, the goal is to make my classes look and work as much like intrinsic types as possible. The include filename, however, is BString.H because the name string.h is already used by the C++ run-time library.*

Rather than getting into String theory, let's just plunge into a sample. The goal is to implement the Visual Basic GetTempFile function. If you read my earlier book, *Hardcore Visual Basic*, you may remember this function. It's a thin wrapper for the Win32 GetTempFileName function. Like most API functions, GetTempFileName is designed for C programmers. GetTempFile is designed for Basic programmers. You call it the obvious way:

```
sTempFile = GetTempFile("C:\TMP", "VB")
```

The first argument is the directory where you want to create the temporary file, the second is an optional prefix for the file name, and the return value is a full file path. You might get back a filename such as C:\TMP\VB6E.TMP. This name is guaranteed to be unique in its directory. You can create the file and fill it with data without being concerned about it overwriting any other temporary file or even a permanent file that happens (incredibly) to have the same name.

A String API Sample

It would probably be easier to write the GetTempFile wrapper in Visual Basic, but we're going to do it in C++ to prove a point. Besides, some of the more complex samples we'll be looking at later really do need C++.

The GetTempFile function is tested by the event handler attached to the Win32 button in the sample program. This code also tests other Win32 emulation functions and, when possible, the raw Win32 functions from which they are created. You can study the Basic code in Cpp4VB.Frm and the C++ code in Win32.Cpp.

Here's the GetTempFile function:

```cpp
BSTR DLLAPI GetTempFile(
    BSTR bsPathName,
    BSTR bsPrefix
    )
{
  try {
    String sPathName = bsPathName;
    String sPrefix = bsPrefix;
    String sRet(ctchTempMax);
    if (GetTempFileName(sPathName, sPrefix, 0, Buffer(sRet)) == 0) {
        throw (Long)GetLastError();
    }
    sRet.ResizeZ();
    return sRet;
  } catch(Long e) {
    ErrorHandler(e);
    return BNULL;
  }
}
```

Exception Handling

This function, like many of the other functions you'll see in this series of articles, uses C++ exception handling. I'm not going to say much about this except that all the normal code goes in the *try* block and the *catch* block gets all the exceptions. The ErrorHandler function is purposely elsewhere so that we can change the whole error system just by changing this function. For now, we're only interested in the normal branch of the code.

You can see that if the GetTempFileName API function returns zero, we throw an error having the value of the last API error. This will transfer control to the catch block where the error will be handled. What you can't see (yet) is that constructors and methods of the String class can also throw exceptions, and when they do, the errors will bubble up through as many levels of nested String code as necessary and be handled by this outside catch block. Instead of handling errors where they happen, you defer them to one place in client code.

In other words, C++ exception handling works a lot like Visual Basic's error handling. Throwing an exception in C++ is like calling the Raise method of the Err object, and catching an exception is like trapping an error with Basic's On Error statement. We'll revisit exception handling again in Article 4.

Initializing String Variables

The first thing we do is assign the BSTR parameters to String variables. This is an unfortunate requirement. It would be much nicer if we could just pass String parameters. Unfortunately, a String variable requires more storage than a BSTR variable and you can't just use the two interchangeably. You'll understand this later when you get a brief look inside the String type, but for now just be aware that the performance and size overhead for this assignment is very low and well worth the cost, especially on functions that are larger than GetTempFile.

The second thing we do is initialize the *sRet* variable, which will be the return value. The String type has several constructors and one of them creates an empty buffer of a given length. The constant *ctchTempMax* is the maximum Win32 file length—256 characters. That's a lot more than you'll need for a temporary filename on most disks, but we're being safe. If you watch the code in a debugger, you'll see that in debug builds the buffer is filled with an unusual padding character—the @ sign. The only purpose is so that you can see exactly what's going on. The data is left uninitialized in release builds.

In the extremely unlikely case that you don't have 256 bytes of memory left in your system, the initialization will fail and throw an out-of-memory exception.

Buffers for Output Strings

Now we're ready to call the Win32 GetTempFileName function. The *sPathName* and *sPrefix* arguments provide the input, and the *sRet* argument is a buffer that the function will fill. There's only one problem. Strings are Unicode internally, but GetTempFileName will usually be GetTempFileNameA and will expect ANSI string arguments. Of course if you're building for Windows NT only, you can do a Unicode build and call GetTempFileNameW. Either way, the String type should do the right thing, and do it automatically.

Well, that worthy goal isn't as easy as you might expect. It's not too bad for the input arguments because the String type has a conversion operator that knows how to convert the internal Unicode character string to a separate internal ANSI character string and return the result. The conversion just happens automatically. But the buffer in the *sRet* variable is a little more difficult because the conversion must be two-way.

The API function has to get an ANSI string, and the ANSI string created by the function must be converted back to a Unicode BSTR. That's why we pass the Buffer object rather than passing the *sRet* argument directly. You might think from the syntax that Buffer is a function. Wrong! Buffer is a class that has a constructor taking a String argument. A temporary Buffer object is constructed on the stack when GetTempFileName is called. This temporary object is destroyed when GetTempFileName returns. And that's the whole point of the object. The destructor for the Buffer object forces the automatic Unicode conversion.

Let's step through what happens if you're doing an ANSI build. You call the GetTempFileName function. The Buffer object is constructed on the stack by assigning the *sRet* String variable to an internal variable inside the Buffer object. But *sRet* contains a Unicode string and GetTempFileName expects an ANSI string. No problem. Buffer provides a conversion operator that converts the Unicode string to an ANSI string and returns it for access by the ANSI API function. GetTempFileName fills this buffer with the temporary filename. Now the ANSI copy is right, but the Unicode buffer is untouched. That's OK because when GetTempFileName returns, the destructor for the Buffer object will convert the ANSI copy of the buffer to Unicode in the real string buffer. Sounds expensive, but all these operations are actually done with inline functions and the cost is acceptable. You can check out the details in BString.H.

Now, what happens during a Unicode build? Pretty much nothing. The Buffer constructor is called, but it just stores the BSTR pointer. The Buffer class also has a conversion operator that makes the buffer return a Unicode character buffer, but it just returns the internal BSTR pointer. The destructor checks to see if anything needs to be converted to Unicode, but nothing does. That's pretty much how the

String type works throughout. It performs Unicode conversion behind the scenes only when necessary.

String Returns

Let's continue with the rest of the function. After calling GetTempFileName, the GetTempFile function has the filename followed by a null in the *sRet* variable. That's what a C program would want, but it's not what a Basic program wants because the length of *sRet* is still 256. If you passed the variable back as is, you'd see a whole lot of junk characters following the null in the Visual Basic debugger. So we first call the ResizeZ method to truncate the string to its first null. Later we'll see a Resize method that truncates to a specified length. Unlike most API string functions, GetTempFile doesn't return the length, so we have to figure it out from the position of the null.

Finally, we return the *sRet* variable and exit from the GetTempFile function. The destructors for all three String variables are called. At this point, all the temporary ANSI buffers are destroyed, but the destructors don't destroy the internal Unicode strings because they're owned by the caller. Visual Basic will destroy those strings when it gets good and ready, and it wouldn't be very happy if our String destructor wiped them out first—especially the return value.

If this seems hopelessly complicated, don't sweat it. You don't have to understand the implementation to use the String type. It's a lot simpler (and shorter) than doing the same operations with the BSTR type. You just have to understand a few basic principles.

A String Warm-up

Let's take a look at some of the specific things you can do with strings. The most important thing you'll be doing with them is passing them to and receiving them from functions. Here's how it's done in the mother of all String functions, TestString. TestString puts the String class through its paces, testing all the methods and operators and writing the results to a returned string for analysis.

```
BSTR DLLAPI TestString(
    BCSTR bsIn,
    BSTR * pbsInOut,
    BSTR * pbsOut)
{
```

This doesn't mean much without its ODL definition:

```
[
entry("TestString"),
helpstring("Returns modified BSTR manipulated with String type"),
]
BSTR WINAPI TestString([in] BSTR bsIn,
                       [in, out] BSTR * pbsInOut,
                       [out] BSTR * pbsOut);
```

We talked about *in* and *out* parameters in Article 1, but at that point they were primarily documentation. With the BSTR type (as well as with VARIANT and SAFEARRAY) you had better code your DLL functions to match their ODL declarations. Otherwise, your disagreements with Visual Basic can have drastic consequences.

The purpose of an *in* parameter (such as *bsIn*) is to pass a copy of a string for you to read or copy. It's not yours, so don't mess with the contents. The purpose of an *in/out* parameter (such as *pbsInOut*) is to pass you some input and receive output from you. Do what you want with it. Modify its contents, copy it to another String, or pass a completely different string back through its pointer. The purpose of an out parameter (such as *pbsOut*) is to receive an output string from you. There's nothing there on input, but there had better be something there (if only a NULL) when you leave the function, because Visual Basic will be counting on receiving something.

String Constructors

Once you receive your BSTRs, you need to convert them to String. You can also create brand new Strings to return through the return value or out parameters, or just to serve as temporary work space. The String constructors create various kinds of strings:

```
// Constructors
String sTmp;                        // Uninitialized
String sIn = bsIn;                  // In argument from BSTR
String sCopy = *pbsInOut;           // In/out argument from BSTR
String sString = sIn;               // One String from another
String sChar(1, WCHAR('A'));        // A single character
String sChars(30, WCHAR('B'));      // A filled buffer
String sBuf(30);                    // An uninitialized buffer
String sWide = _W("Wide");          // From Unicode string
String sNarrow = "Narrow";          // From ANSI string
String sNative = _T("Native");      // From native string
String sRet;
```

Most of these speak for themselves, but notice the WCHAR casts and the use of the _W macro to initialize with a wide-character constant. When initializing Strings with constants, you should always use Unicode characters or strings. The String type will just have to convert your ANSI strings to Unicode anyway. Conversion is a necessary evil if you have an ANSI character string variable, but if you have a constant, you can save run-time processing by making it a Unicode string to start with.

Unfortunately, you can't just initialize a String with a Unicode string like this:

```
String s = L"Test";
```

The problem is that the String type has a BSTR constructor and a LPCWSTR constructor, but what you'll get here is an LPWSTR and there's no separate constructor for that. There can't be a separate constructor because to C++, a BSTR looks the same as an LPWSTR, but of course internally it's very different. Any time you assign a wide character string to a String, you must cast it to an LPCWSTR so that it will go through the right constructor. The _W macro casts to LPCWSTR unobtrusively. C++ is a very picky language, and the String class seems to hit the edges of the pickiness in a lot of places. You have to develop very careful habits to use it effectively.

> **NOTE:** *Extending Visual Basic with C++ DLLs Many of the problems in writing a String class are caused by Unicode confusion, and much of that confusion comes from the fact that in most current compilers the wchar_t type (called WCHAR in this article) is a typedef to an unsigned short rather than an intrinsic type. Overloaded functions are a critical part of designing a safe, convenient class in C++, but when overloading, C++ considers a typedef to be a simple alias rather than a unique type. A constructor overloaded to take a WCHAR type actually sees an unsigned short, which may conflict with other overloaded integer constructors. Debuggers won't know whether to display a WCHAR pointer as a string or as an array of unsigned shorts. Compile-time error messages will display confusing errors showing unsigned short rather than the character type you thought you were using. If you're fortunate enough to use a compiler that provides wchar_t as an intrinsic type, you won't see these problems. Unfortunately, Microsoft Visual C++ is not yet among those compilers.*

String Assignment

As you already know (or had better find out soon if you're going to program in C++), initialization is a very different thing from assignment, even though the syntax may look similar. The String type provides the assignments you expect through the operator= function:

```
// Assignment
WCHAR wsz[] = L"Wide";
char sz[] = "Narrow";
sTmp = sIn;                    // From another String variable
sTmp = _W("Wide");            // From Unicode literal string
sTmp = WCHAR('W');            // From Unicode character
sTmp = LPCWSTR(wsz);          // From Unicode string variable
sTmp = LPCSTR(sz);            // From ANSI string variable
```

Again, you have to jump through some hoops to make sure your wide-character string assignments go through the proper const operator. C++ can't tell the difference between a wide-character string and a BSTR, so you have to tell it. Generally, you should avoid doing anything with ANSI character strings. The String type can handle ANSI strings, but you just end up sending a whole lot of zeros to and from nowhere. The only reason to use ANSI strings is to pass them to API functions or to C run-time functions, and you normally shouldn't do the latter either, because it's much more efficient to use the ws*cxxx* versions of the run-time functions.

String Returns

Let's skip all the cool things you can do to massage String variables and go to the end of TestString where you return your Strings:

```
// Return through out parameters.
sTmp = _W("...send me back");
*pbsInOut = sTmp;
*pbsOut = _B("Out of the fire");

// Return value
return sRet;

} catch(Long err) {
  HandleError(err);
}
}
```

In the first line we assign a wide string to the temporary variable (*sTmp*) and then assign *sTmp* to the BSTR out parameter (*pbsInOut*). A BSTR conversion operator in the String type enables you to perform the assignment of the wide string stored in *sTmp* to the BSTR out parameter, *pbsInOut*. The second assignment does the same thing, but uses the _B macro to create and destroy a temporary

String variable on the stack. The _B macro uses a double typecast and token paste to hide the following atrocity:

```
*pbsOut = String(LPCWSTR(L"Out of the fire"));
```

Finally, the return value is set to the *sRet* variable containing the string that we'll build in the next section. Internally, the return works exactly like the assignment to an out parameter and in fact calls the same BSTR conversion operator. Think of the Basic syntax:

```
TestString = sRet
```

This gives you a better picture of what actually happens in a C++ return statement.

A String Workout

There's a lot more to the String type than initialization and assignment. It's designed to be a full-featured string package—duplicating most of the functions you find in the C run-time library or in popular string classes such as MFC's CString. You won't find everything you could ever need, but conversion operators make it easy to pass Strings to run-time string functions. Or better yet, whenever you want to do something that isn't directly supported, add it to the library and send me the code. Be sure to use the wsc*xxx* version of run-time library calls.

The TestString function uses the iostream library to build a formatted string that tests the String methods and operators, and then assigns that string to the return value. Here's how it works:

```
ostrstream ostr;

ostr << endcl << "Test length and resize:" << endcl;
sTmp = _W("Yo!");
ostr << "sTmp = _W(\"Yo!\"); // sTmp==\"" << sTmp
    << "\", " << "sTmp.Length()==" << sTmp.Length() << endcl;
.
.
.
ostr << ends;
char * pch = ostr.str();
sRet = pch;
delete[] pch;
```

The String class defines an iostream insertion operator (<) so that you can easily insert ANSI character strings (converting from Unicode BSTRs) into an output stream. Notice that I also use a custom *endcl* manipulator rather than the standard *endl* manipulator. My version inserts a carriage return/line feed sequence rather than the standard line feed only.

You can study up on iostream and check the code if this isn't clear. The point here is to show off String features, not the iostream library. The rest of this section will show chunks of output that put the String type through its paces.

Length Methods

We'll start with the length-related methods:

```
sTmp = _W("Yo!"); // sTmp=="Yo!", sTmp.Length()==3
sTmp.Resize(20);  // sTmp=="Yo!", sTmp.Length()==20, sTmp.LengthZ()==3
sTmp.ResizeZ();   // sTmp=="Yo!", sTmp.Length()==3
```

The Length() method always returns the real length of the String regardless of nulls, while LengthZ() returns the length to the first null. Normally you'll Resize to truncate a string to a specified length, but you can also expand a string to create a buffer, then truncate back to the first null after passing the buffer to an API function.

Empty Strings and Comparisons

Internally, a String, like a BSTR, can be either a NULL string or an empty string, although Basic treats these the same. The String type provides methods to test and set this state:

```
sTmp = "Empty";   // sTmp=="Empty",sTmp.IsEmpty==0, sTmp.IsNull==0
sTmp.Empty();     // sTmp=="",sTmp.IsEmpty==1, sTmp.IsNull==0
sTmp.Nullify();   // sTmp=="",sTmp.IsEmpty==1, sTmp.IsNull==1
```

In the Basic tradition, the IsEmpty() method returns True if the string is either null or empty. That's generally all you need to know. Many C++ run-time functions can't handle null strings, and some API functions can't handle empty strings. So you can use the IsNull() function to identify a null string. There's no direct way to identify what C++ thinks of as an empty string, but the following expression will work:

```
sTmp.IsEmpty() && !sTmp.IsNull()
```

Of course, you can test equality to empty or any other value with logical operators. If *sTmp* is empty (in either sense), the String == operator will return True for *(sTmp == BNULL)* or for *(sTmp == _B(""))*. Notice how cast macros are used to convert literals to Strings before comparison. You can also test comparisons with expressions such as:

```
(sNarrow >= sWide)
```

String Indexing

The String class provides an indexing operator to insert or extract characters in strings. For example:

```
// sWide=="Wide", i==2, wch=='n'
sWide[i] = wch;      // sWide=="Wine"
wch = sWide[i - 1]; // wch=='i'
sWide[0] = 'F';      // sWide=="Fine"
```

There's nothing to prevent you from enhancing the index operator so that you could insert a string with it or even extract one. I'll leave that to you.

Concatenation

Any string type worth its salt must be capable of concatenation, and String does it as you would expect—with the + and += operators. It can append characters or strings:

```
// sChar=="A", sIn=="Send me in"
sChar += sIn;         // sChar=="ASend me in"
sChar += WCHAR('F'); // sChar=="ASend me inF"
sChar += 'G';         // sChar=="ASend me inFG"
sChar += _W("Wide"); // sChar=="ASend me inFGWide"
sChar += "Narrow";    // sChar=="ASend me inFGWideNarrow"
sTmp = sNarrow + sNative + _W("Slow") + "Fast" + WCHAR('C') + 'D'
// sTmp=="NarrowNativeSlowFastCD"
```

Some of the String methods look and act like Visual Basic string functions. Don't forget that Visual Basic strings are 1-based, not 0-based like C++ strings:

```
sChar = sTmp.Mid(7, 6); // sChar=="Native"
sChar = sTmp.Mid(7);     // sChar=="NativeSlowFastCD"
sChar = sTmp.Left(6);    // sChar=="Narrow"
sChar = sTmp.Right(6);   // sChar=="FastCD"
```

An additional challenge (left as an exercise for the reader) is to add the Visual Basic **Mid** statement to insert characters into a string.

String Transformations

The String class has some transformation functions in both method and function versions:

```
// sWide=="Fine"
sWide.UCase();          // sWide=="FINE"
sWide.LCase();          // sWide=="fine"
sWide.Reverse();        // sWide=="enif"
sChar = UCase(sWide);   // sChar=="ENIF", sWide=="enif"
sChar = LCase(sWide);   // sChar=="enif", sWide=="enif"
sChar = Reverse(sWide); // sChar=="fine", sWide=="enif"
```

There are also similar versions of the Trim, LTrim, and RTrim functions:

```
sChar = Trim(sTmp);  // sChar=="Stuff", sTmp=="    Stuff    "
sTmp.Trim();         // sTmp=="Stuff"
```

String Searching

I always found Basic's InStr function confusing, so I called the equivalent String function Find. It can find characters or strings, searching forward or backward, with or without case sensitivity.

```
// sTmp="A string in a String in a String in a string"
//      "123456789012345678901234567890123456789012345678901234567890"
i = sTmp.Find('S');     // Found at position: 15
i = sTmp.Find('S', ffReverse);  // Found at position: 27
i = sTmp.Find('S', ffIgnoreCase);  // Found at position: 3
i = sTmp.Find('S',
                ffReverse | ffIgnoreCase);  // Found at position: 39
i = sTmp.Find('Z');              // Found at position: 0
i = sTmp.Find("String");     // Found at position: 15
```

```
i = sTmp.Find("String", ffReverse);  // Found at position: 27
i = sTmp.Find("String", ffIgnoreCase);  // Found at position: 3
i = sTmp.Find("String",
              ffIgnoreCase | ffReverse); // Found at position: 39
i = sTmp.Find("Ztring");            // Found at position: 0
```

This method is 1-based, so C++ programmers may need to make a mental adjustment when using it.

It's not too difficult to think of enhancements for the String type. Just look through the Basic and C++ run-time functions and add anything that looks interesting. It's easy to map existing C++ functions to a natural String format, and it's not much harder to write your own functions that provide string features that C++ lacks. But before you spend a lot of time on this, consider how String is used. In most DLLs, you'll be using the constructors, the conversion operators, and maybe a few logical or assignment operators. Basic already provides its own string functionality, so unless you want to replace it with your own more powerful string library, there's not much point in having a full-featured String type. On the other hand, maybe Basic does need a more powerful string library. Be my guest.

How the String Class Works

We've talked a lot about how to use the String type, but not much about how it is implemented. This article is not about how to write class libraries in C++, so I haven't explained the internals. However, you'll probably feel a little more comfortable using the class (and it will certainly be easier to enhance it) if you have some idea how String works, so let's take a look under the hood.

```
class String
{
    friend class Buffer;
public:
// Constructors
    String();
    String(const String& s);
    // Danger! C++ can't tell the difference between BSTR and LPWSTR. If
    // you pass LPWSTR to this constructor, you'll get very bad results,
    // so don't. Instead, cast to constant before assigning.
    String(BSTR bs);
    // Any non-const LPSTR or LPWSTR should be cast to LPCSTR or LPCWSTR
    // so that it comes through here.
    String(LPCSTR sz);
    String(LPCWSTR wsz);
    // Filled with given character (default -1 means unitialized allocate).
```

```
        String(int cch, WCHAR wch = WCHAR(-1));

// Destructor
    ~String();
    .

    .

    .

private:
    BSTR    m_bs;           // The Unicode data
    LPSTR   m_pch;          // ANSI representation of it
    Boolean m_fDestroy;     // Destruction flag

    // Implementation helpers
    void Concat(int c, LPCWSTR wsz);
    void Destroy();
    void DestroyA();

};
```

String Construction

A String consists of three pieces of data: the internal BSTR, a pointer to an array of ANSI characters, and a flag indicating how the String should be destroyed. You can see how this works by looking at a few constructors.

```
inline String::String()
    : m_bs(SysAllocString(NULL)), m_pch(NULL), m_fDestroy(True)
{
}

inline String::String(const String& s)
    : m_bs(SysAllocString(s.m_bs)), m_pch(NULL), m_fDestroy(True)
{
}

// Convert BSTR to String.
inline String::String(BSTR bs)
    : m_bs(bs), m_pch(NULL), m_fDestroy(False)
{
}

inline String::String(LPCWSTR wsz)
```

```
    : m_bs(SysAllocString(wsz)), m_pch(NULL), m_fDestroy(True)
{
}
inline String::String(LPCSTR sz)
    : m_bs(SysAllocStringA(sz)), m_pch(NULL), m_fDestroy(True)
{
}
```

The constructors do nothing but initialize the three members. Notice that the ANSI string constructor (the one with the LPCSTR argument) uses the SysAllocStringA function to create a Unicode BSTR from an ANSI string. Another important point is that the constructors that create an internal BSTR set the *m_fDestroy* flag so that the BSTR will be destroyed by the destructor. The constructor that takes a BSTR parameter just wraps an existing BSTR parameter (usually passed as a parameter). The String doesn't own this BSTR and has no right to destroy it, so the *m_fDestroy* flag is set to false.

String Translation

The *m_pch* member is initialized to null, and it stays that way until someone asks to translate the BSTR to an ANSI string. The translation mechanism is the LPCSTR conversion operator, which is called automatically whenever you pass a String to a parameter that expects an LPCSTR. It looks like this:

```
String::operator LPCSTR()
{
    if ((m_pch == NULL) && (m_bs != NULL)) {
        // Check size.
        unsigned cmb = wcstombs(NULL, m_bs, SysStringLen(m_bs)) + 1;
        // Allocate string buffer and translate ANSI string into it.
        m_pch = new CHAR[cmb];
        wcstombs(m_pch, m_bs, cmb);
    }
    return m_pch;
}
```

If the internal BSTR is not NULL, this operator allocates an ANSI buffer of the proper size and copies a translated string to it. This ANSI string will be maintained for reuse by subsequent calls to LPCSTR until the String is destroyed or until some member function changes the contents of the internal BSTR, thus invalidating the ANSI buffer. Any such member should destroy or update the ANSI buffer.

String Destruction

Here are the String destruction functions:

```
void String::Destroy()
{
    if (m_fDestroy) {
        SysFreeString(m_bs);
    }
    DestroyA();
}
inline String::~String()
{
    Destroy();
}


// Invalidate ANSI buffer.
inline void String::DestroyA()
{
    delete[] m_pch;
    m_pch = NULL;
}
```

The destruction job is broken into parts so that member functions can de-stroy the whole String or just invalidate the ANSI buffer.

For example, here's how the operator= members handle Unicode and ANSI strings.

```
const String& String::operator=(LPCSTR sz)
{
    Destroy();
    m_bs = SysAllocStringA(sz);
    return *this;
}
const String& String::operator=(LPCWSTR wsz)
{
    DestroyA();
    if (SysReAllocString(&m_bs, wsz) == 0) throw E_OUTOFMEMORY;
    return *this;
}
```

One way or another, an operator= function must replace the previous con-tents of the object with the new contents being assigned. The LPCSTR version destroys the whole member and creates a new one, while the LPCWSTR version just destroys the ANSI buffer and reallocates the BSTR member. The only reason for this difference is that I didn't write a **SysReAllocStringA** function.

A String Method

Once you get construction, destruction, and ANSI conversion figured out, the methods and overloaded operators are easy. Most of them are simply calls to the *wsc* versions of C++ run-time functions. For example, let's look at the **UCase** method, which comes in two versions.

Here's the member function:

```
const String & String::UCase()
{
    DestroyA();      // Invalidate ANSI buffer.
    wcsupr(m_bs);
    return *this;
}
```

It simply calls the wcsupr function (which you may know as strupr) to modify the internal BSTR member. Here's the function version:

```
String UCase(String& s)
{
    String sRet = s;
    sRet.UCase();
    return sRet;
}
```

The version above uses a String argument (which it leaves unchanged) and returns a modified String copy. Its implementation creates a new string and uses the method version of UCase on it.

A Challenge

Before I leave you to figure out the rest of the String internals, let me pose a challenge. If the String class had only one member, *m_bs*, it would be the same size and have the same contents as a BSTR parameter. You could pass a BSTR in from Basic and receive a String in your C++ DLL. But this still wouldn't save you from doing Unicode conversion or from cleaning up correctly in destructors. You'd need to use the equivalents of *m_pch* and *m_fDestroy* without actually putting them in the class. How are you going to manage that?

Well, here's an idea. Create a static class member that is an array of data structures, each of which contains a buffer for ANSI conversion and a flag for destruction. Every time you create a String object, you insert one of these items into the array. When you need to use the ANSI buffer, you look up the item in the array and allocate or use the ANSI buffer. You'll probably want to insert each item in sorted order (maybe by the value of the BSTR pointer) for faster lookup. Whenever you destroy a String, you must find and remove its corresponding data structure from the array

Performance would suffer, but probably not by much because you're not going to have that many String variables active at any one time. You would end up with a more intuitive String class. From what I understand, this is how the old OLE2ANSI DLL used to work. Is it worth the extra work? I didn't think it was for this article, but perhaps it would be for your projects.

Index

Note: *Italicized* page numbers locate figures or tables.

C++

Product ID

#1 00018-099-378976

-10069

#2 00018-099-8053113-

68548

Myn's Compac   00018-099-4186934-14814

C++ DOCS

Work IBM
Doc's #1 00018-099-5255693

-74612

Dell work 00018-099-0988494-02392
Docs ID 00018-099-3393003-02500
#2 00018-099-1571554-51548

Mom's Compaq 00018-099-9398715-04064